Tennessee Studies In Literature

Editors
Richard Beale Davis and Kenneth L. Knickerbocker

Managing Editor
Richard M. Kelly

Assistant Managing Editor
Allison R. Ensor

VOLUME XVII

THE UNIVERSITY OF TENNESSEE PRESS · KNOXVILLE · 1972

Tennessee Studies in Literature

Persons interested in submitting manuscripts should address the Managing Editor, *Tennessee Studies in Literature*, McClung Tower 306, University of Tennessee, Knoxville, Tennessee 37916. Contributions from any qualified scholar, especially from this state and region, will be considered. Return postage should accompany manuscripts. Papers should be no longer than five thousand words. Contributors will receive fifty offprints. Other inquiries concerning this series should be addressed to the University of Tennessee Press, Communications Building, University Station, Knoxville, Tennessee 37916.

CONTENTS

Abstract. The vocabulary of the final scene in Congreve's *Love for Love* is as much religious as it is judicial, for its terms refer us to virtue and justice, trial and faith, martyrdom and punishment, accusation and conversion, rewards and good works. The final scene, indeed, helps us to understand that the play is shaped according to a traditional English dramatic pattern of testing and trial and judgment, and that Angelica in some very suggestive ways lives up to the implications of her name and becomes a vicarious agent of a Providential justice. As it was one function of the good angel to do, we are shown that she has brought Valentine along a course whereby he could "be tried, exercised, and made better thereby." (AW)

Abstract. It has been traditionally assumed that the *Wallace* of Blind Harry is much indebted to John Barbour's *Bruce*. An examination of the two poems, however, demonstrates that the similarities between them, except for some minor characterizations and a few scattered episodes, can be accounted for on grounds other than direct influence and are, in any case, less striking than the differences. Both poems deal with essentially the same historical period and their respective heroes are cast in the heroic mold, but, unlike Barbour, Harry utilizes a neo-Chaucerian style in the *Wallace*, and his depiction of Bruce as a virtual traitor is at odds with both historical fact and Barbour's portrayal of the hero of Bunnockburn. By discrediting Bruce, Harry seems to be trying to supplant Bruce with Wallace in public esteem, and if he is not successful, it is not for want of effort. (WS)

Abstract. The seemingly homely gifts of the shepherds spring from the Epiphany tradition as depicted in the scriptural account of the Presentation of the Magi (Matt. ii.1–12). In the crib scene of the *Secunda Pastorum*, the first shepherd (Coll) offers the Christ-child a bob of cherries. Suggesting Christ's redemptive sacrifice as well as the Eucharist and the Resurrection, such a gift is associated with the myrrh of Balthazar—that Epiphany offering which signifies Christ's death and burial for man's spiritual rebirth. The second shepherd (Gib), however, presents Jesus with a bird. Since this gift symbolizes Christ's divinity, it is linked with the frankincense of Caspar—the Epiphany emblem of the godhead of Christ. Daw, the third shepherd, extends to the Infant Jesus a tennis ball. Signifying Christ's regal divinity and sovereignty, Daw's gift evokes Melchior's offering of gold, the conventional Epiphany symbol of Christ as the King of Kings. (RJB)

Gorboduc as Apology and Critique
By William Babula   37

Abstract. Norton and Sackville in *Gorboduc* simultaneously defend one mode of art and criticize another. Insisting upon the Humanist dream of political effectiveness, they create a drama that attempts to influence court affairs. Their method is to dramatize historical events which should teach the dangers of a divided kingdom. In the process, they defend the mode of historical drama through this ability to instruct. At the same time, while they use many of its devices, the dramatists implicitly criticize the Senecan form of tragedy. This criticism is a natural development of their defense of historical art as instructive and politically effective. Senecan drama implies that man is a helpless victim of fate. The joint consciousness behind *Gorboduc*, however, insists that man can shape his destiny. Thus the Humanist dream leads the dramatists to reject the Senecan mode and accept an historical drama that can influence events. (WB)

The Influence of Astrophil's Star
By Ruth Stevenson   45

Abstract. Stella is an important but unrecognized motivating force in Sidney's sonnet sequence. Examination will show that there are three stages in the dramatic development of the sequence, representing Astrophil's three distinct responses to Stella. Through Sonnet 43 she is to Astrophil an ideal—largely passive and impersonal—but in the second stage he discovers in her a real woman who attracts, fascinates, and disturbs him and who strongly influences his actions and attitudes as mutual affection and desire develop. This stage, through the series of songs following Sonnet 85, reaches its climax as Stella, in spite of her clear desire, refuses physical consummation. The remainder of the sequence records Astrophil's initial bitterness because of his rejection and his gradual withdrawal to an attitude of detachment and convention. This process of disengagement is the key to the proper understanding of the songs inserted into the final portion of the sequence. (RS)

Abstract. Although Bussy remains convinced of his uncompromising virtue, in terms of action he becomes little better than the "politicians" he despises. This radical split between what Bussy says and what he does is the most significant feature of the play. It would seem that success in the society which Bussy instinctively avoids is to be gained only at the expense of "natural virtue," and that no man can remain uncompromised if he seeks to act. Yet if Chapman rejects for his hero the possibility of virtuous action, he does not despair about virtue of intent. Intentionally, Bussy is consistently heroic, and though his actions are compromised his motives remain pure. An unpolitic virtue such as Bussy's cannot succeed in changing a corrupt society, but it can succeed as a heroic, if unworkable, ideal. (RTB)

Abstract. Fielding's critics often claim that the happy ending of *Amelia* is inconsistent with the body of the work. The comic resolution, however, is prepared for by three narrative patterns based on the representation of Booth's arrests, the treatment of the hindering characters, and the characterization of Booth. Fielding's comic technique diminishes the serious implications of Booth's three arrests and minimizes the potential threats of the hindering characters. It is felt that, although Booth and Amelia encounter many difficulties, they will ultimately be delivered from their hardships. Their happiness at the end is particularly satisfying when Fielding portrays Booth as a good man whose faults do not make him undeserving of Amelia's love. (SEL)

Abstract. Of Browning's eleven sonnets all but three were written in the 1880s, after his major work was completed. Though, in the main, they are occasional poems uncollected by their author, they are more self-revelatory of Browning's interests and attitudes than he perhaps realized. During his middle years Browning allows his *men and women* to speak surprisingly often and disparagingly of the sonnet as a verse form. Even though he seems to regard the traditional sonnet series as an invasion of privacy, he is aware of the unique qualities of linked comment and oblique narration as he demonstrates in the footnote sequence to "Jochanan Hakkadosh" and in the structure of "James Lee's Wife." Finally, as "The Onlie Begetter" of the most popular sequence of the most prolific age of sonneteering, Browning, in his relationship to that form, is involved in a series of satires of circumstance. (WTG)

Abstract. Many critics of Robert Browning's "Childe Roland to the Dark Tower Came" have argued that Roland's final act ("And yet / Dauntless the slughorn to my lips I set, / And blew. '*Childe Roland to the Dark Tower Came.*' ") is resolute and clear-sighted. It has not been observed previously, however, that Roland's mind is the cynosure of his physical and moral progress, and that the progress is dependent upon the quality of his mind. This paper attempts to demonstrate that to understand Roland's final act, it is necessary to understand his mind; that from his first thought to his last Roland remains a "childe": quick to see, and quick to draw conclusions, basically unreflective, and yet creative, persistently expedient, and rashly principled—a mental novice who pushes hard to bring past, present, and future together; that his analysis of the problem of overwhelming oppression leads him to a distortion of evidence and the unreliable conclusion that the universe is governed by a malicious force; that his final act of defiance must be viewed as an act of impatience and distraction, rather than resolution and clear-sightedness. (PR)

Abstract. The image of Medusa, a beautiful woman endowed with the power to destroy, provided Rossetti, Morris, and Swinburne with an objective symbol of their basic concepts of art. In a poem and in sketches for a painting, Rossetti saw the myth of Medusa as a symbol of the manner in which the artist can reduce the sordidness of reality into the beauty of art. The socialist Morris valued art primarily as an attempt to beautify life for the common people. In trying to make mythology appeal to the masses, he made Medusa a conventional pathetic heroine rather than a monster. Swinburne symbolized his sexual obsessions by the image of Medusa, especially the snaky hair. By stressing their power to fascinate and destroy, he merges Medusa and Cleopatra into a vision of deadly beauty before which the poet is merely a helpless victim. (KP)

Abstract. George Gissing's novel *In the Year of Jubilee* is a valuable satiric commentary on the culture of nineteenth-century England—a subject masterfully treated in Matthew Arnold's critical prose. Gissing begins with the idea of the Jubilee and exposes a misdirected Victorian pride. Through an effective setting and skillful character vignettes of a would-be advertising executive, a self-"educated" businessman, and an untalented young woman whose sole aim is to graduate from London University, Gissing demonstrates that provincialism, ignorance of excellence, self-

Abstract. Although Edward Taylor held that the will, the faculty most associated with the self, depends upon grace for any ability to express itself in pious art, he also always emphasized the importance of the active efforts of that will. Grace does not overpower the will but renews it, giving it a true identity. It follows that though elements of mysticism occur in his verse, the *Preparatory Meditations* actually reveals how Taylor's will or self maintained its distinctiveness and was never abandoned to a mystical union with the divine Will. Rather than transcending the temporal realm, Taylor sought to ferret out of his "Wildred state" and the apparent "Crooked Passages" of his earthly life the essential meaning of and the key to his real identity either as a child of God or as an heir to hell. In the introspective *Preparatory Meditations*, in which the question of Taylor's spiritual fate is kept suspended, we encounter a unique self deriving from its love for and devotion to Christ as much of a sense of regenerate self-identity as one can achieve in this world. (WJS)

Abstract. Although Poe acknowledged Sir John Herschel's *A Treatise on Astronomy* to have been his inspirational source for "Hans Pfaall" and the late Meredith N. Posey showed that Poe indeed owed much to Herschel, others have contended that the chief source of Poe's indebtedness is George Tucker's romance, *A Voyage to the Moon.* However, new evidence derived from accounts of balloon ascensions which occurred during the late eighteenth and early nineteenth centuries and from a further examination of Herschel's *Treatise* indicates that Poe's most significant sources are scientific rather than fictional. New parallels drawn between passages from these works and passages from "Hans Pfaall" not only reveal that Poe was greatly influenced by them but also tend to minimize the importance of *A Voyage to the Moon* as a major source. Even though Poe may well have been originally indebted to Tucker for some suggestions, it is clear that when he sought to impart to his story what he considered to be its distinguishing feature—the illusion of scientific plausibility—he resorted, in developing these suggestions, to nonfictional works that would prove more helpful in the accomplishment of his design. (WHG)

Abstract. Dynasty, the use of land for purposes of familial establishment, is often assumed to have been a major theme in Faulkner's novels. A survey of the appearance of the dynastic theme in the Faulkner canon, however, reveals that while a triple division of dynastic interests occurs in the earlier works (a division which may be labeled dynastic, anti-dynastic, and non-dynastic) and reaches a peak in *Absalom, Absalom!*, the concept of dynastic establishment, especially as the saga of "great families," does not prove as important to Faulkner's thinking as is often supposed. A shift of emphasis from the propertied to the unpropertied occurs, and dynasty later becomes a spiritual heritage that is a metaphor for traditional values. (JMD)

Abstract. James Agee's unpublished notes and manuscript for *The Morning Watch* clarify his emphasis upon the young protagonist's difficulty in sustaining religious emotion. The unused manuscript consists of an alternate beginning and ending for the book and emphasizes the difficulty of an adult's sustaining his religious fervor. Because the novella evokes the immediacy of the imagined moment, and since Agee minimizes character development, incorporation of the excluded manuscript would have made the design of the novella more apparent. (VAK)

Abstract. The writer of fiction and the historian share a problem of "distance" in their work. The historian writes of a time not his own, and the writer of fiction writes about characters other than himself. Each must then move his imagination into a realm removed somewhat from his own experience. The nineteenth century was a period of grandeur in both history and literature. Writers in both fields possessed a Faustian confidence in their power to describe multitudes of characters in a pandemonium of incidents. But in the twentieth century both historians and fictioners have to some degree lost their nerve. The historian writes monographs on a very narrow range of historical experience. The fictioner writes books that are about characters very much like himself, often invariable from book to book and name to name. Some say these trends lead to a more accurate history and a more honest fiction. But though these claims may be partly true, I think the larger reason for these trends is a loss of energy and nerve. It is not the purpose of either history or literature to be "arty," but I think we will have great art in each realm only when their practitioners place a little more distance between themselves and their work and then strive to transcend that distance with their imagination. (RM)

AUBREY WILLIAMS

THE "UTMOST TRYAL" OF VIRTUE AND CONGREVE'S *LOVE FOR LOVE**

I

Very near the end of *Love for Love* there occurs the moment when Valentine, having finally despaired of gaining the love of Angelica, agrees to sign away all rights to his inheritance and thereby demonstrates that he is, in some sense, "mad" enough to sacrifice himself for her sake. Earlier he had pretended a different kind of madness with the quite opposite and selfish aim of both preserving his estate and tricking Angelica into an open confession of love for him, but in this last scene he seems, as Scandal puts it, "mad indeed," so "mad" as to ruin himself for love of another. The confrontation that here reveals the actual depth and sincerity of Valentine's love, we should note, had been cunningly contrived somewhat earlier by Angelica herself, when she proposed to old Sir Sampson that a match be "seemingly carried on" between the two of them in order to make Valentine "throw off his Disguise of Madness" in "Apprehension of losing" her.

Beautiful and witty as Angelica is, the course of the play also demonstrates that she is as tough-minded and crafty as a Restoration heiress in command of 30,000 pounds would very well need to be. But here, in this final scene she has so cleverly brought about, she seems to me to assume a role and perform a function that utterly transcends the notion of the Restoration heroine of comedy as she is so typically and (I would add) mistakenly conceived. For the conclusion of *Love for Love* unmistakably presents us, to my mind, with a trial and judgment

* The John C. Hodges Memorial Lecture at the University of Tennessee, April 16, 1971.

1

scene, one in which Angelica acts as a minister of justice who, once all
the evidence is in and the truth revealed, proceeds to the reward of
virtue and the punishment of wickedness. Consider these words of
stern admonishment she directs to Sir Sampson Legend:

Learn to be a good Father, or you'll never get a second Wife. I always lov'd your
Son, and hated your unforgiving Nature. I was resolv'd to try him to the utmost;
I have try'd you too, and know you both. You have not more Faults than he has
Virtues; and 'tis hardly more Pleasure to me, that I can make him and my self
happy, than that I can punish you.   (V.i.571–78)[1]

These are certainly severe and magisterial words for so young a woman
to use on so much older a man. But then consider also the suddenly
respectful and very suggestive terms used by Scandal in this last address
to Angelica of the play:

Well, Madam, You have done Exemplary Justice, in punishing an inhumane
Father, and rewarding a Faithful Lover: But there is a Third good Work, which
I, in particular, must thank you for; I was an Infidel to your Sex; and you have
converted me——   (V.i.619–23)

The vocabulary of this final scene is as much religious as it is judicial,
for its terms refer us to virtue and justice, trial and faith, martyrdom
and punishment, accusation and conversion, rewards and good works.
This vocabulary, and the actions associated with it, cause me at least
to believe that here Angelica, in some highly emblematic way, quite
lives up to the very apparent implications of her name and thereby
performs certain offices and duties traditionally assigned to angelic
ministers. As Archbishop James Usher defined these offices in a *Body
of Divinity*, reprinted many times during the Restoration period, the
general function of the angels as to the earthly creation is to serve as
"the Instruments and Ministers of God for the Administration and
Government of the whole World."[2] More particularly, in this ministry they "bestow good things" upon the good, and they "execute
Judgments upon the Wicked, and punish them for their sins committed." Or additionally, as Richard Saunders wrote in 1701, in a
statement that has great relevance for Valentine's development in Congreve's play, if a good person suffers while in an angel's hands, "it is
that he may be tried, exercised, and made better thereby."[3]

So close and emphatic an association of Angelica's words and deeds
with the traditional offices of angelic ministers no doubt seems strange,
even extravagant and bizarre, considering the prevailing views about
Restoration comedy. But to me the climactic scene of *Love for Love*,
as well as the course of the play as a whole, is directly related to a
dramatic tradition going back through the Renaissance to the mystery

and morality plays. That tradition is quite specifically one of testing and trial and judgment, and the Renaissance version of it has been finely described recently, by Professor Thomas Stroup, as "the testing pattern," which "involves the trial or proving of a man." Plays in this tradition take something of their shape, says Professor Stroup, "from the testing force of Providence operating within the characters of men," and it matters not whether the plays be tragedies or comedies. In such plays, "Divine Providence does not appear in proper person," but Providence may, "and especially so in comedy, send a vicar in the guise of the king or duke or simply the judge who settles the conflict and metes out justice, rewards, and punishments, in the last scene."[4]

Professor Stroup does not explore English drama beyond the closing of the theaters in 1642, and one gathers that he would consider the themes and patterns he describes to have waned immensely after that time. I would argue, on the other hand, that the themes of his book, particularly the testing pattern he defines so well, could be copiously illustrated in much of Restoration and eighteenth-century drama, and for evidence of this I would mention offhand the development and re-peated testings of Almanzor in *The Conquest of Granada*, the fierce trial of Amanda's virtue in *The Relapse*, the proving of Jane Shore's repentance in *The Tragedy of Jane Shore*.[5]

The play before us, however, seems sufficient to make my point, for its last scene conforms closely to the last scenes of comedies in the testing pattern defined by Professor Stroup. In *Love for Love* we have a vicar or deputy of Providence who has tested the good and the bad, who has artfully contrived a trial and permitted testimony, who has searched hearts and knows them well, who has pronounced judgment and who has distributed rewards and punishments. In this play the vi-carious agent of Providence is no king or duke, as he so often is in the plays of Shakespeare and others, but a rich and clever young woman whom Sir Sampson quite correctly describes, at one point, as a "cun-ning, a wary Baggage." Indeed she is that, but then her name is An-gelica, and we should not forget (though we seem to have done so), that even more than kings and dukes, angels were regarded, by St. Thomas Aquinas as well as by Congreve's contemporaries, as "the prime Instruments of God's Providence."[6] Herself by no means an angel, she yet performs the function of one in conducting Valentine to what she calls an "utmost Tryal" of his virtue. That performance, moreover, suggests to me that the shape and meaning of this play may be governed by that "testing force of Providence" found by Professor Stroup to be so common a fact of earlier English drama.

II

The reward of virtue and the punishment of wickedness and folly in the last scene of *Love for Love* inevitably suggests, to me at least, a fundamental principle of Restoration drama and criticism—the principle of poetic justice. I have argued elsewhere,[7] and I must argue here, that most of Congreve's work is shaped by this principle: all of his plays, except his first youthful one, *The Old Batchelour*, seem to me to end with the unmistakable terminology, as well as the unmistakable distributive procedures, that was conventional to the employment of poetic justice.

The principle of poetic justice has been considered by the generality of modern scholars and critics to be an arbitrary and unworkable principle, as requiring a wrenching of reality to make things work out to some neat and happy solution. Such were not the implications of the principle, however, for most of the writers and critics of the Restoration and early eighteenth century. To them, and I cannot emphasize this too strongly, the principle involved nothing less than an attempt to mirror in art something they considered to be an actual and metaphysical reality: that is, the very real government of the world by Divine Providence. Poetic justice, in other words, must be understood as the dramatic analogue for Providential Justice, as this blunt statement by the critic John Dennis should make clear:

Poetick Justice would be a Jest if it were not an Image of the Divine, and if it did not consequently suppose the Being of a God and Providence.[8]

The operations of God's Providence in the real world were often described in the ancient metaphor of the world as a stage, another theme that Professor Stroup has explored in his study of Elizabethan drama. In this metaphor God the Divine Dramatist and Director fills the stage of His world with a multitude of players of all degrees in rank and character, contrives the plots and actions by which they may be tried and proven, and finally distributes among them, by His providential justice, their most suitable rewards and condign punishments. Examples of the continued and even prevalent use of this metaphor in theological writings of the Restoration could be endlessly multiplied, but here I shall simply cite one instance as it appeared in a sermon of the Rev. George Hickes, preached on an anniversary of the restoration of Charles II to the throne. Emphasizing that the restoration he celebrates "was the Consult of a special Providence, since it was contrived in a manner so apparently worthy of the Divine Wisdom," Hickes then develops his metaphor:

Certainly the seasonable Contrivance of so many wonderful Scenes into every Act, and of so many curious Acts into one harmonious Play, must needs have been the Study and Invention of a very skilful Author, even of the All-wise, and Almighty Dramatist; who hath the World for his Theatre, and seldom less than a Kingdom for his Stage.[9]

If the larger world was envisioned as a stage, then it was most easy and natural to invert that vision and see the stage as a world,[10] and something of the interchange of vision can be seen in Act IV of *Love for Love* when Valentine says to Angelica: "The Comedy draws towards an end, and let us think of leaving acting, and be our selves. . . ." And as the larger stage of the world had its highly dramatic ordering principle in the concept of Providential Justice, so the smaller world of the stage formulated for itself the highly dramatic counterpart of that ordering principle, the concept of poetic justice. Neither principle of justice was considered to require, moreover, a violation of the laws of natural causation or probability in their realization. In the larger world, Providence was thought to exercise an "Absolute Government over Mankind, who are Free Agents, without destroying the Liberty and Freedom of their Choice, which would destroy the nature of Vertue and Vice, of Rewards and Punishments."[11] And on the world of the stage, said Thomas Rymer (the man who of course invented the phrase "poetical justice"), it is the duty of the poet to observe "that constant order, that harmony and beauty of Providence, that necessary relation and chain, whereby the causes and the effects, the vertues and rewards, the vices and their punishments are proportion'd and link'd together; how deep and dark soever are laid the Springs, and however intricate and involv'd are their operations."[12]

In the contemporary discussions of the operations of God's Providence in the larger world, great emphasis is placed upon the way God contrives things so that the wicked and vicious are "snared in the work of their own hands,"[13] or "fall into the pit themselves have digged for others."[14] The contrivance of such justice as this has intrinsic dramatic and ironic possibilities of a high order, and the seventeenth and eighteenth centuries were fascinated by narrations, from the press as well as from the pulpit, in which vicious and treacherous men were betrayed by themselves or their accomplices, were trapped in their own devices and plots. For example, Thomas Beard's *Theatre of God's Iudgments . . . Wherein is represented the admirable justice of God against all notorious sinners both great and small* was reprinted at least twelve times after its first publication in 1597 (right on up to 1704 and 1708 and 1770), and it is not only filled with such highly ironic instances of Providential Justice but the use of the word "Theatre" in its title illustrates again the metaphorical stage on which God's justice was enacted. And from the pulpit the congregations of Restoration London were hearing time and again such words as these from one of the most admired preachers of the day, the Rev. Isaac Barrow: "when bloudy Oppresours have *bloud given them to drink* [Rev. 16:6], and come to welter in their own gore," or "when Treacherous men" are betrayed "by their own confidents [sic], or by themselves," by "such Occurrences the finger of God doth point out and indicate itself."[15]

The relevance for Congreve's work of such ironic operations of God's Providence in the larger world seems clear to me. The Latin epigraph of his tragedy, *The Mourning Bride*, goes like this in translation: "there is no juster law than that contrivers of death should perish by their own contrivances";[16] and among the concluding lines of the same play one finds these words addressed to Almeria, the mourning bride:

> Thy Father fell, where he design'd my Death.
> *Gonsalez* and *Alonzo*, both of Wounds
> Expiring, have with their last Breath, confess'd
> The just Decrees of Heav'n, in turning on
> Themselves, their own most bloody Purposes.

In the comedies the shaping influence of such a vision of Providential Justice also seems evident. In *The Double-Dealer*, as Maskwell moves step by step through his plots he just as surely advances his own destruction, and thereby justifies the admonitory lines which conclude the play:

> Let secret Villany from hence be warn'd;
> Howe're in private, Mischiefs are conceiv'd,
> Torture and shame attend their open Birth:
> Like Vipers in the Womb, base Treach'ry lies,
> Still gnawing that, whence first it did arise;
> No sooner born, but the Vile Parent dies.

And *The Way of the World*, we may recall, concludes with this warning of the wages of adultery:

> From hence let those be warn'd, who mean to wed;
> Lest mutual falsehood stain the Bridal-Bed:
> For each deceiver to his cost may find,
> That marriage frauds too oft are paid in kind.

III

But the play before us is *Love for Love*, and here the lives and lots of even the secondary characters seem to me to exemplify the operations of a justice that is as providential as it is poetic. Most especially and explicitly may the operations of such a justice be seen in what happens to Tattle and Mrs. Frail, who are tricked into marrying one another.

Tattle, of course, is presented throughout the play as an utter coxcomb, eternally preening himself on his ability to keep secret his sexual liaisons, yet always letting a word slip here or there that will reveal his familiarity with the boudoirs of a veritable multitude of ladies both great and not so great. His vanity about knowing the secrets of others, as well as about "knowing" women in the sexual sense, is not, however, mere silly and harmless foppery, for the entire play reveals that at bottom he is utterly mean and self-interested. In the first act he lets it be gathered, though quite without saying it in so many words, that he has possessed the body of Mrs. Frail, only to be mightily embarrassed the next moment when that lady is announced and he is threatened with exposure. To save his own skin, he then readily agrees to sacrifice the reputations of some dozen or so women of quality. With the words "cruel" or "barbarous" or "inhumane" constantly in his own mouth, he is himself utterly callous in his treatment of Miss Prue and utterly treacherous in his plot against Angelica.

Mrs. Frail, for her part, is a woman of so broken a reputation that she is much in need of a husband to mend it. Given to assignations in notorious watering places and to making out in hackney coaches, she and her sister, Mrs. Foresight, first plot to turn Miss Prue over to Tattle and thus make Ben and his estate the means of patching up her name and fortune. Later, when Valentine's pretended madness makes it seem likely that his estate will not revert to Ben, Mrs. Frail coldly breaks off her engagement with the simple-hearted sailor, and then readily enters into a Judas-like plot, hatched by Mrs. Foresight, to get Jeremy "to sell his Master" Valentine to her in marriage.

After Tattle and Mrs. Frail have been married to each other in disguise, and even made a carnal consummation in disguise, we see in the yoking of two such base and treacherous natures a most ironic and appropriate poetic justice. Thinking he has bedded Angelica, Tattle finds to his horror that instead he has taken permanent possession of that body he had so falsely boasted of having "known" earlier. That each of the pair is tricked is made possible, moreover, only by their own most selfish purposes and by the very means by which they take to accomplish those purposes. Tattle wishes to marry Angelica for her 30,000 pounds; Mrs. Frail schemes to marry Valentine in hopes of a monetary settlement. The disguises they put on to trick their intended victims become the very means, finally, by which they trick themselves as well as one another. When Tattle asks Jeremy if he must be hooded during the ceremony, the latter says: "Aye, Sir, hooded like a Hawk, to seize at first sight upon the Quarry." Entering into so vicious a scheme to make another his victim, he finds that he himself has been victimized. The plight of Tattle and Mrs. Frail is most appropriately described, I think, by Ben when he says of their marriage: "Why there's another Match now, as tho'f a couple of Privateers were looking for a Prize, and should fall foul of one another."

The marriage of Tattle and Mrs. Frail seems to me to be an example, in a comic context, of the kind of Providential Justice described in sermons and more vulgar literature which argued that the wicked are "snared in the works of their own hands" or "fall into the pits themselves have digged for others." Support for this view is given, I think, by a most noticeable passage of the play. After Angelica has finally revealed her love for Valentine, the latter addresses Tattle in these words: "*Tattle*, I thank you, you would have interposed between me and Heav'n; but Providence laid Purgatory in your way——You have but Justice."

This bold declaration of the role played by Divine Providence in the affairs of Tattle and Valentine and Mrs. Frail and Angelica is unmistakably there in the text of *Love for Love*, and in my opinion it cannot be dismissed or taken lightly. It is evidence again that Congreve's play is quite in the tradition of those earlier English plays which are said by Professor Stroup to take something of their shape "from the testing force of Providence operating within the characters of men." It is a commonplace of Restoration providential literature and apologetics that Providence is concerned in the affairs of the most ordinary of men, and also a commonplace that Providence does not suspend or deflect the faculties and wills of men but rather that It works in and through their faculties and wills. A clear example of this is Isaac Barrow's statement that "the instruments of Providence being free agents, acting with unaccountable variety, nothing can happen which may not be imputed to them," for "Divine and humane influences are so twisted and knit together, that it is hard to sever them."[17] A clear dramatic illustration of Barrow's words seems to me to occur in another play by Congreve, *The Double-Dealer*, where Maskwell, in the midst of his plottings to gain another young woman and her fortune, is made to utter these striking words: "Was it my Brain or Providence? No Matter which——I will deceive 'em all, and yet secure my self, 'twas a lucky thought!" When Maskwell's "long track of dark deceit" is finally uncovered and his punishment assured, it seems to me we have again a clear theatrical illustration of what Barrow meant when he said that we may recognize the operations of Providence when "ill men by their perverse vileness do notably befool and ensnare themselves, laying trains to blow up their own designs, involving themselves in that ruine and mischief into which they studied to draw others."[18]

When Valentine says to Tattle, "Providence laid Purgatory in your way——You have but Justice," I think we have a valuable expression of the way in which the Restoration world of the stage attempted to reflect the actions of Providence on the larger stage of the real world. The religious vocabulary used by Tattle at this moment of the play seems to enforce the point. When he says that his "Intentions were good" as he hoped "to be sav'd," and that he now believes he will lead Mrs. Frail "a damn'd sort of Life," I think we may detect in his words a hint of a punishment that is beyond Tattle's own mean and meager comprehension but that is not beyond the comprehensive world of the Restoration stage.

IV

It is not merely in the punishments of Tattle and Mrs. Frail, however, that we have intimations of a Providential dimension. The name of Foresight is almost a literal translation of the word "providence," but at the same time his faith in astrology and other kinds of divination would have served to identify him to Congreve's age as a man not only foolish but also actually impious. I do not think it has previously been noticed, but the idea for one of the more bawdy and amusing scenes of the play, the seduction of Mrs. Foresight under her husband's very nose, could have had a particular source which may help us to understand more fully the implications of Foresight's absurd faith in the stars.[19] In Henry Cornelius Agrippa's *The Vanity of Arts and Sciences* (I use the English translation published in 1676), in the chapter entitled "Of Judicial Astrology," there occurs a passage which seems remarkably suggestive of the character Congreve defined in his Dramatis Personae as "an illiterate Old Fellow, peevish and positive" and "superstitious." Agrippa writes that the judicial astrologers are

A perverse and preposterous generation of men, who profess to foreknow future things, in the mean time altogether ignorant of past and present; and undertaking to tell all people most obscure and hidden secrets abroad, at the same time know not what happens in their own houses, and in their own chambers: Even such an Astrologer as [Sir Thomas] *Moore* laught at in his Epigram.

Agrippa then conflates two of More's epigrams on the cuckolding of an astrologer in this composite set of verses:

> The Stars, Ethereal Bard, to thee shine clear,
> And all our future Fates thou mak'st appear.
> But that thy Wife is common all men know,
> Yet what all see, there's not a Star doth show.
> *Saturn* is blinde, or some long journey gone,
> Not able to discern an infant from a stone.
> The Moon is fair, and as she's fair she's chast,
> And won't behold thy Wife so leudly embrac't.
> *Europa Jove, Mars Venus*, she *Mars* courts,
> With *Daphne, Sol*, with *Hirce Hermes* sports.
> Thus while the Stars their wanton Love pursue,
> No wonder, Cuckhold, they'll not tell thee true.[20]

Angelica has a great deal of impudent fun with her uncle, telling him she is afraid his wife is "a little Retrograde . . . in her Nature" and that she will leave him "to erect a Scheme, and find who's in Conjunction" with her. Foresight is aware, in his own words, that his wife "was born under *Gemini*, which may incline her to Society," and that she "has a Mole upon her Lip," a "moist Palm," and "an open Liberality on the Mount of *Venus*," but even with all these signs from astrology, palmistry, and physiognomy, he is left in querulous uncertainty as to his wife's fidelity, and finally consoles himself with this resigned comment: "Well——Why, if I was born to be a Cuckold, there's no more to be said——."

This resigned and fatalistic comment by Foresight is perhaps designed to recall the most serious charges made against judicial astrology during the Renaissance: that is, the tenets and practice of such astrology seemed to impiously deny not only the operations of God's Providence, but also the freedom of man's will, while at the same time, in Cornelius Agrippa's words, "it teaches, That all things happen by force and vertue of the Stars, and from the Influences of the Constellations, by a kind of fatal Necessity," thereby "excusing Vice as descending from Heaven."[21] This fatalistic strain encouraged by astrology is to be noted several times in Foresight's speech. He says, for example, that "it is impossible that any thing should be as I would have it; for I was born, Sir, when the Crab was ascending, and all my Affairs go backward." Vain of his ability to read signs and faces, he yet is enslaved by dreams and tokens. A "Searcher into Obscurity and Futurity," as Scandal calls him, as well as an anxious and peevish inquirer into his wife's purity, his superstitious credulity seems to receive a most poetic justice when his wife acquiesces in an assignation while he pores over his own face in a mirror. Seeking an impossible certainty from stars and faces, he becomes the dupe and victim of his own astrological calculations, for we know that at the time when the old nurse will bring him his urinal ("within a quarter of Twelve . . . just upon the turning of the Tide"), Scandal will have erected his own scheme within "his Wives Circle."

V

Foresight, however, is not alone in his attempts at physiognomy, for nearly every character in the play is vitally concerned in reading the faces of others while hiding his own egoistic wishes and purposes under a mask of his own making. One cannot stress too much that the world of *Love for Love* (rather like our own world) is one in which people are ruled by the most self-interested motives and that in pursuit of their own interests they seem, as Ben says, "to look one way, and to row another." Everyone seems to have a secret, moreover, some hidden purpose or desire, that someone else wishes to know or reveal. Mrs. Foresight charges her sister with indiscretions at inns and other resorts, and in evidence produces a gold bodkin found in a room at one such place; but then Mrs. Frail points out that the bodkin could only have been found by one who had been taken to bed in the same place, and Mrs. Foresight confesses peevishly: "O Devil on't, that I cou'd not discover her, without betraying my self." Sir Sampson at one point says that he neither knows nor believes that Valentine is his son, while Tattle indoctrinates Prue in the well-bred art of lying, of making her words contradict her thoughts, and her actions contradict her words. Mrs. Foresight, after having lain with Scandal all night, the next morning denies that fact to his face with more impudence than she had granted him her person a few hours before. Valentine finds Angelica harder to read than "a Piece of *Ægyptian* Antiquity, or an *Irish* Manuscript."

The characters of this world, even the best of them, reveal a callousness and selfishness that scarcely support, to my mind, the notion that Congreve's plays represent a move toward sentimentality. Ben, for example, has totally forgotten the fact that his brother Dick had died two years before his return, and Tattle leaves Prue to come off as best she can from the room in which she was striving to be rid of her virginity. Sir Sampson is not, as he says himself, one to "turn Pelican" and feed his son out of his own vitals, and Valentine is enough his father's son to wish, in the first act of the play, that the strumpet who had presented him with a bastard had smothered the boy in its infancy. Indeed, the quite evident flaws and vices that Congreve has attributed to Valentine sent the Rev. Jeremy Collier, in his *Short View of the Immorality, and Profaneness of the English Stage*, into this sarcastic expostulation:

This Spark the *Poet* would have pass for a Person of Virtue. . . . 'Tis true, He was hearty in his Affection to *Angelica*. Now without question, to be in Love with a fine Lady of 30,000 Pounds is a great Virtue! But then abating this single Commendation, *Valentine* is altogether compounded of Vice. He is a prodigal Debauchee, unnatural, and Profane, Obscene, Sawcy, and undutiful, And yet this Libertine is crown'd for the Man of Merit, has his Wishes thrown into his Lap, and makes the happy *Exit*. I perceive we shall have a rare set of *Virtues* if these *Poets* had the making of them! How they hug a Vitious Character, and how profuse are they in their Liberalities to Lewdness.[22]

Collier's evaluation of Valentine is a typical instance of the way his attack on the stage proceeds by distortion and exaggeration, and Congreve put his hero in a better perspective when he answered Collier by saying that Valentine "is a mix'd Character; his Faults are fewer than his good Qualities; and as the World goes, he may pass well enough for the best Character in a Comedy; where even the best must be shewn to have Faults, that the best Spectators may be warn'd not to think too well of themselves."[23]

Nevertheless, we can understand, both from the evident flaws in Valentine's character and from the nature of the world depicted at large in the play, the necessity Angelica is under of testing and proving the sincerity of his love for her. With so large a fortune attached to her person, Valentine is only one of many young men who have pursued her, and how is she to tell, considering his bankrupt status and the world in which she moves, that his motives are any less sordid than those of Tattle? The squandering of his estate in his courtship of her is no certain expression of his love, for that could be merely the act of a gamester who ventures his stake to win a larger prize. Sir Sampson, moreover, at one point tells Angelica that his own son "has not a Drachm of Generous Love about him: All Interest, all Interest; he's an undone Scoundrel, and courts your Estate: Body o' me, he does not care a Doit for your Person."

It is very clear, furthermore, that Valentine *is* capable of wearing a mask for very selfish and mercenary reasons, for his feigned madness is in the main a device to procure him time "to preserve the right" of his inheritance. In addition, he "has a mind," as Jeremy tells Scandal, "to try, whether his playing the Madman, won't make [Angelica] play the Fool, and fall in love with him; or at least own that she has lov'd him all this while, and conceal'd it." But when Angelica visits Valentine in his rooms, out of real concern over the reports of his madness, she proves to be too shrewd an observer of faces for such a trick; when she sees Jeremy and Scandal exchange a wink and a smile, she vows to herself: "if I don't play Trick for Trick, may I never taste the Pleasure of Revenge."

A short time later she does ensnare Valentine in his own contrivance, for when he tries to persuade her that his madness is only feigned, she insists on treating him as if he were indeed a lunatic—to his utter frustration. But amusing as the scene is, we still can see that Valentine has fallen, in a fine moment of poetic justice, into the pit he has dug for another, and also that the underlying element of mercenary self-interest is an important feature of it. For when Valentine confesses to Angelica that his so-called madness had been a device to preserve his estate, he is neatly trapped by her in this exchange:

> *Angelica.* How! I thought your love of me had caus'd this Transport in your Soul; which, it seems, you only counterfeited, for mercenary Ends and sordid Interest.
> *Valentine.* Nay, now you do me Wrong; for if any Interest was considered, it was yours; since I thought I wanted more than Love, to make me worthy of you.
> *Angelica.* Then you thought me mercenary——But how am I deluded by this Interval of Sense, to reason with a Madman?

VI

The pervasive vocabulary of madness and folly, sense and reason, brings us back to the ethical center with which we started, for *Love for Love* in the end seems to be an extremely witty and sophisticated exploration of a traditional Christian paradox: the idea that worldly wisdom may actually be a form of folly or madness, and that some kinds of madness or folly may be of the highest order of wisdom. Certainly by the end of the play nearly everyone has been declared as suffering from one or other form of madness.[24] When Tattle is so foolishly confident of his scheme to marry Angelica, he spurns Prue and arrogantly scorns Foresight, who exclaims: "Mercy on us, what do these Lunacies portend? Alas! he's Mad, Child, stark Wild." Ben considers Angelica to be "mad for a Husband," and his father, Sir Sampson, to be "Horn-mad." Angelica tells Valentine that she is not the fool he takes her for, and that he is mad and doesn't know it.

The wisdom of this world is primarily concerned, of course, with self-interest and the acquisition of material goods and power, and out of such wisdom it is scarcely possible for characters such as Tattle, Sir Sampson, Mrs. Frail, and (initially at least) Scandal to conceive of anyone so mad as to sacrifice himself for another. As Scandal says at the end of the play, when Valentine agrees to sign away his inheritance, " 'S'death, you are not mad indeed, to ruine your self?" But from the very beginning of the play Valentine has introduced us to concepts that, however inadequate his own understanding of them at the time, will eventually provide the best insight into his own salvation and the resolution of the play as well. These concepts are repeated in various terms and ways throughout *Love for Love*, but they all seem ultimately illustrative of such Biblical paradoxes as this one: "There is that maketh himself rich, yet hath nothing; there is that maketh himself poor, yet hath great riches."[25]

We find such paradoxical concepts to be a prominent and pervasive feature of the first act of the play, which opens with Valentine's putting down the writings of Epictetus, whom he shortly identifies to Jeremy as a "very rich Man.——Not worth a Groat." Jeremy himself a moment later describes Seneca and Epictetus as "poor rich Rogues" whose writings are of little help in paying one's debts or filling one's belly. Variations on such paradoxes are continued when Valentine tells Tattle that "to converse with *Scandal*, is to play at *Losing Loadum*; you must lose a good Name to him, before you can win it for your self." And when Scandal concludes Act I in terms that have a dimension of truth neither he nor Valentine comprehends at the moment:

If Indiscretion be a sign of Love, you are the most a Lover of any Body that I know: you fancy that parting with your Estate, will help you to your Mistress.——In my mind he is a thoughtless Adventurer,
    Who hopes to purchase Wealth, by selling Land;
    Or win a Mistress, with a losing hand.

Valentine's allusion to the card game of Losing Loadum is a good example of the play's rich array of paradoxes, and it can be used as another way of describing developments in his character as well as the course of the play. The nearest modern counterpart to Losing Loadum is the game of Hearts, where the idea is to give away hands rather than to take them, and so the winner of the game is actually the one who loses the most tricks containing hearts. Losing Loadum is a bit more complicated than Hearts, and seems to have derived from the French game called *Reversis* or the Spanish game called *La Gana Pierde* (i.e., the winner loses). A signal feature of the game, moreover, seems to have been the progressive surrender of the cards of value in such a way that the players try to bring forth at the very last the cards "that are most price."[26]

At the beginning of the play Valentine has tried to buy the love of Angelica by a silly squandering of his estate. In the middle of the play he tries to play upon her sympathies and arouse her love through a pretended loss of his senses. His plots and stratagems seem a perfect illustration of Scandal's observation that the mind of a wit is "always contriving its own Ruine": Valentine is "more perplex'd to find Evasions" than he would be "to invent the honest means of keeping" his word. Only at the end of the play, when Valentine puts aside all his plots and pretenses and contrivances, and demonstrates that he is willing to "die a Martyr to Sense in a Country where the Religion is Folly," only then does he escape the "Confinement" and the "Restraint" in which he was seen to be locked at the start. That "Confinement," like so many other situations of confinement or imprisonment in the literature of the time, is to be understood not merely as a confinement of the body, but also, I think, as a confinement of the mind and spirit. Circumscribed as much by his disguises and stratagems as by his prodigality and debts, Valentine gains release only when he plays his last card of "most price"—a plain and simple act of self-sacrifice.

The "Blessing" Valentine receives at his moment of self-ruin is quite obviously set off against the "curse" that old Sir Sampson would place upon himself as well as everyone else. Hard, selfish, and unforgiving, he too exemplifies the play's procedures of poetic justice. Warned earlier by Angelica to "Have a care," lest like the "strongest *Sampson*" of his name, he pull "an old House over his Head," he seems a fine illustration of the man who has made himself rich, yet hath nothing. Casting aside both his sons, and engaging in a scheme to deny one of them his chosen love, he is finally ensnared in his own devices, for his vaunted "Fire," in Ben's words, turns out to be "little better than Tinder" which serves "to light up a Match for some body else." That mean and selfish nature which sought the destruction of his son's only hope leads him to contrive the very situation by which that son's "Generosity and Sincerity"[27] can be conclusively demonstrated in an "utmost Tryal" of his virtue.

As for Angelica, she has been wise enough not to give Valentine hope amidst his prosperity and prodigality, tough enough not to give him pity amidst his poverty and constraint, shrewd enough not to yield to his counterfeit madness. She has brought him along a course, as it was one function of a good angel to do, so that he might, in the words of Richard Saunders again, "be tried, exercised, and made better thereby." Through her ministrations and stratagems, and by working, as angels were also supposed to do, on his "Imaginations, and Affections (presenting things to the Mind, and pressing them with some vehemency),"[28] she seems to me to become, in some sense, the theatrical analogy for St. Thomas Aquinas' statement that it is the angels who "execute the divine plan for human salvation; they are our guardians, who free us when hindered and help to bring us home."[29] Certainly she has helped Valentine become an illustration of the man described in Proverbs: the man "that maketh himself poor, yet hath great riches."

VII

One of the passages in *Love for Love* which most infuriated Jeremy Collier was that in which Valentine says: "*Tattle,* I thank you, you would have interpos'd between me and Heav'n; but Providence laid Purgatory in your way——You have but Justice." The language here excited Collier into this outburst: "Thus Heav'n is debas'd into an Amour, and Providence brought on to direct the Paultry concerns of the Stage!"[30] A more recent commentator on the play, Professor Charles Lyons, finds this and other instances of Christian imagery to be "extremely witty," but he does agree with Collier that Congreve's usage is profane, for he says that the emphasis his essay places upon

the significance of religious imagery in the determination of the structure of values does not assume that this image pattern derives from a Christian conception of the action. It is rather the opposite: in Christian terms the application of these images is profane.[31]

In short, Professor Lyons finds *Love for Love* to be written from a "naturalistic perspective."

Now I know of no historical or biographical evidence that shows Congreve to have been atheistic or naturalistic or un-Christian in any way. At the same time, his plays abound with allusions to Providence and to an Eye or Hand of Heaven that intervenes in human affairs, and I see no reason to say these allusions do not derive from a Christian conception of his plots; indeed, to me his plots do not make much sense outside such a conception. I find nothing profane in having Providence brought on to direct the paultry concerns of the stage, or in having a young woman named Angelica act as the vicarious agent of Providence; after all, as Professor Stroup has shown, Providence, and vicars of Providence, had been active on the English stage quite some time before Congreve. In addition, as all providentialists of the Restoration would have argued, there is no event or person too paultry for Providence, for Its eye is on the sparrow (two of which, according to Matthew, are worth a bare farthing), and It numbers each hair on a multitude of human heads.

It seems to me that *Love for Love* presents us with a very witty dramatization of some basic Christian truths and paradoxes. On the stage of Congreve's world we see demonstrated those Christian ironies which affirm that the wicked and foolish do often fall into the pits they have dug for others or become snared in the works of their own hands. We find there superb illustrations of the paradox that the wisdom of this world may really be folly and madness, and that the foolishness of this world may finally lead to blessedness. We find also that a man no better than most, for all his errors and vices and mistakes and stumblings, may have his affections so worked upon and exercised by his "good angel" that he can be led to prove himself in an "utmost Tryal" of his virtue. I find, eccentric as it may seem, nothing profane or naturalistic in Congreve's dramatization of these matters. I rather find that he has entertained us well, and instructed us finely, and shown by the language and the actions of his plays that God's Providence intervenes not merely in the affairs of princes and principalities, but also in the kinds of affairs that take place in drawing rooms and at cocktail parties, at country clubs as well as in the walks of St. James's Park.

NOTES

1. The text cited throughout is that of Herbert Davis, *The Complete Plays of William Congreve* (Chicago: Univ. of Chicago Press, 1967).
2. I cite the 8th ed. of *A Body of Divinity: Or, the Sum and Substance of Christian Religion* (London, 1702), pp. 104–105.
3. Ἀγγελογραφία, sive Πνεύματα λειτυργικά, ΠΝΕΥΜΑΤΟΛΟΓΙΑ: *Or, A Discourse of Angels: Their Nature and Office, or Ministry* (London, 1701), p. 168.
4. *Microcosmos* (Lexington: Univ. of Kentucky Press, 1965), pp. 179–80.
5. Three recent dissertations explore dimensions of trial and testing in these works: Gail H. Compton, "The Metaphor of Conquest in Dryden's *The Conquest of Granada*," Diss. Univ. of Florida 1968; Marianne K. Mayo, "John VanBrugh's *The Relapse*: A Study of Its Meaning," Diss. Univ. of Florida 1968; and especially John Douglas Canfield, "Nicholas Rowe's Christian Tragedies," Diss. Univ. of Florida 1969.
6. See the title page of Saunders' *Discourse of Angels* and St. Thomas' *Summa Contra Gentiles*, III, 79. See also Don Cameron Allen, *The Star-Crossed Renaissance* (New York: Octagon Books, 1966), p. 28, where Pico della Mirandola is cited as arguing that "all authority has shown that God directs men through the angels."
7. See "Poetical Justice, the Contrivances of Providence, and the Works of William Congreve," *ELH*, 35 (1968), 540–65.
8. *The Critical Works of John Dennis*, ed. E. N. Hooker, I (Baltimore: The Johns Hopkins Press, 1939), 183.
9. *A Collection of Sermons* (London, 1713), II, 39.
10. Professor Stroup makes this point (*Microcosmos*, p. 32).
11. William Sherlock, *A Discourse Concerning the Divine Providence* (London, 1694), p. 48.

12. *The Critical Works of Thomas Rymer*, ed. Curt A. Zimansky (New Haven: Yale Univ. Press, 1956), p. 75.
13. John Tillotson, *Works* (London, 1748), III, 111.
14. Richard Kingston, *A Discourse on Divine Providence* (London, 1702), p. 146.
15. *Sermons Preached Upon Several Occasions* (London, 1678), p. 437.
16. I use the Loeb trans. of the Ovid. See *Artis Amatoriae*, ed. J. H. Mozley (Cambridge, Mass.: Harvard Univ. Press, 1939), I, 655–56: "neque enim lex aequior nulla est, / Quam necis artificis arte perire sua."
17. *Sermons Preached Upon Several Occasions*, p. 413.
18. Ibid., p. 424.
19. Davis, *Complete Plays* (p. 206), says the "character of Foresight and the use of the jargon of astrology owes something to Ben Jonson's *Alchemist* and perhaps also to [Thomas] Tomkins's *Albumazar*."
20. Pp. 93–94.
21. Ibid., p. 97.
22. London, 1698, pp. 142–43.
23. "Amendments of Mr. Collier's False and Imperfect Citations," in *The Mourning Bride, Poems, & Miscellanies*, ed. Bonamy Dobrée (London: Humphrey Milford, 1928), p. 453.
24. The "increasing frequency" of images of madness in the course of the play has been noted by Charles R. Lyons, "Congreve's Miracle of Love," *Criticism*, 6 (1964), 331–48. My own understanding of *Love for Love* is quite different from that of Norman Holland in ch. 14 of *The First Modern Comedies* (Cambridge, Mass.: Harvard Univ. Press, 1959).
25. Proverbs xiii.7.
26. S. W. Singer, *Researches Into the History of Playing Cards* (London, 1816), p. 259.
27. These are the words used by Congreve himself in defense of Valentine's character: "he has Generosity and Sincerity enough, in the last *Act*, to sacrifice every thing to his Love." See the "Amendments of Mr. Collier's False and Imperfect Citations," p. 452.
28. Saunders, pp. 266–67.
29. *Commentary on the Four Books of the Sentences*, II, xi, i.1, as trans. by Thomas Gilby in *St. Thomas Aquinas: Theological Texts* (London: Oxford Univ. Press, 1955), p. 91.
30. *A Short View*, p. 76.
31. "Congreve's Miracle of Love," p. 346.

University of Florida

BARBOUR'S *BRUCE* AND HARRY'S *WALLACE*:
THE QUESTION OF INFLUENCE

John Barbour's *Bruce* (1375) has often been cited as the most important source of Blind Harry's *Wallace* (ante 1488). George Neilson, for example, calls the *Wallace* "a rib out of Bruce's side,"[1] and J. T. T. Brown suggests that the scribe of the fifteenth-century manuscript containing both poems has taken elements from the *Bruce* and added them to the *Wallace*.[2] That such views should come to be accepted is not surprising. Both Harry and Barbour deal with the same period in Scottish history. Also, Harry directly cites Barbour's poem (e.g., VII.757–58).[3] That Harry knew the *Bruce* cannot be questioned, but the extent to which he used incidents from it in the *Wallace* and, equally important, the nature of Barbour's influence upon him have yet to be ascertained. It is with these problems that this study will be concerned.

We might begin by summarizing the major points of contact between the *Bruce* and the *Wallace* as given by Brown and Neilson. If they are correct, Harry has taken a passing allusion to the Barns of Ayr in the *Bruce* (IV.36–38)[4] and has expanded it into a wholly fabulous episode in the *Wallace* (VII.25ff., 205ff.). Longueville (*Wallace*, IX.86ff.; *Bruce*, IX.391) and Boyd (*Wallace*, III.52; *Bruce*, II.244), companions of Bruce, become followers of Wallace. Bruce's battle of Loudon Hill is a victory for Wallace (*Wallace*, III.99ff.; *Bruce*, VIII. 207). Crystal of Seton, an adherent of Bruce, becomes a supporter of Wallace (*Wallace*, VII.1276; *Bruce*, II.243). Malcolm, Earl of Lennox, an opportunist at best, according to the historians, is praised effusively in the *Bruce* (II.482ff.); he is treated in the same way in

19

the *Wallace* (IV.156ff.). Aymer Walling, who was English, not Scottish, and who had no land in Scotland until Edward I gave him Bothwell,[5] is one of Bruce's adversaries in Barbour's poem; in the *Wallace* he is called a "fals traytour strange" (III.261) and a "suttell terand knycht" (VI.273). Bruce's bishop, Sinclair of Dunkeld, is appropriated by Harry (*Wallace*, XI.1417; *Bruce*, XVI.575). The use of a sleuth-hound is described similarly in the *Bruce* (VI.36ff., 475ff.) and in the *Wallace* (V.23ff.). Furthermore, Harry attributes to Wallace an invasion of England which reached York, when in fact the only Scottish invasion to penetrate so deeply was led by Bruce in 1322, during the reign of Edward II.[6]

What should be noted first of all is that many of these "borrowings" cannot be proven. It is not unlikely that sources of information available to Barbour and Harry have since been lost; conversely, many of the documents at our disposal, especially those written by the English, were unknown to the Scottish poets. It is unreasonable to accuse Harry of "borrowing" or of deliberate historical tampering simply because his account of an event (e.g., the Barns of Ayr) is fuller than Barbour's. The appropriation of Bruce's bishop and of his victory of Loudon Hill is perhaps the result of confusion on Harry's part. As for those supporters of Bruce who become part of Wallace's force in Harry's poem, we know so little about their activities that it is inadvisable to claim that because they served Bruce they cannot have served Wallace earlier. In the depictions of Lennox and Walling, however, Harry seems to be influenced by Barbour; the sleuth-hound incidents are very similar and also seem to indicate Barbour's influence on Harry.

In ordrr to ascertain the extent of Harry's indebtedness to Barbour, we might begin by examining the personal names and poetic allusions in the respective poems. Such an examination reveals several significant facts. Although, as might be expected, several of the more important characters, like Percy and Comyn, appear in both poems, Wallace is never mentioned by Barbour. Furthermore, those characters who are among Wallace's closest compatriots—John Blair, Thomas Gray, John Graham, Grimsby, Tom Halliday, Kneland, Edward Little, Andrew de Moray, and Steven of Ireland—are likewise ignored by Barbour, as are Wallace's personal enemies—Corspatrik, Hesilrig, Hugh de Cressingham, and John Menteith. Since Barbour fails to mention Wallace, he need not mention Wallace's beloved, Marion Bradfute. These characters are the chief personages in Harry's poem; it is difficult to find twenty consecutive lines in which none of them is mentioned. Thus it would appear that in regard to the characters upon whom Harry is to concentrate most of his attention, he is not very much indebted to Barbour.

But what of Harry's manner? Is he influenced by Barbour stylistically? The answer again seems to be negative. Barbour, the Archdeacon of Aberdeen, fills his narrative with Biblical allusions (David, Jeremiah, Joel, Laban, Philistines, Babylon, Judas, Judas Machabeus, Samuel, Satan, Isaiah); Harry mentions only Samson and Herod. Similarly, Barbour's poem contains many learned references to medieval and classical authors and to characters both real and fictive from antiquity (Adrastus, Aristotle, Fabricius, Hannibal, Eteocles and Polynices, Aristaeus, Dionysius, Cato, Dares, Dictes, Pyrrhus, Scipio the Younger, Tydeus, Ptolemy) but only one allusion to a pagan god or goddess (i.e., Minerva, IV.263).[7] In all of Barbour's poem there is not a single astrological allusion.[8]

In the *Wallace*, on the other hand, references to antiquity are of the vaguest and most general nature imaginable. Harry mentions Achilles, Hector, Thebes, Troy, Alexander the Great, and Julius Caesar; these names hardly suggest any specialized knowledge on Harry's part. His pantheon, however, is more nearly complete than is Barbour's. Harry refers to Bacchus, Juno, Jupiter, Venus, and Saturn, both as deities and as astrological powers. He also speaks of Aries, the Bull (Taurus), Cancer, Capricorn, Luna, Pisces, and Titan. If these astrological allusions can be thought of as being part of the medieval poet's stock of commonplaces, even more so are names like Flora, Zephirus, and Phoebus. None of these is used by Barbour, but all appear in the *Wallace* (e.g., VIII.1187; V.8; IX.23).

It should be clear by now that whatever substantive influence Barbour exerted on Harry is limited to specific incidents and character portrayals and does not permeate the *Wallace* as a whole. Part of the difference between the two poems may be accounted for by Barbour's vocation, although it has sometimes been suggested that Harry, too, was a cleric.[9] As an archdeacon, Barbour would be expected to eschew all references to pagan deities (including Phoebus, Zephirus, and Flora) and to originally pagan systems of divination, like astrology. Unlike Harry,[10] Barbour cannot possibly be subject to Chaucerian influence. His poem is therefore less consciously poetical and much less stylized than Harry's.

The relationship between the two poems is, I believe, clarified if we examine Harry's portrayal of Robert Bruce in the *Wallace*.[11] In the *Bruce*, Barbour had depicted his hero as a model of chivalry, courage, and wisdom. In the *Wallace*, Bruce is a totally different character.

There are several references to King Robert and the *Bruce* through-out the *Wallace*, but it is not until Book VII that these references begin to form a recognizable pattern. In line 755 Harry speaks of "Brucis wer" (this, as the context indicates, refers to Edward I's in-vasion of Scotland, in which Bruce and his father fought on the side of the English king against Wallace) and says, in lines 757–58,

> Mencione off Bruce is oft in Wallace buk;
> To fend his rycht full mekill payne he tuk.

It is difficult to interpret these lines as anything but ironic. There is no mention of Wallace in *"Brucis buk,"* but the "rycht" Harry speaks of, which could refer either to Bruce's claim to the Scottish throne or to his lands in England, makes the comparison to Wallace invidious. In a previous passage Harry had said,

> All worthi men, that has gud witt to waille,
> Be war that yhe with myss deyme nocht my taille.
> Perchance ye say, that Bruce he was none sik.
> He was als gud, quhat deid was to assaill,
> As off his handis, and baulder in battaill.
> Bot Bruce was knawin weyll ayr off this kynrik;
> For he had rycht, we call no man him lik.
> Bot Wallace thriss this kynrik conquest haile,
> In Ingland fer socht battaill on that rik.
> (II.351–59)

W. H. Schofield, who sees this passage as posing a question similar to that asked by Chaucer's Franklin, says, "Bruce was indeed the 'heir' of the kingdom and had the 'right' but Wallace was 'baulder in bat-taill' and thrice saved the realm by his might. . . ."[12]

When Harry next speaks of Bruce and Wallace, he says that Wal-lace has "lawta and trouth" and implies that Bruce is lacking in these qualities.

> Thai [the English] gert him [Bruce] trow
>   that Wallace was rabell,
> And thocht to tak the kynryk to hym sel.
> Ful fals thai war, and evir ȝeit has beyn;
> Lawta and trouth was ay in Wallace seyn;
> To fend the rycht all that he tuk on hand,
> And thocht to bryng the Bruce fre till his land.
> (VIII.141–46)

The difference between Bruce's "rycht" and Wallace's is obvious.

Harry tells us that Bruce fought "contrai his natiff men" (VIII. 341), and he gives Wallace's reaction:

> Off Brucis deid he was agrewit far mar
> Than all the laiff that day at semblit thar.
> (VIII.243–44)

Instead of leading his countrymen against the English invaders, Bruce "sa cruelly wrocht [that] . . . throuch strenth off hand feill Scottis he gert de" (VIII.259–60). Throughout the remainder of the poem (VIII.639–44, 1611–13; IX.1872–73; X.205–16, 252–53, 357–60, 405–407), Bruce is presented in the worst possible light, until finally Wallace, in a face to face meeting with Bruce on the banks of the Carron (X.442ff.), points out to him the tragic consequences of his defection. Bruce is converted to Scotland's cause and breaks his bond with Edward, whereupon Wallace transfers his allegiance from John Baliol to Bruce (X.595ff.) in the hope that Scotland can yet be saved.

Schofield says, "The spirit of hate animates the *Wallace* throughout, and no power on earth can cast it out, so as to make its body wholly clean."[13] Schofield here is speaking of Harry's hatred of the English which is reflected in his characterization of Wallace. I believe that this hatred extends either to Barbour, to the *Bruce*, or to both. Harry does everything in his power to discredit Bruce; whether his animosity is personal or is representative of a desire on Harry's part to supplant Bruce with Wallace and the *Bruce* with the *Wallace*, in public esteem, is conjectural. That this hatred exists, however, is apparent, as when Harry acidly remarks,

> For my labour na man hecht me reward;
> Na charge I had off king nor othir lord[.]
> (XI.1434–35)

Although Harry had no reward for the *Wallace*, Barbour was paid handsomely for the *Bruce*.[14]

If there is yet some doubt concerning Harry's attitude towards Barbour, there is no ambivalence whatever in his portrayal of Bruce. In the *Wallace* we see Bruce as a vacillating, opportunistic individual whose immaturity and insouciance are shocking; with the very fate of Scotland in the balance, Bruce laughs at Wallace's "ernystfulnas" (X.497). Harry's attempts to establish the "suthfastnes" (e.g., VII. 917) of his narrative take on additional significance when we consider his depiction of Bruce.

There are no extant historical authorities who substantiate Harry's portrayal of Bruce. History tells us only that Bruce fought for Edward I against Wallace. If Harry's poem were accepted as fact—and he constantly asks for just such acceptance—the inevitable result would be the removal of Barbour and Bruce from national esteem and their replacement with Harry and Wallace.

Harry's virulent hatred for the English cannot be denied. That he considered Bruce's defection to Edward an act of treason is likely. By making Wallace instrumental in persuading Bruce to join the Scottish patriots, Harry gives Wallace a share in Bruce's later greatness. Apparently Harry's disdain for Bruce included King Robert's biographer, John Barbour, as the ironic references to Barbour in the *Wallace* indicate. The comparison of Bruce and Wallace is inevitable, but in his poem Harry heavily weights the scales. We must remember that when Wallace berates Bruce (X.442ff.) it is with Harry's words, and, if the author of the *Wallace* has not succeeded in completely discrediting the hero of Brannockburn, it is not for want of effort.

NOTES

1. "Blind Harry's Wallace," *E&S*, 1 (1910), 98.
2. *The "Wallace" and the "Bruce" Restudied* (Bonn: P. Hanstein, 1900).
3. This and all future references to the *Wallace* are to *The Actis and Deidis of . . . Schir William Wallace . . .* , ed. James Moir, *STS*, OS 6, 7, 17 (Edinburgh and London: Blackwood & Sons, 1889); hereafter cited as *Wallace*.
4. This and all future references to the *Bruce* are to *The Bruce . . .* , ed. W. W. Skeat, *STS*, OS 31, 32, 33 (Edinburgh and London: Blackwood & Sons, 1895); hereafter cited as *Bruce*.
5. *Wallace*, p. 395n.
6. Neilson, p. 104.
7. See *Bruce*, pp. lxvi–vii.
8. Barbour inveighs against astrology (IV.674) and necromancy (IV.747), yet he seems to believe in the fulfillment of old prophecies (IV.639, 772; X.740; XV.292).
9. See especially James Paterson, *Wallace, the Hero of Scotland* (London: W. P. Nimmo, 1876). Harry himself seems to deny this (V.233–34).
10. See W. W. Skeat, "Chaucer and Blind Harry," *The Modern Language Quarterly*, 1, 2 (1897), 49–50. (This journal, printed in London from 1897 to 1904, should not be confused with the American journal published at the University of Washington.)
11. It is probable that during his career Wallace found arrayed against him three men all named Robert Bruce. The youngest of these, the future king of Scotland, assisted his father in the service of Edward I; King Robert's grandfather had made his claim to the Scottish throne in 1290. From the nature of the references to Bruce in the *Wallace*, it seems that Harry is unaware of these distinctions.
12. *Mythical Bards and "The Life of William Wallace"* (Cambridge, Mass.: Harvard Univ. Press, 1920), pp. 130–31.
13. Ibid., p. 167.
14. See *Bruce*, pp. xxxi–vi.

Ohio State University

ROBERT J. BLANCH

THE SYMBOLIC GIFTS OF THE SHEPHERDS
IN THE *SECUNDA PASTORUM*

With the resurgence of scholarly interest in medieval drama within the past thirty years, the Wakefield *Secunda Pastorum* has received unprecedented attention. Viewing the *Secunda Pastorum* as the efflorescence of the medieval miracle play, modern critics have justly praised this Wakefield drama for its organic unity, an artistic fusion of the comic and the serious;[1] its skillful use of folklore sources in the depiction of Mak the sheep-stealer;[2] its rich panoply of symbolism and paradox;[3] and its subtle ironic overtones.[4] Strangely enough, although many features of the *Secunda Pastorum* have been illuminated by modern scholarship, only token attention has been given to the gifts of the shepherds. With perhaps two exceptions,[5] critical interpretations of the gifts have been superficial, irrelevant, or one-sided.[6] The purpose of this paper, then, is to show that the gifts of the shepherds in the *Secunda Pastorum* are symbolic offerings—gifts rooted in the lore of the Epiphany as suggested by the scriptural account of the Presentation of the Magi (Matt. ii.1–12). To illustrate this symbolic affinity between the gifts of the shepherds and the Epiphany, I shall examine, first, the background of the Epiphany, especially the traditional interpretations of the gifts of the Magi, and second, the symbolic meanings underlying the gifts of the shepherds.

According to medieval Christian tradition, the feast of the Epiphany, "an Apparition or Manifestation"[7] of Christ's divinity and glory, commemorates three events in the life of Christ[8]—the Adoration of the Magi, the baptism of Christ by St. John,[9] and Christ's transformation of water into wine at the marriage feast of Cana.[10] Since the

25

Epiphany is frequently called Theophany, suggesting the appearance of each member of the Trinity at the baptism of Christ—the Father in His voice, the Son in the flesh, and the Holy Spirit in the form of a dove[11]—the Epiphany celebration of this particular event in Christ's life gains a special significance.

In traditional accounts of the Adoration scene, the focal point of this discussion, the Wise Men are called Magi because of the greatness of their knowledge[12]—knowledge which springs from occult powers frequently attributed to the priestly caste in ancient Persia. Conventionally depicted as oriental kings,[13] at least from the fifth century on,[14] the Magi signify the Gentiles:[15]

on this day [Epiphany] our Infant King, so soon after His nativity, was revealed by the guiding star to the first-fruits of the Gentiles.[16]

Although the Gospel of Matthew and the Apocrypha contain no specific references to the number of Magi, the Church Fathers eventually set the number at three,[17] perhaps to correspond with the three gifts of the Magi (Matt. ii.11).[18] Following an old custom which demanded that no one should appear before God or a king without a gift in his hand,[19] the Magi thus offer their gifts to the Christ-child.

Melchior,[20] the first of the Magi, is conventionally represented in medieval iconography as an old man with white hair and a long beard.[21] Declaring Christ to be a true king, the King of the Jews,[22] he offers gold, an appropriate symbol of Christ's regal power:[23]

Aurum ei offertur, dum rex omnium et principium postrae redemptionis creditur.[24]

Although Melchior's gift is ordinarily interpreted as a fitting tribute to a king, gold also suggests wisdom,[25] faith,[26] love,[27] and the human soul.[28] When such meanings are assigned to gold, they represent what human beings ought to offer to Christ the King.

The second Wise Man, Caspar (Gaspar), is generally depicted as a young, beardless man with a ruddy complexion.[29] Coming to adore Him as the true God and Creator of all things,[30] Caspar presents frankincense to the Christ-child. Identified with the priesthood,[31] especially with the priestly sacrifice of Christ for man's redemption,[32] frankincense suggests His divine majesty.[33] Since frankincense emits an aroma when it is burned, this gift signifies for humanity the sweetness of a holy life[34] and the need for prayer and devotion to God.[35]

Balthazar (Balthasar), the last of the Magi, is traditionally portrayed as a brown-skinned man with a full beard.[36] Associated with the Biblical phrase suggesting Christ's humanity, "Where is He who is born?"[37] Balthazar offers myrrh to Christ. Often used in embalming the bodies of the dead,[38] myrrh symbolizes Christ's mortality—His ultimate death and burial for the salvation of man.[39] On a tropological level of interpretation, the level of moral instruction for mankind, the bitter myrrh is a penitential sign of mortification of the flesh, for penance and self-denial protect man's soul from the corruption of evil.[40]

The foregoing discussion of the complex of symbols drawn from the Epiphany tradition discloses the substructure of the final scene of the *Secunda Pastorum*. Before I examine the significance of each gift in the *Secunda Pastorum*, I will trace briefly some general parallels between the Magi and the shepherds in the Wakefield pageant. Although the Gospel account of the Adoration of the Shepherds (Luke ii.8–20) fails to record the number of shepherds present at the crib in Bethlehem and to specify any gifts that they offered to the Christ-child, the traditional analogy between the Magi and the shepherds prompted the inclusion of three shepherds and three gifts in the *Secunda Pastorum*.[41] Furthermore, the rustics in the *Secunda Pastorum*, like the Wise Men, are associated with the Trinity,[42] and the symbolic gifts they offer are similar in significance to the gifts of the Magi.[43] As I will point out later, the gifts of the shepherds also are identified with the three events in Christ's life commemorated on the feast of the Epiphany (see above).

In the final tableau of the *Secunda Pastorum*, the crib scene, the doctrine of the Trinity is evoked when the first shepherd greets the Christ-child.[44] Acknowledging the Infant Babe's beauty and purity, Coll addresses Him as "maker" (711),[45] a term that suggests the creative energy of God the Father, and alludes to Christ's destruction of Satan's power through the Redemption (712–13). Coll then offers the Infant Jesus a "bob of cherys" (718), a gift commonly associated with Christ in religious art and in literature. Erwin Panofsky, for example, reproduces two paintings which employ the cherry motif in connection with the Holy Family. In the first picture, Joseph takes respite from his reading to observe Mary nursing the Christ-child while on a table in front of them stands a tray of fruits containing grapes, an apple, a pomegranate, and a cherry.[46] The second painting focuses on Joseph reading Holy Scripture while Mary nurses Jesus; the fingers of Mary's left hand touch a bob of cherries on a table.[47] In religious art, whenever a cherry is depicted in the hands of the Christ-child, it is identified with the joys of the blessed in heaven, for "the red, sweet fruit of the cherry symbolizes the sweetness of character which is derived from good works."[48]

Additional evidence which serves to link the bob of cherries with the Christ-child may be found in medieval legend and literature. Since the cherry tree is an evergreen, a symbol of fertility within the harsh season of winter, the traditional Christmas miracle of the offering of cherries is normally associated with death and resurrection and represents "a parallel in the world of nature to the miraculous birth of Christ."[49] Furthermore, cherries are identified with the blood of Christ, especially the blood shed by Christ during the Passion and Crucifixion. In one fifteenth-century medieval poem, "Dispute between Mary and the Cross," the anonymous author notes that Jesus shed His first blood at the Circumcision for Man's salvation: "Dropes rede as ripe cherrees . . . from his flesshe gan laue" (219).[50] Since Christ's Circumcision is a prototype of His redemptive sacrifice, the connection between cherries and the Crucifixion is clearly established.

Perhaps the most fertile source of evidence for a symbolic affinity between cherries and the Christ-child is the traditional "Cherry Tree Carol" (ca. sixteenth century). An offshoot of the legend in the Gospel of Pseudo-Matthew concerning a palm tree which bent down in humble obedience to Christ's command during the flight into Egypt,[51] the "Cherry Tree Carol" is set against the backdrop of Mary's pregnancy.[52] Suddenly craving cherries "So red as any blood" (8), a constant refrain in the poem, Mary asks Joseph to pick her some. Joseph, however, unkindly suggests that the man who made her pregnant should pluck the cherries. Then the unborn Christ, speaking from Mary's womb, orders the tallest cherry tree to bow down so that His mother may gather some cherries. Although cherries, in this instance, are clearly identified with Christ's blood shed during the Crucifixion, another version of the "Cherry Tree Carol" suggests additional layers of meaning for the cherry motif. In this particular version, cited by William Hone,[53] the poet notes that Mary "shall gather cherries / By one, by two, by three," perhaps an oblique allusion to the Trinity. This version also focuses on Christ's divinity, the Eucharist, and His death and resurrection.

Furthermore, the cherry-tree incident assumes dramatic form in *The Birth of Christ*, Pageant XV (Cotton MS.) in the *Ludus Coventriae* cycle (ca. fifteenth century).[54] In this particular play, the only pageant in any cycle of medieval drama to depict the miracle of the cherry tree, Mary asks Joseph if he knows the name of a particular tree standing on a hill. After Joseph replies, " . . . it is clepyd A chery tre / In tyme of ȝere · ȝe myght ffede ȝow þeron ȝour ffylle" (25–26), terms suggesting fertility and abundance, Mary marvels at the sudden appearance of cherries on the tree. Once Mary reveals her craving for cherries, Joseph again suggests, as in the "Cherry Tree Carol," that the man who made her pregnant should pluck some cherries for her. Unlike the incident depicted in the "Cherry Tree Carol," however, Mary's prayer to God rather than Christ's speech from her womb impels the tree to bow down before her. The incident concludes with Joseph's awareness of having "offendyd [his] god in trinyte" because of his harsh words to Mary.

Rooted in Christian iconography, legend, and literary tradition, the bob of cherries offered by the first shepherd thus suggests Christ's redemptive sacrifice, the Eucharist, a source of new spiritual life for mankind, and His triumphant Easter Resurrection. Since cherries are clearly identified with such symbolic meanings, Coll's gift to the Christ-child mirrors in significance Balthazar's offering of myrrh in the Epiphany tradition, for myrrh underscores Christ's ultimate death and burial for the spiritual fruitfulness of man (see above). Furthermore, the first shepherd's gift is linked symbolically with the third event in Christ's life commemorated on the feast of the Epiphany—Christ's transformation of water into wine at the marriage feast of Cana. The miracle of Cana, a prototype of the Transubstantiation of Eucharistic wine into Christ's redeeming blood, foreshadows Christ's ultimate death on the Cross. Finally, cherries as fruit represent an especially appropriate symbol for Christ because the unborn infant is described as the fruit of Mary's womb (Luke i.42).[55] Even the Magi, present at the Nativity, are usually termed "the first-fruits of the Gentiles" (see above).

Recognizing the Christ-child's nobility and sovereignty, the second shepherd greets Him as "sufferan sauyoure" (719) and as "full of fauoure, that made all of noght" (721), phraseology suggesting the creative power of God the Father. Gib presents Jesus with a bird, a gift invested with profound significance in the Middle Ages. In early Christian art, the bird was a symbol of the winged soul,[56] "blanchie par la pénitence ou purifiée par la mort."[57] Later on, artists employed the bird form to signify the lofty aspirations of the human spirit, man's spiritual thought which soars beyond material bounds.[58] In medieval iconography, the Christ-child is commonly depicted as holding a bird in His hand[59] because the bird is an emblem of His divinity. For the Church Fathers, also, the bird is identified with Christ's divinity because the earthly body which He assumed rose into the air at the Ascension, the final proof of Christ's divine majesty.[60] Whenever the bird assumes the form of a dove, it represents the Holy Ghost, the creative spirit of love which appears at the Annunciation and at the baptism of Christ.[61] Inasmuch as the bird offered by Gib signifies the divine nature of the Lamb as God the Son, this gift is associated with the frankincense of Caspar—that Epiphany offering which suggests the godhead of Christ and the sweetness of holiness.[62]

Daw, the third shepherd in the *Secunda Pastorum*, hails the Infant Babe as "derlyng dere, full of Godhede" (728), thus attesting to His divinity, and requests Christ to "Put furth thy dall!" (733). Offering the Christ-child a ball, Daw advises Him to "play the withall, / And go to the tenys" (735–36). Since the tennis ball is an orb, a conventional symbol of perfection and eternity, its spherical shape is identified with God the Father, the omnipotent agent in the work of Creation.[63] When the ball is placed in the hands of the Christ-child, it signifies the world,[64] specifically His regal dignity and sovereignty over the earth.[65] This symbolic affinity between the ball and the Holy Infant is clearly suggested in numerous representations of the Nativity in medieval iconography. Philip Nelson, for example, reproduces one alabaster panel depicting the Christ-child with an orb in His left hand.[66] Another alabaster carving, also reproduced by Nelson, illustrates the Adoration of the Magi (museum at Dieppe), a scene in which the Holy Infant is shown as resting His feet upon an orb.[67] Perhaps the best iconographical example of the ball as an emblem of Christ's imperial dignity and sovereignty is the *Quicumque vult*, a fourteenth-century English miniature which depicts Christ enthroned with a sphere in His left hand.[68]

Additional evidence underscoring the connection between the symbolic ball and the Christ-child may be found in English social customs. Tennis, a popular game in France throughout the fourteenth and fifteenth centuries, was well known in England by the end of the fourteenth century. Since tennis courts were expensive to construct, tennis became known as a royal sport, for only kings and noblemen could afford to play the game.[69] With such suggestions of royalty and nobility attached to tennis, Daw's gift is thus a tribute to Christ's imperial power. In this particular context, the third shepherd's tennis ball evokes the Epiphany tradition, for Melchior's offering of gold to the Christ-child is conventionally interpreted as an emblem of Christ as the King of Kings.

From this examination of the final tableau of the *Secunda Pastorum*, it seems clear that the gifts of the shepherds are artistically woven into the symbolic texture of the play. Although it must be granted that the gifts, homely baby gifts on the most literal level of interpretation, characterize the rustic donors, even more significantly such offerings complement symbolically the gifts of the Magi. Since the Magi traditionally signify the Gentiles and the apex of human wisdom and regal dignity, whereas the shepherds represent the Jews and the humble peasantry, together they constitute "a symbol of the homage of mankind to the Incarnate God."[70] Furthermore, the shepherds in the *Secunda Pastorum*, like the Wise Men of the Epiphany, suggest the doctrine of the Trinity,[71] and the shepherds' offerings point toward the eternal truth of the Divine Plan. These gifts—the bob of cherries, a form of vegetation; the bird, a representative of animal life; and the tennis ball, an inanimate object—emphasize the miraculous reality and variety of God's creation. Like the play itself, the shepherds' gifts also represent a timeless fusion of rural England of the fifteenth century and the historical birth of Christ.

As a pageant designed for presentation on Corpus Christi, the feast-day commemorating the Real Presence of Christ in the Eucharist, the *Secunda Pastorum* thus underscores the eternal fact of Christ's sacrifice for the redemption of mankind. With this ritual representation of the Crucifixion in mind, the first shepherd's bob of cherries, with its suggestion of the Son of Man's imminent death, plays a singular role in the *Secunda Pastorum*. This gift, a symbolic adumbration of the Messiah and His function in man's salvation, is identified ultimately with the spiritual life and joy flowing from the Incarnation. That the three shepherds in this Wakefield pageant have embraced Christ as the true fount of grace and delight may be clearly illustrated by their final speeches:

> *1 Pastor.* What grace we haue fun!
> *2 Pastor.* Com furth; now ar we won!
> *3 Pastor.* To syng ar we bun—
>   Let take on loft!   (751–54)

The shepherds' cold preoccupation with the flux of worldly events— their unhappiness over the weather, social injustice, and marital difficulties—has melted into an awareness of the miracle of Christ's birth. They have been truly illuminated by the inner radiance and warmth of the Lamb of God.

NOTES

1. On the organic unity of the *Secunda Pastorum*, see Homer A. Watt, "The Dramatic Unity of the *Secunda Pastorum*," in *Essays and Studies in Honor of Carleton Brown* (New York: New York Univ. Press, 1940), pp. 158–66; Francis J. Thompson, "Unity in *The Second Shepherds' Tale*," *MLN*, 64 (1949), 302–306; Donald F. Peel, "The Allegory in *Secunda Pastorum*,"

Northwest Missouri State College Studies, 24, No. 4 (1960), 3–11; and William M. Manly, "Shepherds and Prophets: Religious Unity in the Towneley *Secunda Pastorum,*" *PMLA,* 78 (1963), 151–55.

2. R. C. Cosbey, "The Mak Story and Its Folklore Analogues," *Speculum,* 20 (1945), 310–17.

3. Joseph A. Longo, "Symmetry and Symbolism in the *Secunda Pastorum,*" *Nottingham Mediaeval Studies,* 13 (1969), 65–85. On the use of paradox, Margery M. Morgan, " 'High Fraud': Paradox and Double-Plot in the English Shepherds' Plays," *Speculum,* 39 (1964), 676–89.

4. Eugene E. Zumwalt, "Irony in the Towneley *Shepherds' Plays,*" *Research Studies of the State College of Washington,* 26 (1958), 37–53.

5. Eugene B. Cantelupe and Richard Griffith, "The Gifts of the Shepherds in the Wakefield *Secunda Pastorum*: An Iconographical Interpretation," *MS,* 28 (1966), 328–35; and Longo, pp. 65–85.

6. See, for example, Eleanor Prosser, *Drama and Religion in the English Mystery Plays: A Re-Evaluation,* Stanford Studies in Lang. and Lit., No. 23 (Stanford, Calif.: Stanford Univ. Press, 1961). Miss Prosser views the gifts of the shepherds to the Christ-child as a demonstration of "carefully controlled humor adding tenderness and intimacy to the adoration" (p. 82). Other critical accounts meticulously avoid explication of the gifts and merely establish the shepherds' naiveté in offering these homely gifts.

7. St. Bernard, "On Imitating Herod and the Magi and on the Virtues Commended in the Different Manifestations," in *St. Bernard's Sermons for the Seasons and Principal Festivals of the Year,* trans. a Priest of Mount Melleray, II (Dublin: Browne and Nolan, 1923), 22.

8. See William Durandus, *Rationale divinorum officiorum* VI.xvi (Naples: J. Dura, 1859), 426–30; Ludolphus de Saxonia, *Vita Jesu Christi,* ed. L. M. Rigollot, 9th ed. (Rome: Libraria S. Congreg. De Propaganda Fide, 1870), I, No. 1, pp. 102–103; and Emile Mâle, *The Gothic Image: Religious Art in France of the Thirteenth Century,* trans. from 3rd ed. by Dora Nussey (1913; rpt. New York: Harper, 1958), p. 180. For a fourth event celebrated on the feast of the Epiphany, the miracle of the loaves and fishes, see Ch. 14 in Jacques (Jacobus) de Voragine, *La Légende Dorée,* trans. Teodor de Wyzewa (Paris: Perrin et cie, 1925), p. 73.

9. For the tradition that the baptism of Christ took place on the anniversary of the Epiphany, see *Speculum Sacerdotale,* ed. Edward H. Weatherly, *EETS,* OS 200 (1936), 19: "And in the same day a xxx.ti yere that he was so worschipped of the kynges it is red that he was baptysed of John Baptist in the Flom Jordan, where the Holy Gost come vpon hym in the lyckenes of a doufe." See also the gospel for the octave of Epiphany (Matt. iii.13–17) in *The Sarum Missal,* ed. J. W. Legg (Oxford: Clarendon Press, 1916), p. 39.

10. Durandus, p. 427. Alluding to patristic commentary and to the Epiphany Mass of the *Missale Gothicum,* Julius Baum, "Symbolic Representations of the Eucharist," in *Pagan and Christian Mysteries,* ed. Joseph Campbell and trans. Ralph Manheim and R. F. C. Hull (New York: Harper, 1963), p. 75, interprets the miracle of Cana as a prototype of the transformation of wine into Christ's blood in the Consecration of the Mass—the daily re-enactment of Christ's redemptive sacrifice.

11. See Durandus, p. 427; and Voragine, p. 73. In a 15th-century ME poem on the Epiphany, "Illuminare Jherusalem," all three persons of the Trinity are mentioned in the context of Christ's baptism; cf. Richard L. Greene, ed., *A Selection of English Carols* (Oxford: Clarendon Press, 1962), pp. 90–91, no. 31.

12. Ludolphus, p. 101.
13. See Voragine, pp. 73–74; Durandus, p. 426; and "In epiphania Domini," in *Old English Homilies of the Twelfth Century*, ed. Richard Morris, *EETS*, OS 53 (London, 1873), 45. According to Jules Lutz and P. Perdrizet, the modern editors of *Speculum Humanae Salvationis* (Mulhouse: E. Meiniger, 1907), a 14th-century Latin work, the Magi (p. 195) were transformed into kings (not in Matthew) because the Church Fathers wanted to apply to them the words of the Psalmist: "Tibi offerent reges munera" (Ps. lxvii. 30); and "reges Tharsis et insulae munera offerent" (Ps. lxxi.10).
14. Hardin Craig, *English Religious Drama of the Middle Ages* (Oxford: Clarendon Press, 1955), p. 51.
15. Mâle, *Gothic Image*, pp. 180–81; Ludolphus, p. 101; and *Speculum Humanae Salvationis*, IX.20–21.
16. St. Bernard, p. 22. Durandus, p. 426, points out that the star was the Holy Spirit who afterwards descended in the form of a dove on the baptized Christ.
17. Origen was the first Church Father to speak of three Magi; cf. *In Genesim. Homilia* XIV.iii (*PG*, XII, 238). Other writers following Origen's interpretation include Durandus, p. 426; Voragine, p. 73; and *Speculum Humanae Salvationis*, IX.20–21.
18. Karl Young, *The Drama of the Medieval Church* (Oxford, Oxford Univ. Press, 1951), II, 31; and G. McN. Rushforth, *Medieval Christian Imagery* (Oxford: Clarendon Press, 1936), p. 284.
19. See *A Stanzaic Life of Christ*, ed. Frances A. Foster, *EETS*, OS 166 (London, 1926), 68; and Ludolphus, p. 108. Ludolphus maintains (p. 108), further, that the offering of gifts by the Magi served to unveil the divine mysteries, especially the mystery of the Trinity: "hoc [offering of gifts by the Magi] tamen divina inspiratione est factum, ut aliquid mysterii muneribus demonstrarent, et fidem suam mysticis rebus profiterentur: tum scilicet Trinitatis fidem et mysterium revelantes, et in Christo Trinitatem adorantes."
20. For the traditional names of the Magi, see Pseudo-Bede, "Excerptiones Patrum, Collectanea" (*PL*, XCIV, 541). A convenient translation of this part of the "Collectanea" is found in Emile Mâle, *Religious Art* (New York: Pantheon, 1949), p. 81.
21. M. D. Anderson, *The Imagery of British Churches* (London: J. Murray, 1955), p. 107.
22. Denis the Carthusian, *Enarratio in Evangelium Secundum Matthaeum* II.iv, *Opera omnia* (Monstrolii: Typis Cartusiae Sanctae Mariae de Pratis, 1900), XI, 22; and Ludolphus, p. 108.
23. See Irenaeus, *Adversus Haereses*, III.ix (*PG*, VII, 870–71); Walafrid Strabo, *Glossa ordinaria* (*PL*, CXIV, 75); Durandus, p. 427; and *Stanzaic Life*, p. 69. The liturgy was greatly influenced by symbolic interpretations of the gifts of the Magi. In the *Sarum Missal*, p. 37, the procession for the feast of the Epiphany includes the following explication of gold: "In auro ut ostendatur regis potencia." For gold as royalty in medieval iconography, see Louis Réau, *Iconographie de l'art chrétien*, II, 2 (Paris: Presses Universitaires de France, 1955), 241. For the traditional homiletic application, see *Old English Homilies*, p. 45, and *Speculum Sacerdotale*, p. 20.
24. Honorius of Autun, *Speculum Ecclesiae* (*PL*, CLXXII, 845).
25. Denis the Carthusian, XI, 25; and Hugh of St. Cher on Matt. ii.11, *Opera Omnia in universum Vetus et Novum Testamentum* (Venice: Nicolaum Pezzana, 1732), VI, fol. 7^n.
26. Ludolphus, p. 109.
27. *Stanzaic Life*, p. 70; Voragine, pp. 75–76; and Denis the Carthusian, XI,

25. See also *Speculum Humanae Salvationis*, IX.21: "Aurum, quia in valore suo praecellit omne metallum, / Significat caritatem, quae mater est omnium virtutum."

28. Ludolphus, p. 109.

29. Pseudo-Bede, XCIV, 541.

30. Ludolphus, pp. 108–109; and Denis the Carthusian, XI, 22.

31. Ludolphus, p. 108; *Sarum Missal*, p. 37; and *Stanzaic Life*, p. 69. For a reference in medieval drama to frankincense as priesthood, see the remarks of the second King (ll. 706–708) in *The Pageant of the Shearmen and Taylors*, in *Two Coventry Corpus Christi Plays*, ed. Hardin Craig, *EETS*, ES 87, 2nd ed. (London, 1957), 24–25.

32. Durandus, p. 427; *Speculum Humanae Salvationis*, IX.21; and Honorius, CLXXII, 845.

33. *Glossa ordinaria*, CXIV, 75.

34. Denis the Carthusian, XI, 25.

35. Hugh of St. Cher, VI, fol. 7^n; *Old English Homilies*, p. 45; and *Stanzaic Life*, p. 70.

36. Pseudo-Bede, XCIV, 541.

37. Denis the Carthusian, XI, 22; and Ludolphus, p. 108.

38. *Speculum Humane Salvationis*, IX.21; and Réau, II, 2, pp. 241–42.

39. St. Bernard, p. 15; *Glossa ordinaria*, CXIV, 75; Honorius, CLXXII, 845; *Cursor Mundi*, ed. Richard Morris, *EETS*, OS 59 (London, 1875), ll. 11492–506; *Speculum Sacerdotale*, p. 20; and *Sarum Missal*, p. 37.

40. Hugh of St. Cher, VI, fol. 7^n; Denis the Carthusian, XI, 25; and *Old English Homilies*, p. 45.

41. For the development of the tradition of three shepherds and three gifts in liturgical drama and in the English shepherd plays, see Millicent Carey, *The Wakefield Group in the Towneley Cycle* (Baltimore: The Johns Hopkins Press, 1930), pp. 116–21; and Mary Hatch Marshall, "The Dramatic Tradition Established by the Liturgical Plays," *PMLA*, 56 (1941), 968.

42. A 15th-century ME poem on the Epiphany, "Reges de Saba venient," juxtaposes the Magi with the Trinity. See *English Carols*, pp. 87–90, no. 29.

43. See John Speirs, *Medieval English Poetry: The Non-Chaucerian Tradition* (London: Faber and Faber, 1957), p. 334; "The gifts of the Three Shepherds (as of the Three Kings) have surely some relation to the magical or otherwise rich gifts which are bestowed on a newborn child . . . and which often have to do with the ultimate recognition of his supernatural or royal origin and status." Although Speirs's statement is directed toward the gifts in the *Prima Pastorum*, it is equally applicable to the gifts in the *Secunda Pastorum*.

44. All quotations from the *Secunda Pastorum* are taken from *The Wakefield Pageants in the Towneley Cycle*, ed. A. C. Cawley (Manchester, Eng.: Manchester Univ. Press, 1958).

45. For the influence of the medieval "Hail" Lyrics on the shepherds' salutations to Christ, see the note for 458ff. of the *Prima Pastorum*, in Cawley's edition of *The Wakefield Pageants*. See also A. C. Cawley, "The Wakefield First Shepherds' Play," *Proceedings of the Leeds Philosophical and Literary Society (Literary and Historical Section)*, 7 (1953), 117. On the term "maker" as an allusion to the Holy Spirit, see Cantelupe and Griffith, pp. 329–30.

46. *Early Netherlandish Painting* (Cambridge, Mass.: Harvard Univ. Press, 1958), II, fig. 494. On the symbolism of the fruits, see Panofsky, I, 144.

47. II, fig. 495. Both paintings, normally attributed to the Master of the Death of the Virgin, hang in the Metropolitan Museum of Art, New York.

48. George Ferguson, *Signs and Symbols in Christian Art* (1955; rpt. New York: Oxford Univ. Press, 1966), p. 29.
49. Cawley, *Wakefield Pageants*, p. 113, n. 718. See also Martial Rose, ed., *The Wakefield Mystery Plays* (New York: Norton, 1969), p. 303; and Speirs, p. 331.
50. See *Festivals of the Church*, XX, in *Legends of the Holy Rood*, ed. Richard Morris, *EETS*, OS 46 (1871), 217.
51. *Évangiles Apocryphes*, ed. and trans. Charles Michel (Paris: Librairie Alphonse Picard, 1911), pp. 116–19; and Edgar Hennecke, *New Testament Apocrypha*, ed. Wilhelm Schneemelcher, trans. R. Mc L. Wilson, I (Philadelphia: Westminster Press, 1963), 411–12. The Gospel of Pseudo-Matthew, compiled around the 8th or 9th century, was written in Latin.
52. *The Oxford Book of Carols*, ed. Percy Dearmer, R. Vaughan Williams, and Martin Shaw (London: Oxford Univ. Press, 1928), pp. 87–89. For a similar incident in Christian art, see *Rest on the Flight into Egypt* (Baltimore: Walters Art Gallery), reproduced in Panofsky, II, fig. 191.
53. *Ancient Mysteries Described* (London: Wm. Hone, 1823), pp. 90–93.
54. *Ludus Coventriae*, ed. K. S. Block, *EETS*, ES 120 (1922), 135–45, esp. ll. 23–51.
55. Significantly, *fructus* symbolizes both "body of Christ" and "eternal beatitude," perhaps variant forms of the death and resurrection motifs associated with cherries. See, for example, the 12th-century *Allegoriae in Sacram Scripturam* (*PL*, CXII, 937–38), formerly attributed to Rabanus Maurus.
56. Ferguson, pp. 12–13; and J. E. Cirlot, *A Dictionary of Symbols*, trans. Jack Sage (New York: Philosophical Library, 1962), p. 27.
57. Réau, I, 80–81.
58. Ferguson, pp. 12–13; Cirlot, pp. 25–27; *Allegoriae*, CXII, 871; and *Clavis Melitonis*, in *Spicilegium Solesmense*, ed. J. B. Pitra (Paris: Firmin Didot Fratres, 1855), II, 470.
59. See, for example, the miniature painting, "The Virgin and Child," from *The Psalter of Robert de Lisle* (East Anglian illumination, early 14th century), British Museum Arundel MS. 83, fol. 131B.
60. Alanus de Insulis, *Distinctiones* (*PL*, CCX, 716); and *Allegoriae*, CXII, 871.
61. Réau, I, 80–81; and Cawley, *Wakefield Pageants*, p. 113, n. 722. In this context, the second shepherd's gift is linked with the Epiphany, for that feast commemorates the baptism of Christ.
62. In *Clavis Melitonis*, II, lxxx, *aves* signify "the holy" as well as "the Saviour."
63. M. Didron, *Christian Iconography*, trans. E. J. Millington (London: H. T. Bohn, 1851), I, 222.
64. Alanus, CCX, 883–84; and *Allegoriae*, CXII, 1012.
65. See, for example, Ferguson, p. 175; Fr. Charles Cahier, *Caractéristiques des Saints dans l'Art Populaire* (1867; rpt. Bruxelles: Culture et Civilisation, 1966), p. 449; and Msgr. X. Barbier de Montault, *Traité d'Iconographie Chrétienne* (Paris: L. Vivès, 1890), I, 54.
66. "Some Fifteenth-Century English Alabaster Panels," *Archaeological Journal*, 76 (1919), pl. IV, fig. 2, and p. 135. For additional examples associating the ball with Christ in Adoration of the Magi scenes, see W. L. Hildburgh, "English Alabaster Carvings as Records of the Medieval Religious Drama," *Archaeologia*, 93 (1949), pl. XIa and p. 62.
67. "Some Additional Specimens of English Alabaster Carvings," *Archaeological Journal*, 84 (1927), pl. V, fig. 2, and p. 121.
68. *Queen Mary's Psalter*, ed. George Warner (London: Trustees of the Brit.

Museum, 1912), pl. 293, fol. 298ᵛ. Warner's edition is reproduced from British Museum Royal MS. 2B.vii.

69. Christina Hole, *English Sports and Pastimes* (London: B. T. Batsford, 1949), p. 39. See also Cawley, *Wakefield Pageants*, p. 113, n. 736.

70. Alan W. Watts, *Myth and Ritual in Christianity* (London: Thames & Hudson, 1954), p. 124.

71. Significantly, Mary's concluding speech in the play underscores the doctrine that all three members of the Trinity play instrumental roles in the Incarnation: "The fader of heuen, God omnypotent, / That sett all on seuen, his son has he sent. / My name couth he neuen, and lyght or he went. / I conceyuyd hym full euen thrugh myght, as he ment; / And now is he borne" (737–41).

Northeastern University

GORBODUC AS APOLOGY AND CRITIQUE

I

In his study of John Lyly, G. K. Hunter writes of two closely related aspects of early Renaissance Humanism: "The dream that the centre of power [the court] was the natural home of learning . . . " and the "dream of learning as politically effective."[1] Yet under Elizabeth, though something of a Humanist herself, the Humanist became the provider of witty diversions, of entertainments for the court. Or as Hunter puts it: "The Humanist ideal had shrunk to that of 'the courtier' who . . . was to use his learning as decoration."[2] Nothing could be further from the hope for political effectiveness.

Joseph Kramer takes similar comments by Hunter to shape a context for Richard Edwardes' *Damon and Pithias* (1564–1565).[3] In his article, he focuses on this play "because it is specifically in this drama that the entertainer appears to have given form to an apprehension of the function of his art to ameliorate and transform."[4] Kramer continues, "The self-conscious artist presents a deliberate apology for his art and gives imaginative substance to the Humanist dream of effectiveness at the center of society the Court."[5] Kramer then goes on to demonstrate convincingly how Edwardes has fashioned through his play a defense of art. Yet Kramer ignores part of Edwardes' own apology. In the Prologue the dramatist writes of the play to follow: "It is no legend-lie, / But a thing once done, indeed, as histories do descry . . . " (31–32). Edwardes calls upon a history that is allied to the tradition of *The Mirror for Magistrates* (1559) for support. This concept of history is described by Amyot as "a certain rule and instruction, which by examples past, teacheth us to judge of things present and to foresee things to come: so we may know what to like of, and what to follow; what to mislike and what to eschew."[6] Art and history function to instruct the present in *Damon and Pithias*.

This Humanist dream, this sense of art as politically effective, this self-consciousness on the part of the artist are, however, equally relevant to an earlier drama by Norton and Sackville, *Gorboduc* (1561–1562). Hunter writes of certain speeches in this play which are concerned with the need for an heir: "The advice of Eubulus is direct advice to the Queen."[7] In contrast, Irby B. Cauthen, Jr., comments: "To have admonished her in specific terms would have been impolitic and impertinent."[8] He continues: "If there is a subject for any admonition the play contains, it is Parliament and the Queen's council."[9] The particular target, however, is not that important. What matters is that Norton and Sackville are not writing an entertainment, but exerting artistic and historical pressure upon a specific political situation involving court and Parliament.

Their concern is to present an historical example which "teacheth us to judge of things present." And within their play a major theme is the importance of example. The target of the play *Gorboduc* is admonished to learn from history; within the play itself King Gorboduc is admonished to learn from it as well. Thus a crucial point in the play is the failure of history to convince Gorboduc his actions are unnatural. He is not a good audience. Undoubtedly, Norton and Sackville hoped to find a better one in the Inner Temple.

The only real opponent among the counselors to Gorboduc's plan to divide the kingdom is Eubulus, a proper historical artist who uses the past to instruct the present. The story of Brutus who divided the realm is not glossed over as it had been by another counselor, but is emphasized as an example. He parallels Brutus' decision to Gorboduc's intention and reminds the king of the slaughter that followed (I.ii.269–83).[10] He notes, in fact, how recent these civil wars were: "Ruthful remembrance is yet raw in mind" (I.ii.281). Eubulus also refers to the story of Phaeton as a moral exemplum from mythology against letting these unprepared youths guide the kingdom (I.ii.330–31). Similarly, the Chorus picks up the myth of Phaeton and Apollo for the same instructive purpose (I.ii.16–18). In fact, the Chorus itself closes the act with a return to the idea of the history as an exemplum when it states that Gorboduc "A mirror shall become to princes all, / To learn to shun the cause of such a fall" (I.ii.23–24).

Although the action is slow on stage because of the dramatic techniques, the story moves rapidly. The kingdom is divided, the brothers war, Porrex kills Ferrex, and Videna kills him in revenge. The Chorus interprets this last action as Jove's proper and inevitable justice.

> The times before record, and times to come
> Shall find it true, and so doth present proof
> Present before our eyes for our behoof.
> (IV.ii.20–22)

The exemplum is not only concerned with the division of a kingdom, but with the ability to profit from history (as it is shaped by art) in general. As the Chorus comments: "And happy he, that can in time beware / By other's harms, and turn it to his good" (IV.ii.25–26). The Queen and Parliament are being urged to settle the current question of succession. But at the same time the dramatists defend the play as an embodiment of an historical record that instructs.

At the start of the last act the audience learns that "the people" in rebellion have slain their king and queen. Obviously we have an example of what happens in a divided kingdom. But there are more lessons in history. If the rebels do not surrender, Eubulus says:

> Then do I wish such slaughter to be made,
> As present age, and eke posterity,
> May be adrad with horror of revenge
> That justly shall then on these rebels fall.
> (V.i.118–21)

The just revenge that will fall on the rebels will teach both present and future generations the outcome of rebellion.

When the rebels cannot be won over, he insists that they are fools who have ignored the obvious lessons history offers. Their response parallels Gorboduc's; now it is the rebels who should have before them all that the king rejected. But, like Gorboduc, the rebels ignore "so many books, so many rolls / Of ancient time" (V.ii.34) that could instruct them in the folly of their course. As Gorboduc ignored the warnings of Eubulus, the people ignore the words of "their aged fathers." While the memory of the last civil wars should still be "raw" in Gorboduc's mind, while the rebels should remember the punishments they have seen others receive, neither has learned by example nor by history—exactly what this play is (V.ii.1–14). For a good part of the last act, these traitors against nature replace another traitor to nature and history, Gorboduc, as the erring protagonists of the play.

In their defeat they are transformed into examples by Eubulus: "Their carrion carcasses do preach / The fruits that rebels reap of their uproars" (V.ii.53–54). This idea of current example is picked up by Clotyn: "I think the world will now at length beware / And fear to put on arms against their prince" (V.ii.58–59). Arostus generalizes the fate of rebels back in time with implications for the future: "Such as all times before / Have ever lotted to those wretched folks" (V.ii.65–66). Neither Gorboduc nor the rebels learned.

Thus in the closing speech of Eubulus, there is not only concern for the succession, but a desire that the subjects of the admonition learn from it. Throughout the play, the necessity of such a response has been stressed. Thus each exemplum in the play comes to form part of an insisting whole that asserts the validity of history and art itself. The materials, properly organized by the artists, are there. While Gorboduc and the rebels did not learn from history, it is hoped that the objects of this play's message will indeed learn "by other's harm." The historical artifice is the Humanist assertion of the dream of political effectiveness. What it did not do for Gorboduc, and what by implication it can do for England in 1561, is its defense. The problem is why the historical exemplums within the play failed to instruct Gorboduc.

II

While *Gorboduc* defends itself as instructive art, it is critical of another mode of drama. In certain ways it is a Senecan tragedy: there are the act divisions, the chorus, the messengers. However, as Cauthen points out: "The unities, an integral part of the Senecan technique, are here almost ignored . . . and we particularly miss the Senecan ghost."[11] But the dismissals of the ghost and of the unity of time in particular are for a purpose: Norton and Sackville are removing those parts of the Senecan machinery that they find inimical. And thus they criticize certain of the assumptions about existence that are implied by those elements. Ultimately, though they use a good number of Senecan devices, *Gorboduc* is a criticism of the Senecan conception of life.

As the tragedy unfolds, Gorboduc blames the fates for events: "O cruel fates, o mindful wrath of gods . . . " (III.i.1). He continues to say that the gods will never be satisfied until all the issue of Troy has been destroyed. His sentiments are Senecan, though he never reaches the stoical remedy relied on by the Roman. As Hardin Craig writes: "With Seneca the very nature of things was disastrous, and calamity was irresistible and inescapable."[12] This attitude defines every reaction by Gorboduc. When things may still be salvaged, all Gorboduc can do is foolishly hope: "The gods send joyful news!" (III.i.59). When it seems too late, in despair he laments: "Their death and mine must pease the angry gods" (III.i.103). After Porrex kills his brother, the king complains: "What cruel destiny, / What froward fate hath sorted us this chance . . . " (IV.ii.142–43). Gorboduc's intellectual position, his attitude towards experience, is out of step with the consciousness that created the history play *Gorboduc*. The Senecan king cannot learn from history.

That consciousness is part of the Judaeo-Christian sense of history, and it is very different from Seneca's. Tom F. Driver writes of this distinction:

The importance of time and the importance of the unique combine to place an importance upon human personality in its capacity for decision which the classical world did not show. Christianity allows for, even demands, a certain internationalization of history.[13]

Thus Norton and Sackville delete from the play those elements that conflict with their historical consciousness. The unity of time, if Driver is correct, is useful for classical tragedy because it expresses "the limits of the action"—all that is shown are the usually destructive cosmic powers in operation upon a helpless man.[14] The ghost itself is often only an agent of the laws of *nemesis*. Both elements suggest that man is simply a victim, that he has no say in his destiny. But these Humanists cannot agree. Thus they alter the Senecan form and in fact challenge the Senecan attitude towards life as embodied in King Gorboduc.

This Christian consciousness is emphasized by the presence of other than Senecan influences. Willard Farnham argues that the play is related to the moralities.[15] Good and evil forces struggle to control an individual, in this case the commonwealth, as they did in *Respublica*. Cauthen suggests that *Gorboduc* may even look back to the earlier *King John* (1538) by Bale.[16] Not only have the dramatists inherited elements of medieval forms, however, but also the consciousness that shaped those forms. Man is presented as a creature that decides: ultimately the result of his decision means heaven or hell—the difference between Dr. Faustus and Everyman. As obvious as it may be, it is impossible to be truly Senecan and truly Christian.

Erich Auerbach writes: "The dramatic occurrences of human life were seen by antiquity predominantly in the form of a change of fortune breaking in upon man from without and from above."[17] So Gorboduc has defined what happened to him. But surely he is wrong. As Cauthen points out: "By acting wisely and morally . . . the tragedy that Gorboduc brings upon himself, his family, and his country could have been averted."[18] Unlike the Senecan presentation of life, calamity is not in this context irresistible. Throughout the play Gorboduc is urged to take responsibility, to see the likely effects of his decisions. When he falls, it is not because of fate, but because of his *choice* to rebel against nature.

Thus the Senecan figure Gorboduc can hardly speak for Norton and Sackville. Gorboduc, who only speaks of destiny, sees no significance in Eubulus' warnings against dividing the kingdom: "Give no beginning to so dreadful end" (I.ii.299). He refuses to see the fact of "cause and effect that lies behind all of life."[19] The king denied his internal power to shape history and affirms an external nexus over which he presumes he has no control. For Gorboduc the future is closed.[20]

He speaks of "angry gods" while Philander warns: "Yield not, o king, so much to weak despair" (III.i.104). Similarly Eubulus urges the king, "Now is no time / To wail and plain, and waste your woeful life" (III.i.135–36). Gorboduc is urged not to take the Senecan stance. Men can alter history. Without such an assumption the play *Gorboduc* would make no sense, nor would the Humanist dream of being politically effective. The king unleashed the possibilities for destruction implicit in the first scene of the play. His unnatural act created "murders, mischief, or civil sword." Videna stresses the burden upon Gorboduc for the tragedy as she speaks of events to come in the conditional language of "if," "and if," and "when" (I.i.54–59). What Gorboduc decides matters. Such a consciousness is the opposite of the Senecan. To accept the Senecan view of life is to deny the validity of history as exemplum; for Seneca there is nothing to learn but that the human condition is always bad.

Norton and Sackville, as a corollary to their defense of historical drama, criticize the Senecan mode of tragedy. Eubulus' admonition at the end of the play asserts that history depends upon human decisions (V.ii.180–279). The concept is neither Senecan nor classical. In fact, the entire last act functions as a rejection of Senecan attitudes, while it keeps some of the Senecan machinery. With Gorboduc dead, the chronicle history play emerges out of the Senecan rhetoric. No one speaks of fate; there is only danger and opportunity. Fergus is ready to seize the crown: "If ever time to gain a kingdom here / Were offer'd man, now is it offer'd me" (V.i.132–33). In contrast the counselors must decide how to reorder the kingdom. But there is no one who says "O cruel fates." Instead, political figures on stage attempt to be politically effective. To be so, they must deny the Senecan view of man as victim and assert the Christian view of man as destiny-maker. Thus Norton and Sackville have given shape to the Humanist dream by defense and criticism of the two artistic modes. They become one with the non-Senecan counselors in their attempt to shape politics. Ironically, their Humanism leads them to reject the implications of Senecan tragedy while they build their historical exemplum upon its form.

NOTES

1. *John Lyly: The Humanist as Courtier* (Cambridge, Mass.: Harvard Univ. Press, 1962), p. 30.
2. Hunter, p. 31.
3. Joseph E. Kramer, "*Damon and Pithias*: An Apology for Art," *ELH*, 35 (1968), 475–90.
4. Kramer, p. 476.
5. Ibid.
6. Quoted in Lily B. Campbell, *Shakespeare's Histories: Mirrors of Elizabethan Policy* (San Marino, Calif.: Huntington Library, 1947), p. 47.
7. Hunter, p. 146.
8. In his introduction to the Regents Renaissance Drama edition of *Gorboduc* (Lincoln: Univ. of Nebraska Press, 1970), p. xxiii.
9. Cauthen, p. xxiii.
10. References to *Gorboduc* in my text are to *Five Elizabethan Tragedies*, ed. A. K. McIlwraith (London: Oxford Univ. Press, 1938), pp. 69–129.
11. Cauthen, p. xvii.
12. Hardin Craig, "The Shackling of Accidents: A Study of Elizabethan Tragedy," *PQ*, 19 (1940), rpt. in *Elizabethan Drama: Modern Essays in Criticism*, ed. T. J. Kaufmann (New York: Oxford Univ. Press, 1961), p. 33.
13. *The Sense of History in Greek and Shakespearean Drama* (New York and London: Columbia Univ. Press, 1960), p. 65. Driver, as he states (pp. 44–49), develops ideas presented by Erich Auerbach in "Odysseus' Scar," in *Mimesis: The Representation of Reality in Western Literature*, trans. Willard R. Trask (Princeton: Princeton Univ. Press, 1953), pp. 3–23. Both writers, however, do not place Seneca in "the classical world" which they define as Hellenic. Driver suggests that the Senecan and the Roman historical consciousness parallels that of the Judaeo-Christian tradition (p. 63, n. 71). Auerbach, in "The Arrest of Peter Valvomeres" in *Mimesis*, states that Seneca helped create "a sombre and highly rhetorical realism which is totally alien to classical antiquity" (p. 60). I maintain, however, that both ignore those implications of Senecan tragedy which do align him with the Greek tragic writers.
14. Driver, p. 208. He speaks of Greek tragedy.
15. *The Medieval Heritage of Elizabethan Tragedy* (Oxford: Oxford Univ. Press, 1956), pp. 353ff.
16. Cauthen, p. xviii.
17. In "The Weary Prince," in *Mimesis*, p. 318.
18. Cauthen, p. xix.
19. Ibid.
20. Driver, p. 37. Again Driver speaks of the Hellenic historical consciousness.

University of Miami

RUTH STEVENSON

THE INFLUENCE OF ASTROPHIL'S STAR

There seems to be little doubt in any critic's mind that Astrophil dominates Sidney's sonnet sequence. William Ringler conveniently summarizes this basic assumption in his introduction to the most recent edition of Sidney's poems. "Astrophil is the central figure," he points out; "everything is presented from his point of view, and he addresses a variety of persons . . . or things . . . , or personifications . . . , or he communes with himself. The poems, then, are a series of conversations or monologues which the reader overhears."[1] Similar specific emphasis on Astrophil is placed by virtually all of the Sidney critics. Hallett Smith, it is true, does allow for some consideration of Stella as "audience,"[2] and thereby suggests her human presence, but her role is incidental; indeed, Mr. Smith represents the prevailing critical attitude explicitly: "the most vivid thing in Sidney's sonnet cycle is the personality of Astrophel."[3]

It would be foolhardy to challenge this assumption directly; but the discovery that Astrophil's personality dominates the sequence can be misleading, for it tends to confuse the voice of the sonnets with their actual development. Astrophil's voice is indeed pervasive; it fills every poem and touches every mood. But it does not direct the whole sequence. Stella, I think, does that.

Stella's actual identity has occasioned a good deal of critical speculation. Some have argued that the sequence is not autobiographical and that Stella is little more than imagined mistress and thus only an ideal occasion for the poem. Others find sonnets in the sequence circumstantial enough in their details (see Sonnets 30, 41, 53) to indicate a biographical significance throughout the entire work. Malcolm Wallace, Jean Robertson, and Roger Howell represent modern critical opinion that Stella was Penelope Devereux Rich,[4] a very real woman, as her relationships with Lord Rich and Lord Mountjoy (later Earl of Devonshire) attest.

Stella's sixteenth-century identity is interesting, but not, I think, crucial. Those who seek it generally do so without clear reference to the whole development of the sequence in which they find only isolated clues (particularly in the Rich sonnets) to establish biographical certainty. What matters is not so much Stella's identity as her reality. The fact that she is a real woman becomes progressively clear as the sequence unfolds. The first, rather unearthly, Stella whom we meet may well be imaginary, but she becomes incarnate; and she does this not so much through Astrophil's vision of her as in spite of it. Her reality finally becomes a stubborn thing, and Astrophil's friction with and reaction to it provide the real dramatic vitality of the sequence.

The dramatic structure of *Astrophil and Stella* has been considered in various ways. W. J. Courthope sees no dramatic progression but only a loose design of theme and variation, a kind of artistic exercise undirected by genuine feeling.[5] C. S. Lewis also denies a dramatic development.[6] Sherod Cooper perceives no overall structure.[7] Malcolm Wallace makes a simple division at Sonnet 32, affirming that all the preceding poems concern Penelope before her marriage and that those following deal with Lady Rich.[8]

Various other critics, including William Ringler, Roger Howell, Richard Young, and Neil Rudenstine,[9] have analyzed the structure more thoroughly and find a three-part development. The specific bases for their divisions of the sequence often vary sharply, but each of these writers responds to three distinct tones within the sequence, and their focus is directed towards Astrophil.

But the different tones are not merely facets of Astrophil's personality or aspects of his singular dramatic presence. The three parts are distinguished, in my view, by Astrophil's three distinct responses to Stella. The first part extends from Sonnet 1 to Sonnet 43. In this section Astrophil beholds an ideal which is abstract, passive, and impersonal and which inspires him to spirited self-analysis as he contemplates it. He has a delightful time in these sonnets; and his exuberance, whimsy, and sportiveness—what Myrick calls his *sprezzatura*[10]—have free play. He experiences love *in vacuo*; there is no context in which to define the emotion, and Stella is exactly what he wants her to be. Section two extends from Sonnet 44 to the end of the series of songs which follow Sonnet 85 and which are transitional. In this portion of the sequence Stella has achieved flesh and blood. She is no longer an abstraction but a warm, insistent presence who both delights and flusters Astrophil. She has a distinct will of her own, and her attitudes not only thwart his desires but also unsettle his principles. This creature is far more complicated than the early Stella. Part three, which extends from Sonnet 85 to the end of the sequence, presents Astrophil's direct reaction to the Stellas encountered in parts one and two. His notion of love has been expanded, filled out, rubbed against reality. Whereas he began by exploring his new emotions through testing them against convention, by exploring its formalities, he ends as the Petrarchan lover he initially (though of course not fully) rejected.

Even Veronese, who is said to have painted Sir Philip, would have had trouble sketching the early Stella. The only human features we are sure she possesses are eyes and lips, and we do not learn much about them. Her eyes are Nature's chief work (Sonnet 7), Cupid shines in them (12), they are like stars amid the universe (26), and they are, of course, devastating weapons (43). Her lips receive the highest individualization, for they swelled "so full" (12). Her face is mentioned twice, but we learn only that it is a place for love to perch (8) or that it is "Queene *Vertue's* court" (9), bedecked with alabaster, gold, red porphir, pearl, and red and white marble.

Like other Elizabethan maidens, Stella had to undergo periodic dissection or (perhaps more accurately) dismemberment. In Sonnet 13, for example, her hair lies on Cupid's chest, "her face he makes his shield." In a frivolous sonnet (17) her brows are turned into bows, and her eyes become arrows.

Occasionally Stella is given specific roles. In Sonnet 22, for example, Mythical Stella confidently marches out to meet the sun, totally unimpressed by her companions' timorous efforts to shield their tender skins. Such "meaner beauties parcht," but the Sun, "which others burn'd did but her kisse." On another occasion (36) Stella, as a military commander, directs a vigorous assault against her trembling-happy foe.

Otherwise Stella remains a chaste, formless vision who is worth more than reason to Astrophil (18), who makes even learning irrelevant by comparison (21), who incites his ambition only for her grace (27), who haunts his dreams (32, 38, 39), who inspires him to victory in the lists (41), and who, of course, is rich (24, 37). She is the center, the pervading principle, of the innocent world which she slowly ("Not at first sight, nor with a dibbed shot"—Sonnet 2) fills with an abstract presence. Her distance enables the poet to debate basic principles of "will and wit" (4), Sense and Love (10), and to surrender himself almost complacently to a conception which other "dustie" wits (26) could not appreciate. It is Stella's meek passivity which accounts for the high spirits and untroubled contemplation of part one. She is hardly more than a name ("Stella; now she is nam'd, need more be said?"—Sonnet 16) in this section, but in part two the word is made flesh.

At Sonnet 44 Stella rather abruptly takes on human characteristics. She maintains her docility ("Her heart, sweet heart, is of no Tygre's kind"), but she also reveals obduracy ("And yet she heares, yet I no pitty find; / But more I crie, lesse grace she doth impart") and even an elegant sadism:

> . . . when the breath of my complaints doth tuch
> Those daintie dores unto the Court of blisse,
> The heav'nly nature of that place is such,
> That once come there, the sobbes of mine annoyes
> Are metamorphosd straight to tunes of joys.

Her humanness is further revealed through three principal roles which she actively adopts and which Astrophil slowly discovers in her.

The first and certainly most conspicuous role is that of a studious female pedagogue. Stella has a compulsion to teach, and poor Astrophil continually exposes himself to the professorial gleam in her eye. In Sonnet 46, he learns that he must love to look on Stella not with desire but with a more scholarly detachment. He addresses Love:

> Alas poore wag, that now a scholler art
> To such a school-mistresse, whose lessons new
> Thou needs must misse, and so thou needs must smart.

As early as Sonnet 51, Astrophil has already had enough. Her tongue has proceeded fluently against his ears; her "grave conceits" need a Hercules to bear them—not poor Astrophil, who is already exhausted by "your wisedome's heav'nly sway." Astrophil needs some respite, but Stella pays him no heed; her persistence is exemplary, and he fidgets:

> No more, my deare, no more these counsels trie.   (64)

He doesn't care what the intellectuals or anyone else thinks about him:

> Let folke orecharg'd with braine against me crie,
> . . .
> Let all the earth with scorne recount my case,
> But do not will me from my Love to flie.   (64)

We get a glimpse of the curriculum:

> I do not envie *Aristotle's* wit,
> Nor do aspire to *Caesar's* bleeding fame,
> Nor ought do care, though some above me sit,
> Nor hope, nor wishe another course to frame.

We notice that she is interested in the elevation not only of his mind but also of his rank. Hers is not an ivory tower.

Occasionally she makes concessions, but they are only slight. In Sonnet 62, in order to comfort him, she confesses that he will find true love in her; but she waters his wine by forbidding him to decline "From nobler course, fit for my birth and mind." Therefore, she again advises Astrophil to "anchor fast . . . on Virtue's shore."

One aspect of Virtue is Patience, and Stella, in her "schoole of Patience" (56), is a good disciplinarian. In Sonnet 56 she seems to have sent Astrophil off on a course of independent study. He would far prefer to be in her classes:

> Fy, schoole of Patience, Fy, your lesson is
> Far far too long to learne it without booke:
> What, a whole weeke without one peece of looke,
> And thinke I should not youre large precepts misse?
> When I might reade those letters faire of blisse,
> Which in her face teach vertue, I could brooke
> Somewhat thy lead'n counsels. . . .

But without her presence, can he ever take "In thy cold stuffe a flegmatike delight?"

In Sonnet 61 Astrophil, having assayed her eyes and invaded her ears, discovers that Stella is imperturable. Her "sweet breath'd defence" is this:

> That who indeed infelt affection beares,
> So captives to his Saint both soule and sence,
> That wholly hers, all selfnesse he forbeares,
> Thence his desires he learnes, his live's course thence.
> Now since her chast mind hates this love in me,
> With chastned mind, I straight must shew that she
> Shall quickly me from what she hates remove.

Occasionally, however, she does slip, and Astrophil loses no opportunity to crow. Her zealous double negative provokes his delighted assertion that "Grammar sayes . . . / That in one speech two Negatives affirme" (63). But such a triumph only accentuates her inflexible determination. In Sonnet 71, Astrophil, quite ruefully by this time, summarizes Stella's intention:

> . . . not content to be Perfection's heire
> Thy selfe, doest strive all minds that way to move.

This remark has more truth to it than Astrophil seems at first to comprehend. For Stella vigorously plays another role closely allied to that of teacher. She is an Independent Thinker. One of the discoveries he eventually makes about this flesh-and-blood Stella is that she has will and desire of her own. Early in part two (Sonnet 57), he flatters himself that "Her soule, arm'd but with such a dainty rind" will fall to his assault if he can only get his every sense poised and primed, ready to pounce on her with a sudden expression of woe so that she "should soone be pierced with sharpnesse of the mone." But she is tougher than she looks. Against his will and best laid plans she can turn his intentional sorrow to joy; she is so beguiling that Astrophil's woes, in spite of his intent, now

> sweetly sing,
> With that faire breast making woe's darknesse cleare:
> A prety case!

What is more, he discovers that she, too, is a dreamer who has vague imaginings of her own; her own idealizations interfere with her appreciation of flesh-and-blood Astrophil. She is capable of quick sympathy for those who are not part of her real world; she deliberately avoids making any connection with herself:

> Yet hearing late a fable, which did show
> Of Lovers never knowne, a grievous case,
> Pitie thereof gate in her breast such place
> That, from that sea deriv'd, teares' spring did flow.
>   (45)

Her reaction leads Astrophil to a realistic and playful adjustment of his position: "I am not I, pitie the tale of me." We may see the same tendency in operation in Sonnet 60. When Astrophil is actually present, she can swell to such force and fierceness that even Hippolyta might envy her:

> That heav'n of joyes throwes only down on me
> Thundred disdaines and lightnings of disgrace.

But when Astrophil is absent,

> then sweetly she
> With words, wherein the Muses' treasures be,
> Shews love and pitie to my absent case.

Just as Astrophil has built and tries to develop an idea of Stella which her intractable humanness directly opposes, so she has a specific idea of what she wants her courtier to be. Her mind is filled with notions of honor and ambition and fame; and she molds a part of him, momentarily at least, to her own desire. We glimpse the result fleetingly in the model, immaculate, and rueful Astrophil; he tells Desire that they must part, for

> *Venus* is taught with *Dian's* wings to flie:
> I must no more in thy sweet passions lie;
> *Vertue's* gold now must head my *Cupid's* dart.
> Service and Honor, wonder with delight,
> Feare to offend, will worthie to appeare,
> Care shining in mine eyes, faith in my sprite,
> These things are left me by my only Deare.
>
> (72)

The strongest evidence of Stella's independence lies in the fact that Astrophil never diminishes or even influences her will power. Her own wishes are never overcome. Occasionally she expresses feelings in spite of herself, but these are merely reflections of her interest or desire. In Sonnet 51, for example, underneath the grave conceits heaved back and forth between the two of them, Astrophil's "heart confers with Stella's beames." And sometimes there is spontaneous emotional and physical response:

> And yet amid all feares a hope there is
> Stolne to my heart, since last faire night, nay day,
> *Stella's* eyes sent to me the beames of blisse,
> Looking on me, while I lookt other way:
> But when mine eyes backe to their heav'n did move,
> They fled with blush, which guiltie seem'd of love.
>
> (66)

But generally Stella is vigilant and in full command. Astrophil never really wins a kiss from her, for the first, crucial one is merely stolen while she sleeps (*Second song*). And when she has declared her love for him, it is not because he has stormed any fortresses; she has made a cool decision and the rules are hers:

> ... she give but thus conditionly
> This realme of blisse, while virtuous course I take.
>
> (69)

The two Stellas we have just examined are far more human than the passive creature of the first section, and Astrophil must make deliberate but certainly not startling adjustments to these two facets of her personality. The third Stella is more delightful and more disconcerting: she is a Sensualist.

The first hint of sensuality comes as early as Sonnet 59, where

Stella quite coyly plays with her dog. "Deare, why make you more of a dog than me?" her lover asks. The dog becomes an unwelcome rival, and Stella worries Astrophil with her casual preference:

> Yet while I languish, him that bosome clips,
> That lap doth lap, nay lets, in spite of spite,
> This sowre-breath'd mate tast of those sugred lips.

Her sensual instincts are indeed most prominent in those sugred lips, for they—not her eyes nor her ears, nor any other part of her—are the portals to her delight. Once Astrophil has surreptitiously brushed them in the night (*Second song*, which follows Sonnet 72), it is as though a lock is sprung. Even her anger at the presumption of her lover is less than it might be. In *Second song* he fears her wrath ("Now will I alas refraine, / Love fears nothing else but anger"), but her reaction does not intimidate him: as he flees, he has time to mutter to himself, "Foole, more foole, for no more taking." And once the kiss has been taken, she decides (and her practical spirit is evident) that the no-kissing game is over. Right after *Second song*, at the conclusion of Sonnet 73, we suspect that even in her anger she allows him another kiss: "That Anger's selfe I needs must kisse againe." Sonnet 74 confirms the suspicion: "My lips are sweet, inspired with *Stella's* kisse." Her active participation is explicit: "Sweet swelling lip, well maist thou swell in pride" (Sonnet 80). She becomes, in fact, an expert, but she is a bit shy at his praise:

> How faine would I paint thee [the kiss] to all men's eyes,
> Or of thy gifts at least shade out some part.
> But she forbids, with blushing words, she sayes,
> She builds her fame on higher seated praise.
>
> (81)

At times the playful sensuality edges to passion. In Sonnet 82 he must swear "even by the same delight, / I will but kisse, I never more will bite."

Astrophil is obviously delighted in these new developments, and the pace of the sonnets quickens as he grows more and more enrapt. Sonnet 83 through *Fift song* (which follows Sonnet 86) reflects the enthusiasm of his reactions to the new physical Stella whom he has discovered. But his new knowledge is disconcerting as well as pleasing. He has come a long way from his reverence of the old celestial Stella, for he knows now that underneath all the talk about Virtue there lies her very real desire. Therefore, he does not easily accept her rejection of his advances. He reacts to her in a variety of ways in this crucial final section of part two, and its emotional range from fascinated delight to deep bitterness is the broadest in the entire poem. The intense development of this section begins with Sonnet 83. Here we have a situation like that of the dog earlier, but intensified by recent physical contact. With a direct glance at John Skelton, Sidney writes about a sparrow who enjoys what impatient Astrophil cannot. His rejection here is treated whimsically and playfully, but the last line contains more than humorous tension:

> I bare (with Envie) yet I bare your song,
> When in her necke you did *Love* ditties peepe;
> Nay, more foole I, oft suffered you to sleepe
> In Lillies' neast, where *Love's* selfe lies along,
> . . .
> Cannot such grace your silly selfe content,
> But you must needs with those lips billing be?
> And through those lips drinke Nectar from that toong;
> Leave that sir *Phip*, least off your necke be wroong.

He suspends his jealousy and impatience momentarily in order to savor the idea of her physical reality. Thus, in *Third song*, which follows, he emphasizes her impact on inanimate objects, like stones and trees. In the next two sonnets he remains acutely (though playfully) aware of everything that touches her; he envies the highway, which may kiss Stella's feet (84), and he nearly bursts at seeing her house (85), where he will see her in private that night. His own desire has been growing all the while, and, at their meeting in her bedroom (*Fourth song*), he actually makes an open attempt at seduction. Her reply seems firm (" 'No, no, no, no, my Deare, let be' "). Evidently he did not fully believe her, for in the following sonnet (86) he has incurred her wrath ("Alas, whence came this change of lookes?"). There can be no doubt that her refusal is firm. At this point Sidney reveals Astrophil's reactions in an unexpected, very important series of songs.

The five songs (the *Fift, Sixt, Seventh, Eighth,* and *Ninth*) which follow Sonnet 86 have puzzled critics such as Sidney's modern editor, William Ringler, for two reasons. First, why place them all together in an unusual lyric succession? Theoretically, they were intended to relieve the strict formality of the sonnets: why not disperse them judiciously? Second, when there are already four successive songs, why include at the beginning of the series an additional one which had been written for an entirely different occasion?[11]

If the emotional reaction and development which we have traced so far have any validity, then it is not difficult to suggest answers to these questions. Astrophil's passion has been mounting; along with it has grown his expectation, for he knows very well that Stella loves and desires him. Her rejection, therefore, highly complicates an already intense emotional state: the feeling pours out beyond the form of the sonnet into the looser, more lyric expression of song. And one song is not enough; nor are two or three. The reasons for this are two-fold. First, the range of emotion here is too broad for a single, fragile lyric; second, Sidney wants to make a transition through the convenient, receptive medium of song to the new attitude which will characterize the third and final section of his sequence. Thus the *Fift song* forms the climax for Astrophil's strong feeling. Sidney obviously employed it because it forcefully expresses the intense bitterness—even hatred—that Astrophil must now feel. The transition to a new state begins immediately afterwards.

The opening three stanzas of the *Fift song* reflect the painful disillusionment.

> While favour fed my hope, delight with hope was brought,
> Thought waited on delight, and speech did follow thought:
> Then grew my tongue and pen records unto thy glory:
> I thought all words were lost, that were not spent on thee:
> And all ears worse than deafe, that heard not out thy storie.

> I said, thou wert most faire, and so indeed thou art:
> I said, thou wert most sweet, sweet poison to my heart:
> I said, my soule was thine (ô that I then had lyed)
> I said, thine eyes were starres, thy breasts the milk'n way,
> Thy fingers *Cupid's* shafts, thy voyce the Angels' lay:
> And all I said so well, as no man it denied.

> But now that hope is lost, unkindnesse kils delight,
> Yet thought and speech do live, though metamorphosd quite:
> For rage now rules the reynes, which guided were by
>   Pleasure.
> I thinke now of thy faults, who late thought of thy praise,
> That speech falles now to blame, which did thy honour
>   raise,
> The same key op'n can, which can locke up a treasure.

The rejection itself, despite her clear desire, provokes his particular contempt:

> Lo you grow proud with this, for tyrans make folke bow:
> Of foule rebellion then I do appeach thee now;
> Rebell by Nature's law, Rebell by law of reason,
> Though, sweetest subject, wert borne in the realme
>   of Love,
> And yet against thy Prince thy force dost dayly prove:
> No vertue merits praise, once toucht with blot of Treason.

> But valiant Rebels oft in fooles' mouthes purchase fame:
> I now then staine thy white with vagabunding shame,

> Both Rebell to the Sonne, and Vagrant from the mother;
> For wearing *Venus'* badge, in every part of thee,
> Unto *Dianae's* traine thou runaway didst flee:
> Who faileth one, is false, though trusty to another.

His inner turmoil is also explicit:

> For I protest, my sight never thy face enjoyeth,
> But I in me am chang'd, I am alive and dead:
> My feete are turn'd to rootes, my hart becometh lead,
> No witchcraft is so evill, as which man's mind destroyeth.

This marks the depth of his anguish. We feel that the old conventional statements about loving-hate and joyful-woe are for the first time real to him; it is therefore appropriate, I think, that Astrophil slides towards convention in the following songs and poems to explore the new relevance and to withdraw and to shelter himself. In the *Sixt song* we may feel him moving away into the conventional framework of a debate between Music, which appeals to reason, and Beauty. Music seems to win. The *Seventh song* extends the convention even further; in the last stanza the ideal lady has returned:

> Heare you this soul-invading voice, and count it but a
> voice?
> The very essence of their tunes, when Angels do rejoyce.

The *Eighth song* has puzzled critics because of its unusual use of the third person. I suspect that Sidney chose this form as part of the gradual, soothing process of withdrawal. The song itself is cool, and its tone of distance and objectivity is calmly announced in the first two stanzas:

> In a grove most rich of shade,
> Where birds wanton musicke made,
> May then yong his pide weedes showing,
> New perfumed with flowers fresh growing,
> Astrophil with Stella sweete,
> Did for mutuall comfort meete,
> Both within themselves oppressed,
> But each in the other blessed.

In contrast to the recent violent pressures of the sequence, this song unwinds gently and leisurely, as though the past hectic scenes were rerun in slow motion and framed in soft eloquence. Astrophil suggests that Nature in all of her beauty and freshness encourages them to union; he approaches her; she resists, even while showing that ever-present desire:

> While such wise she love denied,
> As yet love she signified.

She addresses him directly, admits her love, explains her own conception of honor and virtue that forces her to refuse him; and she leaves him. Thus is the crisis reworked, reordered, reinterpreted. The withdrawal reaches its peak in the *Ninth song*, for we find ourselves in the quintessence of convention, in the midst of a pastoral scene. But at least by now Astrophil has gained some perspective, and he can face his pain and perhaps smile.

> No, she hates me, wellaway,
> Faining love, somewhat to please me:
> For she knowes, if she display
> All her hate, death soone would seaze me,
> And of hideous torments ease me.
>
> Then adieu, deere flocke adieu:
> But alas, if in your straying
> Heavenly *Stella* meete with you,
> Tell her in your piteous blaying,
> Her poore slave's unjust decaying.

When Astrophil finally turns back to the sonnets, he brings his perspective with him. Thus, in Sonnet 87, the first poem in the final section of the sequence, Stella weeps at their parting ("I saw that tears did in her eyes appear"), but he himself turns the sorrow into a light formality: "I had been vext, if vext I had not beene." His new distance is particularly well shown in Sonnet 89, which is a mere conventional exercise.

Throughout the remainder of the sequence we witness a counterpoint between Stella, a real human being, and distant but lovingly conventional Astrophil. In Sonnet 92, like the old Astrophil he wants to know every detail about her; in 93 we sense an indignant Stella, vexed by his inadvertent blunder. We witness Stella sick in bed (101) and boating on the Thames (103); occasionally we hear Astrophil still maintain "that I / Do *Stella* love" (104). But most of the time he is distant from her: his statements filter through the convention. He assures her in Sonnet 90 that he does not desire either fame or immortality but wishes only Stella's praise. In Sonnet 94 he adopts the Petrarchan stance of the wretched lover. Sonnets 95, 96, and 97 are laden with Sighs, Joy, Sorrow, Thought, and a conventional handling of Night and Diana. In Sonnets 98 and 99 he is the conventional sleepless lover, and in Sonnet 105 he once more beholds "the heav'n of Stella's face." Even when he describes her sorrow (100), he seems rather detached. In the final two sonnets he achieves his final distance. In Sonnet 107 he actually leaves Stella, courteously and discreetly assuring her that he wants to save his reputation so that people will not laugh at his loving her. The final sonnet combines traditional and homely imagery and concludes with a conventional and significant couplet which restates the mysterious, inextricable elements of joy and woe as they mutually infold the complexity of love:

> That in my woes for thee thou art my joy,
> And in my joys for thee my only annoy.

Sidney's last words in the sequence are appropriate, I think, in their emphasis on the complex dramatic relationship between the two lovers. Throughout the whole poem the dramatic interest was sustained not primarily by the vivid accents of Astrophil's monologues but by the progressive stages of experience that unfold like intricate figures in a courtly dance. The tension which flowed between Astrophil and Stella inspired the dance and gave it grace and drama. The finest steps and most graceful leaps and bows were certainly Astrophil's; but Stella led the figure and at her own pace brought it to a close.

NOTES

1. William Ringler, ed., *The Poems of Sir Philip Sidney* (Oxford: Clarendon Press, 1962), p. xliv.
2. Hallett Smith, *Elizabethan Poetry: A Study in Conventions, Meaning, and Expression* (Cambridge, Mass.: Harvard Univ. Press, 1966), p. 147.
3. Smith, p. 166.
4. Malcolm Wallace, *The Life of Sir Philip Sidney* (Cambridge, Eng.: The Univ. Press, 1915), pp. 244ff.; Jean Robertson, "Sir Philip Sidney and his Poetry," in *Elizabethan Poetry*, Stratford-Upon-Avon Studies 2, eds. John Russell Brown and Bernard Harris (New York: St. Martin's Press, 1960), p. 116; Roger Howell, *Sir Philip Sidney: the Shepherd Knight* (Boston: Little, 1968), pp. 182–83.
5. W. J. Courthope, *A History of English Poetry*, II (London: Macmillan, 1904), 228.
6. C. S. Lewis, *English Literature in the Sixteenth Century, Excluding Drama* (Oxford: Clarendon Press, 1954), p. 328.
7. Sherod Cooper, *The Sonnets of Astrophel and Stella: A Stylistic Study* (Paris: Mouton, 1968), pp. 26–46.
8. Wallace, p. 249.
9. Ringler, pp. xliv–ix; Howell, pp. 194–98; Richard B. Young, "English Petrarke: A Study of Sidney's 'Astrophel and Stella,'" in *Three Studies in the Renaissance: Sidney, Jonson, Milton*, ed. B. C. Nangle (New Haven: Yale Univ. Press, 1958), pp. 40–88; Neil Leon Rudenstine, *Sidney's Poetic Development* (Cambridge, Mass.: Harvard Univ. Press, 1967), pp. 217–87.
10. Kenneth Orne Myrick, *Sir Philip Sidney as a Literary Craftsman* (Cambridge, Mass.: Harvard Univ. Press, 1935), pp. 298–315.
11. "Internal evidence indicates that this song [the *Fift*] was composed earlier than the *Astrophil and Stella* sonnets, and that 'Stella' of line 31 was originally 'Mira.'"—Ringler, p. 484.

Duke University

ROGER TRUSCOTT BURBRIDGE

SPEECH AND ACTION IN CHAPMAN'S
BUSSY D'AMBOIS

Early in the first act of *Bussy D'Ambois*, Bussy justifies his entering the corrupt world of the court by announcing:

> I am for honest actions, not for great:
> If I may bring up a new fashion,
> And rise in Court with virtue, speed
> his [Monsieur's] plough.
> (I.i.128–30)[1]

In the rest of this speech Bussy prepares the audience for a struggle between his virtue and the "policy" of Monsieur and other politicians of the court. As the play progresses, however, this conflict between good and evil is blurred by the action, as well as by the inaction, of the hero. We are told by everyone in the play that Bussy has superior strength and virtue, yet his actions fall far short of the standards indicated by the various comments made about him both by others and by himself. He becomes, in fact, a murderer and an adulterer, and he is exposed by the very people he has determined to purge from the court. Yet trapped though he is by circumstances, everything that is said by and about Bussy makes his death seem a glorious one, his spirit "made a star." The play seems to move, as Eugene Waith says, on two parallel lines, one the adventure of the historical Bussy, the other the progressive revelation of a mythic figure, "a Herculean disguised as Bussy."[2]

It is essential to keep this discrepancy between the language and the action of the play in mind. If we see Bussy's fall in terms of the action alone we will be tempted, as others have been, to interpret the

59

play as an exemplum, condemning Bussy for not living according to Christian virtues.[3] If we focus on language alone, we will tend to see Bussy as a stoic hero, master of his fate. Neither of these interpretations represents the impression made on us by the play as a whole. We must assume, therefore, that Chapman was only partially successful in coordinating the two elements of the play in achieving his overall purpose. He seems to have had a definite moral in mind, but it remains to be discovered. There are important questions to be asked regarding the moral pattern of *Bussy D'Ambois*. What is the nature of good and evil in the world of the play? Does the moral framework of the play provide Bussy with a satisfactory basis for action? What do his struggle with society, and his failure, mean?

In the opening scene Bussy condemns the evils of society from the safety of his "obscure abodes," his "green retreat." At first he seems a complainer rather than a reformer, and his first words betray the bitter sense of personal injustice and indignity of the typical malcontent:

> Fortune, not Reason, rules the state of things,
> Reward goes backwards, Honour on his head;
> Who is not poor, is monstrous . . . .
>
> (I.i.1–3)

Chapman seems to have made Bussy of lower social status than is warranted by the historical sources to develop in him the rebellious spirit of an outcast. However, Bussy is not discontent with his personal lot alone, but with the very nature of the social system from which he is excluded. It soon becomes clear that the root of society's corruption for Bussy is "policy." This term represents for Bussy, as it would for Chapman's audience, all the vices such as hypocrisy, flattery, and intrigue which further the lawless pursuit of personal ambition at the expense of the common good. Bussy is not really ambitious, and in the speech rationalizing his entry into court society he contrasts the calculating "learning-hating policy" of Monsieur with his own nature, whose ". . . smooth plain ground / Will never nourish any politic seed . . . " (I.i.126–27). From the beginning Chapman takes pains to emphasize the uncorrupted nature of Bussy's virtue and uses it to put his actions in a special light. His relatively minor good actions are enlarged upon and his bad ones minimized, both by himself and by those around him. His blunt, impolitic destruction of court manners is amplified by Monsieur until it becomes proof of Bussy's extraordinary moral courage and elemental passion:

> His great heart will not down, 'tis like the sea,
> That . . . .

>   . . . . never will be won—
> No, not when th' hearts of all those powers are burst—
> To make retreat into his settled home,
> Till he be crowned with his own quiet foam.
>   (I.ii.138–46)

Bussy's deliberate grossness, his discourtesy to the great men at court, and even his murders are finally seen not as blameworthy but as the energetic outpourings of a noble soul. Since policy, as established by both Bussy and the King, is the wellspring of evil, then anything Bussy does which is unpolitic comes to represent a good in itself. Even Monsieur admires him for his refusal to play the politic game.

For the King, Bussy represents a prelapsarian ideal:

> . . . Man in his native noblesse, from whose fall
> All our dissensions rise . . . .
> . . . . kings had never borne
> Such boundless eminence over other men,
> Had all maintained the spirit and state of D'Ambois . . . .
>   (III.ii.91–97)

Yet Henry's characterization is slightly awry. As Edwin Muir has pointed out, Bussy's essential virtue is not innocence but, as the King himself calls it, "native noblesse": "Bussy is like a cross between Adam and Achilles crossed again by something quite different, the Renaissance man stepping out of the Middle Ages into a new world."[4] Bussy is not, after all, content to remain in his uncorrupted garden outside the pale of society but wishes, godlike, to blaze an exemplary path of virtue within it; for

> There is a deep nick in Time's restless wheel
> For each man's good . . . .   (I.i.134–35)

Bussy must, of course, be seen as the moral center of the play. He is the only character besides the King who avoids, in his intentions if not always in his deeds, the use of policy. Significantly, however, Chapman does not provide him with positive moral values by which to act. Bussy's avowed purpose is simply to tear out the rotten heart of society. The difficulty of acting in a world which is entirely corrupt is that positive values are impossible, and good lies only in destruction. Thus Bussy's main virtue has to be a negative one, the defiance not only of policy but of society itself.

Bussy knows, on entering society, that it is ruled by Fortune and Chance and that its values have lost real meaning. Law in this society is what one makes it and is to be used for personal gain. Bussy calls this rapacity "Protean law" and declares that even sacred law is turned

by the lawyers ". . . Into a harpy, that eats all but's own . . . " (III.ii.
54). Yet since this world is the only one in which he can act, Bussy
must have faith that his "destiny" and inner law will win out over
those of the politicians. His opposition of his own "higher" law to that
of society is made clear after the King has pardoned him for the slay-
ing of Barrisor and his comrades:

> . . . since I am free,
> Offending no just law, let no law make
> By any wrong it does, my life her slave:
> When I am wronged, and that law fails to right me,
> Let me be king myself, as man was made,
> And do a justice that exceeds the law . . .
> . . . .
> Who to himself is law, no law doth need,
> Offends no king, and is a king indeed.
> (II.i.194–204)

Bussy sounds at this moment like the self-sufficient Senecan man whose
adherence to the absolute command of reason and virtue places him
above the dictates of others. And, except for the spontaneous and passionate nature attributed to Bussy by the other characters, this is the
view of him that they generally accept. The King's admiring reactions
to Bussy are typical of the other characters throughout the play.

Before exploring the inconsistencies of this picture with Bussy's actions, it is important to determine what Chapman intended by emphasizing the importance of his "inner law." While Bussy's defiance of
policy is essentially a negative virtue it has a positive side, since it
represents a desire to preserve man's freedom. Bussy defies Fortune
by entering a world ruled by her; his assurance of his personal "destiny" is an assertion of his independence from Fortune's caprice. He
defies court conventions to prove this freedom, and the King approves
because he too senses the degree to which the human spirit is stifled
by society.

Bussy's justification for his adulterous affair with Tamyra is simple:
he is furthering his defiance of policy, in this case the policy of false
virtue, by which man's soul is imprisoned. He chides Tamyra for her
"puritan" conscience:

> Sin is a coward, madam, and insults
> But on our weakness, in his truest valour,
> And so our ignorance tames us, that we let
> His shadows fright us . . . .
> . . . .
> . . . . the sly charms
> Of the witch Policy makes him like a monster
> Kept only to show men for goddess money . . . .
> (III.i.18–26)

Rationalization though it seems, this speech is Bussy's sole argument for the major portion of his action in the play. We are left with the distinct impression that he takes Tamyra simply because he wants her. In fact, Bussy's superior law works out to be more or less a license to do what he wants. He is a would-be Marlovian superman trying to exercise absolute freedom. Unlike Tamburlaine, however, Bussy really wants to be morally responsible. Instead of fighting society with its own weapons, he would like to purge it with the aid of virtue and honesty. But Bussy's moral energies are vitiated by the strangely tangential intrigue which occupies most of the play and which brings about his downfall, assuring the survival of the evil forces he has set out to destroy.

The struggle between Bussy and society is, then, a conflict more of words than of deeds. For one thing, there is no one in the play evil enough for Bussy to defy in meaningful dramatic terms. Monsieur is, it must be remembered, unwilling to kill the King to further his ambitions, and it is what Bussy *says* about him that creates the monstrous image rather than anything he does. On the other hand, Bussy himself fails to act in the exemplary fashion which we are led to expect from the language of the play. As many critics have shown, Chapman confuses his moral concerns by having his hero work out his fate through a melodramatic intrigue filled with such hackneyed devices as the letter written in blood, the faithful friar, and the conjuring of spirits.

It is true that Chapman does seem to realize the disparity between speech and action in his hero and makes efforts to pull the two together. He has Monsieur and the Guise plot to trap him in an affair with one of the "greatest women" of the court, which makes Bussy's seduction of Tamyra right under their noses seem like a poetically just foiling of policy, although ironically it is Bussy's spontaneous, passionate, and somewhat careless wooing of Tamyra which finally makes it possible for these two Machiavels to succeed. Chapman also makes Montsurry a monster intent only on saving face and not at all loath to torture his wife. The bond of love between Bussy and Tamyra, which is unconcerned with form, is put in a far more sympathetic light by Montsurry's lack of human feeling and preoccupation with convention. Chapman also minimizes Bussy's faults in scheming with the friar by changing his picture of the friar at the end from that of a religiously hypocritical intriguer to that of a saintly ghost bidding Bussy to forgive his enemies. (Eugene Waith points out that even the earlier friar's traffic with the occult, and thus Bussy's, is never made explicitly evil as is that of Faustus.)

Even at the end of the play, however, Chapman is still unable to resolve the essential conflict between what his hero says and what he does. Bussy's affair involves him deeply in the intrigues of the society with which he is supposedly at odds. He continues to believe until the very end that he has the special privilege of involving himself in society without having to obey its rules, either the traditional values which Tamyra tries unsuccessfully to follow, or the relativistic rules of the Machiavellian court. Even when he is trapped by Monsieur and the Guise, Bussy trusts that "Fate is more strong than arms, and sly than treason, / And I at all parts buckled in my fate" (V.iii.87–88). Bussy is incredulous that his unfettered spirit can be conquered by intrigue, that his "fate" finally becomes the fickle Fortune which mocks society's members. To the end he considers his virtue unassailable. He resolves the dilemma in the only way possible, by realizing that such a virtue as his can exist only as an ideal. His final wish is to keep that ideal alive:

> Oh, my fame,
> Live in despite of murther! Take thy wings
> And haste thee where the grey eyed Morn perfumes
> Her rosy chariot with Sabaean spices!
> . . . .
> And tell them all that D'Ambois now is hasting
> To the eternal dwellers; that a thunder
> Of all their sighs together, for their frailties
> Beheld in me, may quit my worthless fall
> With a fit volley for my funeral.
> (V.iii.145–58)

What does Bussy's fall mean within the context of the extravagant words used to describe his life and death? Bussy's fall is not due to a moral failing, for within the moral framework of the play he is at worst a sincere opponent of the forces of evil. Bussy's failure can only be ascribed, I think, to the practical impossibility of *any* positive ideal action in a society riddled with intrigue and artifice; Bussy is heroic material in the wrong place. Chapman's vision thus presents him with an unresolvable problem. He is well aware of this for he makes Bussy say that ". . . rhetoric yet works not persuasion, / But only is a mean to make it work . . . " (I.i.136–37). In the fallen world he has chosen to depict, however, he can represent the constructive force of virtue only in words, not in deeds. For Tamyra as for Bussy, finally, the only way to realize Chapman's ideal of natural virtue is to defy the norms of society, yet this is both philosophically and dramatically an incomplete fulfillment. Tamyra's irresolution is ours also, because men must live in society. Bussy's failure is in a sense necessary, for any success Chapman could have given him would have become increasingly tainted in action. Bussy's morality could not possibly work in *any* society, but that does not prevent Chapman from holding him up as an ideal.

NOTES

1. All quotations taken from the New Mermaid edition of *Bussy D'Ambois,* ed. Maurice Evans (New York: Hill and Wang, 1966).
2. Eugene Waith, *The Herculean Hero* (New York: Columbia Univ. Press, 1962), p. 93.
3. For example, Ennis Rees in *The Tragedies of George Chapman* (Cambridge, Mass.: Harvard Univ. Press, 1954) sees Bussy's fall as exemplifying the dangers of the active life.
4. Edwin Muir, "Notes on the Tragedies of George Chapman," *Shakespeare's Contemporaries,* ed. Max Bluestone and Norman Rabkin (Englewood Cliffs, N.J.: Prentice-Hall, 1961), p. 234.
5. Waith, p. 103.

Indiana University Northwest

SAMUEL E. LONGMIRE

AMELIA AS A COMIC ACTION

Fielding's critics often claim that the happy ending of *Amelia* "does not necessarily follow from the logic of the novel itself."[1] My intention is to challenge this critical commonplace and to show that the comic ending is consistent with the expectations that the novel creates. *Amelia* does raise serious issues, but, with a few exceptions, critics have put too much emphasis on the seriousness of the work and too little attention on those elements which define it as a comic action.[2] Fielding not only provides several hints that a happy ending will occur, but develops larger narrative patterns that support the comic ending. We can discover these patterns by focusing on three basic problems: (1) the representation of Booth's arrests; (2) the treatment of the hindering characters; and (3) the characterization of Booth.

I

One central theme of the novel is that society fails to reward worthy men like Booth. Because he cannot get his deserved commission, he must find some other way to provide for his family. But in the course of the novel all other avenues are closed to him. As a symbol of Booth's vulnerable position in society, Fielding depicts him as caught in three unjust arrests, approximately at the beginning, middle, and end. Although these arrests are always potentially serious matters, they are represented in such a way that our anxiety for him and Amelia is not allowed to become excessive.

The first arrest, which leads to Booth's imprisonment in Newgate, promises at first to have terrible consequences for him. John Butt

67

believes that the "scene is in fact so sombre that a tragic conclusion seems inevitable."[3] There is, however, a danger in overreacting to the opening scenes. Booth is soon removed from the horrors of the prison by Miss Matthews, and his confinement then turns into an amusing intrigue. There is little attempt by Fielding to maximize the painful aspects of Booth's predicament. Social issues rather than private experiences dominate the early stages of the action. Thus Booth's various discussions with the prisoners are meant to introduce and to expose theories of behavior, prison conditions, and legal anomalies. Our indignation is raised against the system, but our emotional involvement with the inmates is minimal.

Fielding's success in controlling the serious implications of Booth's first imprisonment can be attributed partly to the narrator's role. Unlike the narrator of *Tom Jones*, the narrator of *Amelia* withdraws considerably, and, when he does appear, he generally engages in serious commentary. But this is not the case at the beginning, for there the narrator's ironic presence serves to keep the horrors of the prison at a distance. The narrator is capable of moral outrage, but in these early chapters he treats the undesirable characters less harshly than we might expect in what is ostensibly a novel of social protest. Almost any character or situation is fair game for a jest; and if we sense an incongruity between the scenes of pathos and the narrator's jocular commentary, such an effect is not necessarily a fault. It is reassuring that the narrator can break into the story from his superior position and belittle those who meant to do Booth harm.

The harmless nature of Booth's imprisonment is more evident to us when we consider how terrible it could be for a man in similar circumstances. Fielding conveniently provides a shocking description of the real consequences of such imprisonment in the *Champion* for February 16, 1739–40, where he concludes that a trip to the gallows is perhaps better for the prisoner than life in the dungeon.[4] To recognize the disparity between Booth's experiences and those, say, of the poor soldier whom Booth meets, is essential if the novel is to succeed as a comic action; for we should come to feel that he is a lucky man who is not meant to share the fate of those less fortunate persons.

Booth's second arrest, during which he never leaves the bailiff's house, is even less severe, mainly because he spends his time in diverting conversations with Bondum, the author, and the poor stoic philosopher. Some may feel that Booth's intellectual discussions portray him as inappropriately cheerful at a time when he should, realistically speaking, be grief-stricken by his misfortunes.[5] Booth is remarkably nonchalant about his predicament, but not inappropriately so if we bear in mind that *Amelia* is a comic action and not a realistic tale of hardship. Fielding is more interested in exploring something other than Booth's personal fears. Booth's three debates are both amusing in themselves and relevant to the major themes of the novel. It is comical to see Booth's opponents exposed when they foolishly maintain theories which are incongruous with their actions. And their exposure does, of course, remind us of certain serious problems: Bondum's activity proves that the corrupt system continues to spawn incompetent officials; the bad author's moderate success in society and his extraction of a guinea from James illustrate once again that the social order encourages the wrong people; and the stoic's superficial answers about human suffering suggest the need for a Christian resolution which the novel poses at the end. But these serious concerns emerge only after the process of comic exposure has occurred.

Thus, when Booth is released from Bondum (after a delightful brawl), we are aware that Booth and Amelia live in a deplorable world, but that they are not meant to be victimized by it. We have known that Booth's second arrest could have disastrous results: not only are he and Amelia temporarily alienated from Harrison, but at this point James begins his attempt to ruin Booth while seducing his wife. Amelia suffers greatly when her husband is taken from her, yet her grief, while natural, is somewhat excessive from our point of view; and our point of view, which shifts alternately from Booth to Amelia, should determine the response we make. When we see, on the one hand, that Booth spends his time at the bailiff's talking about philosophy and literature and, on the other hand, that Amelia is drawn under the protection of the shrewd Mrs. Atkinson, we are strongly assured that the worst fears of the heroine will not materialize. Additional assurance is provided when we see that Amelia herself grows stronger as a result of her ordeal. Her declaration to Mrs. Atkinson suggests a new inner strength that may counterbalance the misfortunes she seems destined to meet: "I have sinned against commonsense, which should teach me, instead of weakly and heavily lamenting my misfortunes, to rouse all my spirits to remove them. . . . There is nothing now too difficult for me to undertake" (VIII.iv). We may therefore conclude that since Fielding portrays his heroine as increasingly capable of meeting distress, he has constructed an essential pattern for his comic action.

Another kind of comic assurance is created by the pattern of distress and relief which is evident in Booth's arrests. When he and Amelia are happily reunited after his second incarceration, we realize that although they have suffered misfortunes which tend to culminate in real or potential threats of imprisonment, they have managed to escape their worst predicaments without suffering utter calamity. This pattern may lead us to suspect that because they have so far escaped disaster, they will continue to do so. The security we may begin to feel for them is similar to the kind of assurance we develop for Tom Jones when he continually escapes one complication after another.[6] Although *Amelia* is a more serious work than *Tom Jones*, both novels share unrealistic or improbable plots in which the heroes and heroines lead charmed lives in a realm that is slightly removed from the most painful contingencies of the real world. This suggests that a miraculous happy ending assisted by either Fortune or Providence is not a violation of the premises of their respective narratives.

Thus, when Booth is arrested for the last time, at the climax of the novel, we are mildly but not unduly alarmed for him and Amelia. As the happy ending gains momentum, Fielding does not bother to represent in detail Booth's confinement at Bondum's, and, in retrospect, we learn it has been a redeeming experience, for he has been converted to Christianity. Once again, as we have come to expect, he escapes the real horrors of arrest and imprisonment, this time through the propitious discovery of Amelia's fortune. The means by which the worthy couple finds happiness is doubtless a surprise, but the fact that they are ultimately happy is not.

II

Since Booth cannot secure a place in the social order on his own merit, he and Amelia are particularly dependent on their relationships with other people. But such relationships are usually unstable and hazardous, and much of the seriousness of the novel derives from the problems an innocent couple faces in a world where few can be trusted. Toward the end of the novel the harassment caused by their chief antagonists, Colonel James and the lord, seems quite severe: Booth is arrested by the lord and James sends Booth the much-feared challenge. It takes both the discovery of Amelia's fortune and the intervention of Harrison to extricate them from this final complication. Although the hindering characters pose more and more of a threat to the Booths, we need not conclude that the novel should move toward some catastrophe; on the contrary, we are given good reason to suspect that both James and the lord will be frustrated. Fielding succeeds in diminishing the frightening implications of their villainy by various techniques that contribute significantly to the total comic action.

James's pursuit of Amelia could lead to a serious confrontation, perhaps a fatal duel, between him and Booth. Those who feel that the novel points toward an unhappy ending may be thinking in part of the potentially disastrous duel which never occurs. Fielding is aware that such an encounter would compromise the comic ending, and therefore Booth never fully discovers James's hidden designs. Although Fielding does not want the duel to take place, he does, however, wish to exploit its possibility in order to create the maximum comic suspense, to say nothing of exploring other interests. In one episode, for example, Major Bath, who mistakenly believes Booth and James intend to settle their differences by a duel, concludes after hearing no word of the battle "that both were killed on the spot" (V.viii). His stupidity then takes on comic proportions when he consoles Mrs. James, who is apparently hysterical from the shock of her husband's death. According to Bath, she should be comforted by the thought that her husband "hath behaved himself with becoming dignity, and lies in the bed of honor" (V.viii). Before we become too indignant over Bath's insensitivity, we suddenly discover that Mrs. James is not really lamenting the death of her husband, but the loss of a new suit of brocade which his untimely departure prevents her from purchasing. With the comic exposure of Mrs. James—made comic partly because we feel that James deserves a cynical wife—we find that Fielding has used the possibility of a James-Booth encounter to expose both Colonel Bath's ridiculous sense of honor and Mrs. James's loveless relationship with her husband. But we can enjoy the whole episode without alarm because we are assured in the first part of the chapter that James and Booth are temporarily reconciled to each other. Since the potential confrontation between James and Booth always leads to a kind of suspenseful false alarm, we are not too surprised that Harrison succeeds at the end in convincing James to call off his challenge.[7]

James's willingness to cease his persecution of Booth is quite consistent with Fielding's representation of the complex and unreliable Colonel James. Early in the novel Booth testifies often to Miss Matthews that James is capable of extraordinary acts of friendship. Later, James appears less attractive, but we are disillusioned with him only gradually, mainly because the narrator seems so reluctant to present him in the worst light. There emerges, in fact, a kind of narrative counterpoint, as every disagreeable revelation about James is accompanied by commentary that throws a steady ray of light on his more redeeming qualities. At one point (IV.iv), the truth about his sordid marriage is revealed; however, the remainder of the chapter exists primarily as a testimony to his goodness. He has gained, we learn, a seat in Parliament for his brother-in-law, a fact that is inserted, Fielding admits, because "it serves to set forth the goodness of James, who endeavored to make up in kindness to the family what he wanted in fondness for his wife" (IV.iv). In the next chapter we are told that he is a libertine with women, but we are quickly warned that this is "the principal blemish in his character, which otherwise might have deserved much commendation for good-nature, generosity, and friendship" (IV.v).

Even when James begins his pursuit of Amelia, the narrator gives a balanced and judicious appraisal of his behavior. In a rare rhetorical display, the narrator first offers a lavish description of Amelia's beauty (VI.i) and then carefully points out that James is attracted to her involuntarily, "for he was taken by surprise, and his heart was gone before he suspected himself to be in any danger" (VI.ii). One feels that it is hardly possible, without great moral restraint, for James to resist Amelia's charms, and this opinion is supported by the narrator when he comes to James's defense: "to confess a truth in his favor, however the grave or rather the hypocritical part of mankind may censure it, I am firmly persuaded that to withdraw admiration from exquisite beauty, or to feel no delight in gazing at it, is as impossible as to feel no warmth from the most scorching rays of the sun" (VI.i). Since no reader wants to be in the camp with the "grave or hypocritical part of mankind," he is obliged to consider James's sexual passion with tolerance and understanding.

Fielding's narrator is generous toward James partly because he indirectly illustrates the Christian implications of the novel. James represents what a man can achieve morally without the influence of Christianity, but he also represents the moral limitations of a man whose natural impulses are not controlled by Christian principles. We should not condemn him but only regret that his basic goodness has not been disciplined in a higher school than nature alone. This seems to be the response of Harrison, who, in answer to Amelia's despair about human wickedness, comes to the defense of man in general and James in particular:

The nature of man is far from being in itself evil; it abounds with benevolence, charity, and pity, coveting praise and honor, and shunning shame and disgrace. Bad education, bad habits, and bad customs, debauch our nature, and drive it

headlong as it were into vice. . . . I am convinced there are good stamina in
the nature of this very man; for he hath done acts of friendship and generosity
to your husband before he could have any evil design on your chastity; and in a
Christian society . . . I doubt not but this very colonel would have made a
worthy and valuable member.   (IX.v)

Harrison's statement about the natural goodness of man and the cor-
ruptive influences of society occurs at a crucial point in the novel, just
when James's actions seem most inexcusable. The effect of such Christian judgment is to make him seem less culpable and less frightening.
Amelia accepts Harrison's charitable evaluation of James, and the
reader should too.

The comic thrust of the novel permits us to do more than forgive
James: we ultimately laugh at him. This is why the domestic debate
(XI.i) between the Jameses is so important to the structure of the
work. The quarrel is perfectly balanced as the husband and wife trade
insults about their respective flirtations. We enjoy the episode because
the combatants get what they deserve from each other. Since we may
be inclined to feel more antipathy for the husband, Fielding terminates
the scene so that James, in spite of all his wit, loses the argument. Mrs.
James not only thwarts her husband's plans to send her to the country, but cajoles him into letting her go to Tunbridge and to Bath with
an increased allowance, provided that she invites Amelia to dinner.
As the reader knows, it is a bad bargain for James because Amelia is
already acquainted with his dishonorable intentions.

This domestic scene is amusing in itself, but it is also related struc-
turally and thematically to the comic action. The episode occurs precisely when things begin for the Booths to take a sudden turn for the
worse, and, as a result of its place in the sequence of events, it is
necessarily an obtrusive comic interlude allowing us to laugh at one
of Booth's and Amelia's tormentors. To make us laugh at James, particularly toward the end of the novel, is Fielding's way of reminding
us that James's threat need not be taken too seriously. But James's
capitulation to his wife also illustrates one of the ironic themes of the
work: the libertine paradoxically never finds satisfaction from either
wife or mistress—to say nothing of the virtuous Amelia. And it is
comically satisfying to learn at the end that James is yoked to the fat
and tyrannical Miss Matthews. James's frustrations surely qualify him
as one of the novel's comic blunderers.

It would seem, then, that the reconciliation of the Booths with the
Jameses when they dine together at the end is actually the logical outcome of the portrayal of James. George Sherburn, I believe, is unduly
perplexed about the festive ending: "Whether this is by implication

forgiveness of one's enemies, or whether Fielding is ironically indicating that life goes on as usual even after conversions, or whether it is simply the outburst of exuberant good-nature that frequently affects English authors (even Shakespeare) at a joyful conclusion, it is hard to say."[8] Fielding allows us to see James's goodness and to laugh at his folly. Surely this is enough to prepare us for the "outburst of exuberant good-nature" at the end.

Northrop Frye observes that comedy "often includes a scapegoat ritual of expulsion which gets rid of some irreconcilable character . . . ."[9] It would be too painful for Fielding to repudiate completely either Matthews or the Jameses—their redeeming qualities do not permit such a fate in a comic action—but we are likely to accept the final view of the lord who becomes a victim to his amours, "by which he was at last become so rotten that he stunk above ground" (XII.ix). He is, for some readers, the true villain of the story in his exploitation of women, but we need not overreact to his presence. In fact, the anonymous lord is such an unrealized character that we may describe his role as "a mysterious absence which looks at times almost comical."[10] But more important, we are assured through Mrs. Bennet's tale (Book VII) that Amelia will not become one of his victims. Mrs. Bennet's narrative dilutes considerably any suspense we may feel about the lord's interest in the heroine. She is not only forewarned, but, as we discover in the analogies between her circumstances and Mrs. Bennet's, she is armed with a moral strength and prudence which Mrs. Bennet did not possess when she was tempted by the lord. Indeed, one realizes from her confession that the lord can succeed only with a woman who is willing to compromise her standards, and there is no chance that the virtuous Amelia would encourage a dishonorable flirtation.

Since the lord is nevertheless a despicable character, Fielding gratifies any outrage we may harbor toward him by incorporating several episodes in which he is duped. For our pleasure there is the ruse of Mrs. Atkinson, who, disguised as Amelia, tricks the lord—apparently without granting him what he most desires—into giving her husband the commission. Furthermore, there is the important history of Trent, which, Sherburn admits, abounds in "brilliant and caustic facetiousness."[11] Trent is not a pleasant fellow, but the way he traps the lord and makes his fortune is grimly satisfying. Dudden objects to the whole episode because it is interpolated at a moment of crisis and is therefore "an error of construction."[12] But Dudden's complaint is based on the assumption that *Amelia* is essentially a dark, realistic novel, moving inevitably toward some calamity, and that the comic diversion provided by the story of Trent detracts from the serious mood which Fielding presumably should be trying to sustain. I have tried to indicate, however, that Fielding often is willing in *Amelia* to sacrifice seriousness for other effects. As the story of Trent reveals, Fielding inserts comic episodes involving the hinderers toward the end of the novel as a reminder that, while the Booths' misfortunes multiply, we can anticipate that their tormentors will ultimately be frustrated.

III

"Happy endings do not impress us as true, but as desirable and they are brought about by manipulation."[13] Some readers may accept the contrivances that lead to the happy marital conclusion, but still find it undesirable because they develop a dislike for the husband and consequently lose some sympathy for the wife as well.[14] Booth has had many detractors, and one is tempted simply to say that he is a better man than his critics have recognized. But the problem is not easily dismissed, for we soon discover that what is in question is Fielding's technique of characterization. In the case of Booth, it is a technique that puts unusual demands on the reader. Booth's undesirable traits are generally magnified while his good ones are understated, and Amelia's virtues are always extolled while her faults are minimized. Our attention is on the contrast between the imperfect husband and the exceptional wife. No doubt Fielding meant to glorify the virtuous Amelia (it is her book) and perhaps to emphasize her redemptive role, a function that parallels the beneficent intervention of Divine Providence at the end. But if we are to admire Amelia's acceptance of Booth, we must believe that he is worthy of forgiveness. The comic ending is certainly undesirable if Amelia is forever shackled with a "dumb ox" (to use Allen's phrase). Thus Fielding's problem is to show the disparity between the two without making the distance too great. I find his strategy successful and so does John Middleton Murry, who claims that "however much we deplore some of Booth's weaknesses, we become increasingly convinced that these two creatures, so alike in their congenital incapacity for thinking evil, are really made for each other."[15] But readers have not concurred on this matter, and the problem seems to lie mainly in the portrayal of Booth. Time and again, Fielding sacrifices Booth's image for other interests, and the reader's challenge is to discover all the evidence that Booth is indeed a much better man than a casual reading might suggest.

Let us look first at his courtship. Booth is initially attracted to Amelia's intrinsic worth rather than her physical beauty, for her infamous nose is smashed at the time. As the courtship progresses, however, his noble love for Amelia takes a comic turn when he is forced into the role of a frustrated romance lover who worships his fair but inaccessible lady.[16] Such a role places him in ridiculous situations which can only provoke laughter at his expense. For example, when he delivers his long monologue about the hardships Amelia would face as his wife, the highly stylized speech should end, as it does momentarily, in a scene of tender sensibility; however, the tearful moment is suddenly shattered when the angry Mrs. Harris bursts from her hiding place to upbraid him for his clandestine affair with her daughter. Ironically, the tyrannical mother uses Booth's arguments against him, and she banishes the embarrassed lover from the house (II.iii). But no matter how silly Booth appears, he provokes only good-natured laughter, since his excesses are the result of his devotion to Amelia.

Fielding, of course, has more serious social concerns than the pastoral setting allows him to explore. But his indictment of the London world sometimes leads to a satiric mode that divides our interest between the objects of satiric attack and the principal agents of the action. The difficulties posed by such a method can be illustrated best when Booth is brought before the corrupt Justice Thrasher. Booth's "crime" is that he has tried to save a poor man being beaten by two ruffians. Booth's courageous act should gain him universal applause, but this is not the case. Wilbur Cross, for instance, believes that Booth makes a mistake in obeying his generous impulses.[17] Cross is certainly wrong in his disapproval of Booth's interference in the street fight, but the problem is partly that Fielding has not really played up Booth's generous impulses. The whole trial scene is presented so that his goodness is subordinated to the brilliant exposure of Thrasher's court. Booth is only one of the victims of injustice, and the narrative focus is more on his innocence than his goodness. Furthermore, after the trial only Booth remains a part of the continuing action; all the other characters, including the man whom Booth rescues, disappear once they have served Fielding's satirical purposes. The implications of such narrative procedure can be seen if we compare Booth's plight with that of Tom Jones. Tom's active benevolence is never wasted, since his acts of kindness create a host of friends who step forth to praise him and to save him at the end. But in the more serious world of *Amelia*, Booth performs a good deed which remains an isolated act, leading to no beneficial personal relationships.

Booth is capable of active virtue, but we may forget that fact when we see that much of his role is passive in nature. He is a soldier, but all we know about his performance in battle is that he gets wounded. He obviously loves Amelia, but much of the early portion of the novel shows him being seduced by Miss Matthews. Even when Fielding focuses on the domestic scene, Booth's active goodness is often subordinated to other narrative interests. A good case in point is the important fact that Booth, while still imprisoned, writes two letters to his wife. When Amelia rebukes him for not writing, the narrator defends him in the following passage:

> Booth excused himself, and with truth, as to his not having writ; for, in fact, he had writ twice from the prison, though he had mentioned nothing of his confinement; but as he sent away his letters after nine at night, the fellow to whom they were intrusted had burnt them for the sake of putting the twopence in his own pocket, or rather in the pocket of the keeper of the next gin-shop.
>
> (IV.iii)

We are pleased to learn, after the fact, that Booth does not callously forget about Amelia during his affair with Miss Matthews, but Fielding does not stress that point. The contents of the letters are never revealed (yet other letters are introduced in the course of the story), and the narrator's satirical summary emphasizes more the rascality of the messenger than Booth's consideration in writing.

The reader's challenge, then, is to keep in mind Booth's good traits which are often merely hinted at, or casually stated, without elaboration. For instance, Amelia, after being cruelly denied by Mrs. James, becomes ill. We learn that this illness "confined her several days to her house, during which Booth officiated as her nurse, and never stirred from her" (IV.vi). But Fielding does not expand on Booth's devotion; it is submerged in a context which is meant to show the painful contrast between Amelia's charitable concern and Mrs. James's cruel indifference. Booth is a devoted husband, but he is not allowed to demonstrate it dramatically in the narrative itself.

Once the reader is alerted to Booth's intrinsic goodness, his worthiness as Amelia's husband is unquestionable. Even his undesirable spiritual condition does not create a damaging distance between him and his wife. To be sure, Booth must be converted to Christianity before the marriage is truly harmonious. However, it would be a mistake to attach too much importance to Booth's skepticism, particularly if we believe his religious doubts make him spiritually unfit for Amelia. Indeed, those readers who think that Fielding has thrown together a happy ending, partly by the off-stage conversion of Booth, might keep in mind that the conversion simply does not represent a major change in his personality. At the beginning of the novel Booth is "an extreme well-wisher to religion" (I.iii), and after his conversion he admits that he never was "a rash disbeliever" (XII.v).

George Sherburn may claim that Booth's theory of the passions weakens his moral stamina, but the novel does not adequately support such an inference.[18] Booth's deterministic beliefs do not seem to influence his behavior. He cannot, for example, consider prostituting his wife, and he claims he is free to reject such a course of action (V.ix). Booth's declaration of his moral freedom obviously contradicts his theory, but we are convinced that it is not an empty boast. He is morally incapable of certain evil actions, and his goodness is finally recognized by Harrison at the end of the novel: "Your sufferings are all at an end, and Providence hath done you the justice at last which it will, one day or other, render to all men" (XII.vii).

Whether we agree with Harrison's claims about the role of Divine Providence is not wholly relevant; we can, however, feel at the end of the novel that a satisfying poetic justice prevails and that it is congruous with the expectations of the work. Only after we see how *Amelia* functions as a comic action can we discuss the seriousness of the novel without claiming that the ending is false and artificial.

NOTES

1. Robert Alter, *Fielding and the Nature of the Novel* (Cambridge, Mass.: Harvard Univ. Press, 1968), p. 165. See also F. Homes Dudden, *Henry Fielding: His Life, Works, and Times* (1952; rpt. Hamden, Conn.: Archon Books, 1966), 811–12; and Andrew Wright, *Henry Fielding: Mask and Feast* (Berkeley and Los Angeles: Univ. of California Press, 1966), p. 120.

2. Sheldon Sacks in *Fiction and the Shape of Belief: A Study of Henry Fielding with Glances at Swift, Johnson, and Richardson* (Berkeley and Los Angeles: Univ. of California Press, 1966) argues that all of Fielding's novels are comic actions; however, a stronger case than Sacks has provided can be made in demonstrating how *Amelia* succeeds as a comic action. Recently Arthur Sherbo in *Studies in the Eighteenth Century English Novel* (East Lansing: Michigan State Univ. Press, 1969), pp. 85–103, takes issue with those critics who have neglected the comic side of the novel.

3. *Fielding*, Writers and Their Work, No. 57 (London: Longmans, Green, 1959), p. 25.

4. *The Complete Works of Henry Fielding*, ed. W. E. Henley (1903; rpt. New York: Barnes and Noble, 1967), XV, 206. I am using the Henley edition of *Amelia*; all references to the novel will consist only of book and chapter numbers.

5. See Michael Irwin's complaint in *Henry Fielding: The Tentative Realist* (Oxford: Clarendon Press, 1967), p. 130.

6. See R. S. Crane, "The Concept of Plot and the Plot of *Tom Jones*," in *Critics and Criticism* (Chicago: Univ. of Chicago Press, 1952), p. 635.

7. Fielding raises the possibility of a duel in other episodes which are basically amusing. See both the treatment of Atkinson's farcical nightmare (IX.vi) and the manipulation of the sermon-letter at the masquerade (X.ii–v). For

an analysis of the consequences of the letter, see Maurice Johnson, *Fielding's Art of Fiction* (Philadelphia: Univ. of Pennsylvania Press, 1961), p. 162.

8. "Fielding's *Amelia*: An Interpretation," *ELH*, 3 (1936), rpt. in Ronald Paulson, ed., *Fielding: A Collection of Critical Essays*, Twentieth Century Views (Englewood Cliffs, N. J.: Prentice-Hall, 1962), p. 153.
9. *Anatomy of Criticism* (Princeton: Princeton Univ. Press, 1957), p. 165.
10. Alter, *Fielding and the Nature of the Novel*, p. 153.
11. "Fielding's *Amelia*," p. 146.
12. *Henry Fielding*, II, 811.
13. Northrop Frye, p. 170.
14. George Sherburn in "Fielding's *Amelia*," p. 157, responds to those critics who believe the ending contradicts the narrative premises of the story by pointing out that such a notion is "partly based on a lower conception of the character of Booth than Fielding intended. . . ." For a perfect illustration of Sherburn's point, see Walter Allen, *The English Novel* (New York: Dutton, 1958), pp. 60–61.
15. "In Defence of Fielding," in *Unprofessional Essays* (London: Jonathan Cape, 1956), p. 44.
16. For a discussion of the romance elements in *Amelia*, see Sheridan Baker, "Fielding's *Amelia* and the Materials of Romance," *PQ*, 41 (1962), 437–49.
17. *The History of Henry Fielding* (1918; rpt. New York: Russell and Russell, 1963), II, 318.
18. "Fielding's *Amelia*," p. 150.

Vanderbilt University

WILLIAM T. GOING

BROWNING AND THE SONNET

Of the major Victorian poets Browning wrote the fewest sonnets. Tennyson, who composed no memorable sonnet, is known to have written forty-six, thirty of which were published during his lifetime.[1] Though Arnold wrote only twenty-nine, they represent almost one-fourth of the total number of his poetic titles. In fact, the Victorian age itself, influenced by the quality of Keats's sixty-odd sonnets and the quantity of Wordsworth's more than five hundred, was the most prolific time of the sonnet.[2] And the poetic reputations of Elizabeth Barrett Browning, Meredith, the Rossettis, Wilfrid Scawen Blunt, John Addington Symonds, Hopkins, and Bridges rest to a large degree on their sonnet sequences.

The purpose of this essay is to examine Browning's sonnets and especially his attitude toward this verse form as expressed both directly and indirectly by the poet in his own *persona* and by the *men and women* he wrote about. Prejudiced against sonnet writing, Browning during most of his poetic career seems to denigrate this form of poetry because he associated it with an invasion of privacy, being himself "The Onlie Begetter" of the most popular sonnet sequence of the age—those sonnets he preferred disguised by the title "Sonnets from the Portuguese." For him the form seemed a *bête noire* that would not entirely vanish from his conscience until he finally tamed it into that little something he occasionally had to write "to order" for the ever-popular keepsake albums, public and private.

Browning is known to have written only eleven sonnets, one of which was a translation from the Italian poet, G. B. F. Zappi (1667–1719).[4]

81

Only three of these, which form a sequence, appeared in any collection of his poems published during his lifetime: "Moses the Meek" Browning used in a comic footnote on exaggeration to "Jochanan Hakkadosh." He directed his printer, "Print these sonnets in smaller type, after the Note."[5] All the other sonnets appeared only in magazines, newspapers, or anthologies, and they were never collected by the poet himself. The occasions for writing these sonnets, their dates, and publications have been carefully noted from Arthur Symons' *An Introduction to the Study of Browning* (1886) and *The Browning Society's Papers* to Sir Frederic Kenyon's ten-volume *Centenary Edition* (1912) and *New Poems* (1914) to William C. DeVane's *A Browning Handbook* (1955). For the purposes of this essay, however, a list indicating the date of composition, the first publication, and the subject matter of each will be helpful:

1. "Eyes Calm Beside Thee," 1834 (*Monthly Repository*, 1834), adoration from a speechless lover.
2. The "Moses" of Michael Angelo, translated 1850 (*Cornhill*, 1914), praise of a great work of a great sculptor.
3. "Helen's Tower," 1870 (*Pall Mall Gazette*, 1883), admiration for Helen, Lady Dufferin, and her memorial tower in Ireland as contrasted with the Greek hatred for Helen at the Scaean Gate.
4, 5, 6. "Moses the Meek" ("Jochanan Hakkadosh") I, II, III, 1882 (*Jocoseria*, 1883), exaggerated postscriptal jokes about the size of Moses compared to the giant Og.
7. "Goldoni," 1883 (*Pall Mall Gazette*, 1883), graceful tribute to a graceful writer of eighteenth-century Venetian comedy.
8. "Rawdon Brown," 1883 (*Century*, 1884), memorial account of an Englishman who found Venice so lovely that he "visited" it for forty years.
9. "The Founder of the Feast" (To Arthur Chappell), 1884 (*The World*, 1884), presentational tribute to the impresario of the popular Saturday and Monday Concerts at St. James's Hall.
10. "The Names" (To Shakespeare), 1884 (*Shakespeare Show-Book*, 1884), memorial tribute to a name almost as great as that of the ineffable Jehovah, who "didst create us."
11. "Why I am a Liberal," c. 1885 (*Why I am a Liberal*, ed. Andrew Reid, 1885); "Because all I haply can and do . . . . That little is achieved through Liberty."

From this list certain facts are apparent. Though Browning's use

of the sonnet form extends over a period of fifty years, almost his entire poetic career, all but three were written in the 1880s, after his
major work was completed. Thus the sonnets belong to his apprentice
years and to his years of decline. To see something of the evolution
of his sonnet style one need only place "Eyes Calm Beside Thee" next
to "Rawdon Brown."[6]

Sonnet

Eyes, calm beside thee, (Lady couldst thou know!)
   May turn away thick with fast-gathering tears:
I glance not where all gaze: thrilling and low
   Their passionate praises reach thee—my cheek wears
Alone no wonder when thou passest by;
   Thy tremulous lids bent and suffused reply
To the irrepressible homage which doth glow
   On every lip but mine: if in thine ears
Their accents linger—and thou dost recall
   Me as I stood, still, guarded, very pale,
Beside each votarist whose lighted brow
Wore worship like an aureole, "O'er them all
   My beauty," thou wilt murmur, "did prevail
Save that one only":—Lady couldst thou know!

Rawdon Brown

"Tutti ga i so gusti, e mi go i mii." *Venetian Saying*

Sighed Rawdon Brown: "Yes, I'm departing, Toni!
   I needs must, just this once before I die,
   Revisit England: *Anglus* Brown am I,
Although my heart's Venetian. Yes, old crony—
Venice and London—London's 'Death the bony'
   Compared with Life—that's Venice! What a sky,
   A sea, this morning! One last look! Good-by,
Cà pesaro! No, lion—I'm a coney
To weep! I'm dazzled; 'tis that sun I view
   Rippling the— the— *Cospetto*, Toni! Down
   With carpet-bag, and off with valise-straps!
'Bella Venezia, non ti lascio più!' "
   Nor did Brown ever leave her: will, perhaps
Browning, next week, may find himself quite Brown!

The first is a typical sonnet from an adoring lover who cannot tell
his Lady how his calm eyes belie his feelings for her: Lady couldst
thou know!" Though Browning's delight in drama is in brief evidence
in lines 12, 13, and 14 when the Lady's own words are hazarded, the
spirit of the sonnet is that of the prostrate lover of the Renaissance—
the kind of attitude that Meredith's hero in *Modern Love* sarcastically
castigates in "Lady, this [description of the human being as an intelli-
gent animal] is my sonnet to your eyes." Browning's *Pauline*-like hero
anticipates, when he describes other lovers and imagines the Lady's

own words, the dramatic shorthand of character and place that is later fully evident in the second sonnet that is a little "parleying" with Rawdon Brown. The "Yes, I'm departing, Toni" of the first line sharply delineates Brown's vignette of conversation with his valet Toni as he plans to depart for London. He looks out at Venice's "What a sky"; but he ends by ordering "Down with carpet-bag, and off with valise-straps!" Browning concludes the Petrarchan sonnet with lines that break the mood in Shakespearean fashion, pun on his own name, and warn his hostess, Mrs. Bronson (who had suggested the subject matter and requested the poem), that he may linger like Brown—even die himself in Venice. In this poem Browning reveals how he could make the sonnet a vehicle as dramatically unique as his longer monologues.

Different in style and tone is the "Goldoni" sonnet. In the graceful charm of its strict Petrarchan form it recalls in miniature the Venetian elegance of "A Toccata of Galuppi's," a recollection Browning probably intended since Galuppi wrote music for many of Goldoni's libretti.

> Goldoni
>
> Goldoni— good, gay, sunniest of souls,—
>   Glassing half Venice in that verse of thine—
>   What though it just reflect the shade and shine
> Of common life, nor render, as it rolls,
> Grandeur and gloom? Sufficient for thy shoals
>   Was Carnival: Parini's depths enshrine
>   Secrets unsuited to that opaline
> Surface of things which laughs along thy scrolls.
> There throng the people: how they come and go,
>   Lisp the soft language, flaunt the bright garb— see—
> On Piazza, Calle, under Portico
>   And over Bridge! Dear king of Comedy,
> Be honored! thou that didst love Venice so,
> Venice, and we who love her, all love thee!

These three examples, along with the classic elegance of "Helen's Tower" and the straightforward lines of "Why I Am a Liberal"—

> Why? Because all I haply can and do,
> All that I am now, all I hope to be—....
> That little is achieved through Liberty.

come near to negating Hatcher's opinion that "Browning's genius was not at home in the rigid limits of such a fixed form as the sonnet."[7]

A second apparent observation is that with the possible exception of "Eyes Calm Beside Thee"[8] all of Browning's sonnets are occasional poems: the Marquis of Dufferin and Ava requests a poem honoring his mother, the granddaughter of Sheridan; the Goldoni Committee wishes to honor the "king of Comedy"; seeing the ease with which Browning complies with that request, his Venetian hostess, Mrs. Bronson, asks a poem for herself about a present-day Venetian, Rawdon Brown, who has just died. And so it goes: the presentation album for Arthur Chappell, the Hospital for Women in Fulham Road and their *Shakespearean Show-Book,* Andrew Reid and his anthology for the Liberal Party. Even the sequence "Moses the Meek," appended to the "Note" to "Jochanan Hakkadosh," is occasioned by Browning's own wry after-hope to lend Talmudic mystification and exaggeration to what DeVane calls an "otherwise bald and unconvincing narrative."[9] The occasion of the Zappi translation about Michelangelo's *Moses* is not known, but with the MS., found among the papers of George Smith, Browning's publisher and friend, was the note, "From Zappi, R. B. (Given to Ba 'for love's sake,' Siena, Sept. 27, '50)."[10] Could it be that this sonnet is a peace offering for having "said something against putting one's loves into Verse" and thus discouraging Elizabeth from showing Robert her sonnets about him until 1849, three years after they were written? It was at Lucca, he told Miss Wedgwood, a "strange, heavy crown, that wreath of Sonnets [was] put on me one morning unawares."[11] Could it be that a year later on their summer sojourn in Siena Robert made of the Zappi poem an "occasional" presentation to attest at least his toleration of the sonnet form? If this supposition and that of Griffin and Minchin about the first sonnet's being addressed to Eliza Flower contain any truth, then all Browning's sonnets may rightly be called "occasional." Certainly all were presented to some person, committee, or "occasional" anthology or album. To be sure, many sonnets by many poets have been and will be occasional, but there is a difference with Browning's. Milton's "Avenge, O Lord Thy Slaughtered Saints," for example, was occasioned by the April 1655 "masacher in Piemont." The letters that Milton as Latin Secretary wrote for Cromwell's signature as well as the subscription for the refugees, to which the poet contributed £2,000, were direct occasional actions.[12] The sonnet was written to vent his personal feeling after he had executed professional and public duties. Browning's sonnets, on the other hand, were written to order, on the request of a person or committee. And perhaps because they were in this sense ordered "merchandise," Browning never collected or republished them. Even "Eyes Calm Beside Thee" was signed *Z* and placed in *The Monthly Repository*, where Miss Flower would be sure to see it and know its real author. And the "Moses" sequence in "Jochanan Hakkadosh" was occasioned by the poet as annotator and critic in his desire to heighten the humor of his poem, and was "given" to the curious reader in very small print.

This literal sense of scrupulosity may, according to DeVane, have prevented Browning from collecting "his most successful sonnet," "Helen's Tower,"[13] as Tennyson did his less good one on the same subject in *Tiresias and Other Poems* (1885). This same attitude on the part of Browning seems to be true for the equally successful "Rawdon Brown"; it belonged to his hostess, Mrs. Bronson. And when she asked his permission to publish it, Browning granted the request. But he was, for the same reason, horrified when Longfellow's daughter Edith published, without his permission, in the *Century Magazine*, the ten lines, "Thus I Wrote in London, Musing on My Betters," which he had written in her album after copying out his little poem, "Touch Him Ne'er So Lightly." For Browning there was a consistency in this view, and it was different from the situation of "The Pied Piper," which he wrote for little Willie Macready to illustrate while the child was ill. The idea for this presentation poem was Browning's, not the Macreadys'. Therefore, while Willie could and did illustrate the poem, Browning could and did publish it in *Dramatic Lyrics*.[14]

A third observation is that for a prolific poet Browning wrote extremely few sonnets and these few not in the self-relevatory tradition of Shakespeare, Keats, Mrs. Browning, Meredith, and Rossetti. Yet Browning does "sonnet-sing" about himself more than he perhaps intends, just as his *men and women* are not always entirely *dramatis personae*. The very fact that Browning chose to respond to these particular "occasional" requests and not to others that came his way is somewhat indicative of the tastes of the man. He is, for example, flattered by the request from the Marquis of Dufferin and Ava; as a dramatist himself he has genuine interest in Goldoni; as a lover of Venice he sees something of himself in Brown (he even puns on their names and forecasts his own death in Venice); as a good amateur musician and concert-goer he can send a tribute with grace to one of the great impresarios of London; and Shakespeare had always been for him the archetype of the best and greatest of the "objective" poets. In fact, the subject matter of these *objective* occasional poems furnishes an adequate portrait of Browning the man: a shy young lover, an exalter of women, one who has interest in Italian artists, a lover of jokes and ironies, an admirer of Venice, a lover of drama and music, an idolater of Shakespeare, and a political liberal. To this extent Browning did "sonnet-sing you about myself."

On the other hand, none of these sonnets is revelatory of strong emotions in the way that a poet through art transmutes an autobiographical crisis into great poetry. Moreover, in the short poem "House" Browning gives direct, dramatic expression to the same sort of attitude he had expressed years earlier to E. B. B. after their marriage, when he "happened early to say something against putting one's loves in verse." And whatever that *something* was, it prevented her from showing him her sonnets for about three years. Doubtless, the opinion was close to that expressed in "House" with its point of departure an attack on Wordsworth's "Scorn Not the Sonnet": "Unlock my heart with a sonnet-key?" The controlling image of the poem is a house whose front walls have been knocked down by an earthquake, revealing the interior and the domestic habits of its occupant. For Browning only such a catastrophe as this could open his house to public view; never could it be opened voluntarily by a sonnet-key. And even if the great Shakespeare was willing thus to "unlock his heart," Browning considered him "the less Shakespeare" for doing so. The poem is an aspect of the general theme of the entire *Pacchiarotto* volume (1886): the right of privacy. It belongs to the years of Browning's imagined quarrel with the "British Public, ye who like me not." But DeVane is doubtless right when he says that "something more immediate than Wordsworth's sonnet impelled Browning to write 'House.'"

In 1870 he read the fifty sonnets that then composed "*Sonnets and Songs* Toward a Work to be called 'The House of Life,' " a few of which had literally been dug from the grave of Rossetti's wife, where they had impulsively been buried along with other poems like "Jenny." Though Browning rather liked Rossetti, whom he first met in 1855 on one of his London visits, he apparently felt that the poet-painter had "betrayed the cause of personal privacy." And in describing "the householder's odd furniture, musty old books, his exotic and foreign habit of burning perfumes in his rooms," Browning may have had Rossetti in mind.[15] The very word *House* of the title links the poem with Rossetti, who was long in evolving a suitable title for his sequence, *The House of Life*. On the other hand, Browning is careful to set this earthquake "in a foreign land" so that the parallel circumstances would not be exact, just as he had earlier written of Wordsworth in general terms as "a lost leader," a reference he both denied and affirmed. If reading Rossetti's *The House of Life* was the immediate cause for Browning's "House," the root of that cause lay in the fact that "Poor Rossetti" had lost his wife shortly after the time of Browning's own loss of E. B. B. Knowing few of the actual conditions of that marriage, Browning must have seen Rossetti as something of a traitor to the cause of privacy: not only was he putting his love into verse but into sonnets—and fleshly ones at that.

Another less immediate cause of "House" may well have been Meredith's *Modern Love*. Four months after Mrs. Browning's death[16] Mary Meredith also died, and *Modern Love*, which must have seemed to Browning, as it did to others, a thinly veiled account of the author's unhappy marriage, made its appearance in *Modern Love and Poems of the English Roadside* (1862). Browning read this volume, but what he really thought can only be surmised. In typically gallant fashion he complimented the author. Meredith, who was peculiarly sensitive to unfavorable criticisms, was disturbed by the neglect of reviewers' comments on the chief poem, but he wrote happily to his good friend, Captain Maxse, about *Modern Love*: "I saw Robert Browning the other day, and he expressed himself 'astounded at the originality, delighted with the naturalness and beauty.' "[17] As for its taste Browning surely must have had his doubts. Such lines in "House" as

> You see it is proved, what the neighbors guessed:
> His wife and himself had separate rooms.

could more probably suggest the bedroom scenes of *Modern Love* than the house in Cheyne Walk with its blue china, wombat, and orientalia, where Rossetti moved after his wife's death.

One thing, though, is certain: in 1876 Browning spoke out clearly in "House" against the "confessional" sonnet at a time when he himself was known to have written only two sonnets, translated only one, and published none in a collected volume. And a few years earlier he had written Miss Wedgwood that even the *Sonnets from the Portuguese* "was a strange, heavy crown . . . put on me unawares."

In addition to writing very few sonnets and inveighing against the tradition of "putting one's love" into sonnets, Browning allows his numerous *men and women* to make revealing comments about that form of verse. These references run from *Sordello* (1840) to "The Two Poets of Croisic" (1878). The three instances from *Sordello* are of especial interest because Sordello in "Book the Second" wins a troubador's "Court of Love" contest to become the Count's minstrel at Mantua, where rivals like Bocafoli, with his psalms, and Plara, with his sonnets, strive to outdo him:

> The worse,
> That his [Sordello's] poor piece of daily work to do
> Was—not to sink under any rivals; who
> Loudly and long enough, without these qualms,

Turned, from Bocafoli's stark-naked psalms,
To Plara's sonnets spoilt by toying with,
"As knops that stud some almug to the pith
Pricked for gum, wry thence, and crinkled worse
Than pursed eyelids of a river-horse
Sunning himself o' the slime when whirs the breese"—
(II.764–73)

A hungry sun above us, sands that bung
Our throats,—each dromedary lolls a tongue,
Each camel churns a sick and frothy chap,
And you, 'twixt tales of Potiphar's mishap,
And sonnets on the earliest ass that spoke,
——Remark, you wonder any one needs choke
With founts about!   (III.819–25)

This town, the minister's trust,
Held Plara; who, its denizen, bade hail
In twice twelve sonnets, Tempe's dewy vale.
(III.898–900)[18]

Whether Browning is using the word *sonnet* in a general sense of "madrigal" one cannot be sure. Actually the time of Sordello is almost a century before the fourteen-line sonnet as we know it came into being. But this is shadowy territory at best, and it is not necessary to assume that Browning speaks anachronistically or accepts a date other than the first part of the thirteenth century as the most likely time for the first sonnet. The important point is that he chose the word *sonnet* and furnished a four-line example from Plara in the worst taste of early Renaissance metaphysics. The semantic note that Browning seems to be striking here is that the sonnet form is overwritten, over-ornate, dull and trifling in subject matter, and that twice twelve sonnets on "Tempe's dewy vale" is excessive.

In "Up at a Villa—Down in the City" (1855) the use of the term is similar. At the city "post-office" the news is always wonderfully exciting, thinks "an Italian Person of Quality": notices of three liberal thieves just shot, the Archbishop's fatherly rebukes, some "little new law" of the Duke,

Or a sonnet with flowery marge, to the Reverend Don
So-and-So,
Who is Dante, Boccaccio, Petrarca, Saint Jerome, and Cicero,
"And moreover," (the sonnet goes rhyming,) "the skirts of
Saint Paul has reached,
"Having preached us those six Lent-lectures more unctuous
than ever he preached."

With the mention of Dante, Boccaccio, Petrarca, and the rhyming process, the speaker seems to refer to a sonnet that tries to imitate the exaggerated figures of speech of Renaissance sonneteers. Now in the nineteenth century, Browning intimates, that verse form has fallen into awkward, apprentice hands and is attached to the public bulletin board. The semantic implication is that the sonnet can too easily become an over-flowery, public thank-you note.

In "One Word More" (1855), which Browning wrote somewhat hastily after he arrived in London to oversee the publication of *Men and Women*, he speaks of the sonnet in his own person, as he was to do later in "House." The poem was of course a dedication to E. B. B., and somewhat of a public thank-you for the *Sonnets from the Portuguese*, now no longer known as "translations"—if they ever were. The chief point of the poem is that when one wishes to give a loved one a gift, he gives a unique one: Dante, for example, painted a picture for Beatrice, and Rafael "made a century of sonnets" for Margharita. He, Robert Browning, unfortunately has but one talent, "This of verse, alone," so he here presents E. B. B. "my fifty men and women." The interesting point about the use of the term *sonnet* in this poem is Browning's insistence that Rafael's gift of sonnets was right because while the world might view his pictures, "but one [could view] the volume," that "century of sonnets" now lost to mankind. Even though Robert's dedicatory "verse alone" must serve for both public and private gift, the very use of the sonnet illustration must have made E. B. B. uneasy, wondering if she had been right in publishing her half-century of sonnets. It is true that Browning said that he could not reserve to himself "the finest sonnets written in any language since Shakespeare's,"[19] but the irony of the situation is unmistakable, if unintentional.

The references to the term *sonnet* in *The Ring and the Book* are chiefly centered upon Caponsacchi. In Book I he is "A prince of sonneteers and lutanists"; the rather coarse narrator of "Half-Rome" in Book II finds Caponsacchi, like exiled Ovid, given to "much culture of the sonnet-stave." In Book VI Caponsacchi himself refers to the process of writing and riming—"Counting one's fingers till the sonnet's crowned." In Book VII the sinister Margherita, who believes "All Poetry is difficult to read," whispers to the swooning Pompilia, "Just hear the pretty verse he [Caponsacchi] made to-day! / A sonnet from Mirtillo, 'Peerless fair . . . .' " In Book IX the garrulous Dr. Bottinius digresses to describe the admonition that the Law might give to women like Pompilia "faultless to a fault":

> "And dance no more, but fast and pray! avaunt—
> "Be burned, thy wicked townman's sonnet-book!
> "Welcome, mild hymnal by . . . some better scribe!"
> (IX.1203–1205)

And in a similar vein in Book XI Guido angrily reminds the Abate Panciatichi of a story about the latter's ancestor when some indiscreet soul

> —hitched the joke
> Into a sonnet, signed his name thereto,
> And forthwith pinned on post the pleasantry:
> For which he's at the galleys, rowing now
> Up to his waist in water,—just because
> *Panciatic* and *lymphatic* rhymed so pat!
>   (XI.1251–56)

Thus the references to the *sonnet* by various personages in *The Ring* tend to fall into one of two definitions: a worthless private love song or canzonet, or a libelous public pasquinade.

In *Prince Hohenstiel-Schwangau* (1871) the one use of the word *sonnet* seems merely synonymous with *poem* and illustrative of the "artistic" drain upon its creator:

> That whoso rhymes a sonnet pays a tax,
> Who paints a landscape dips brush at his cost.
>   (1808–1809)

In *The Inn Album* (1875), however, the use of the term is more integral to the drama about the gambling debts the losing player has scribbled in the margin of the verses in the *Inn Album*. The young "polished snob" observes:

> Let's see, however—hand the book, I say!
> Well, you've improved the classic by romance.
> Queer reading! Verse with parenthetic prose—
> *"Hail, calm acclivity, salubrious spot!"*
> (Three-two fives) *"life how profitably spent!"*
> (Five-naught, five-nine fives) *"yonder humble cot,"*
> (More and more naughts and fives) *"in mild content;*
> *And did my feelings find the natural vent*
> *In friendship and in love, how blest my lot!"*
> Then follow the dread figures—five! *"Content!"*
> That's apposite! Are you content as he—
> Simpkin the sonneteer?   (I.128–39)

In the second section of the poem the young man refers again to the words of the Inn-Album sonnet that have come jokingly to stand for the Inn because the countryside itself is "no longer the symbol of natural innocence."[20] By implication the sonnet has become a trite form for trite words:

> For see now!—back to *"balmy eminence"*
> Or *"calm acclivity"* or what's the word!
> Bestow you there an hour, concoct at ease
> A sonnet for the Album, while I put
> Bold face on, best foot forward, make for house.
>   (II.379–83)

Of note here is the fact that the quoted snatches from one Simpkin suggest a legitimate sonnet (rather than a general lyric form) by the meter and rimes, while at the same time the very name of the poetaster "Simpkin the sonneteer" prefigures and underlines the pretentious aridity of the verses. Even the arithmetic scratchings in the margins are more engaging. These and other ironies are woven throughout the long dramatic narrative, which ends:

> " 'Hail, calm acclivity, salubrious spot!'
> Open the door!"
>   No: let the curtain fall!

In "The Two Poets of Croisic" Browning again uses the term *sonnet* to denote the petty verses of small poets. René Gentilhomme, who became a poet of momentary renown by the accident of prophecy,

> Was bound to keep alive the sacred fire,
>   And kept it, yielding moderate increase
> Of songs and sonnets, madrigals, and much
> Rhyming thought poetry and praised as such.
>   (229–32)

And when his fame died, the world was "saved from more sonneteering." Paul Desforges Maillard, who achieved notoriety by passing his verses off on Voltaire and La Roque as those of a feminine-novice, "hoarded" his treasure of "Sonnets and songs of every size and shape."

Though it is often difficult in these poems to be sure of the exact sense of *sonnet* and *sonneteering*, one thing is certain: Browning associates the words with petty poetry and petty poets. When the score is reckoned up and allowances are made for the customary uses and denotational changes in the England, France, and Italy his *men and women* inhabit, for Browning the term *sonnet* implies opprobrium. When he speaks in his own person in "House" or "One Word More," the emphasis is on the impropriety of sonnet-singing about oneself or on the propriety of the private, unpublished sonnets of Rafael's unique gift.

The second conclusion to be drawn from these references is that they occur during the years when Browning himself wrote no sonnets. His 1850 translation of Zappi aside, he wrote "Eyes Calm Beside Thee" in 1834 and "Helen's Tower" in 1870; the other eight sonnets were written in the 1880s. The allusions made by and about his dramatic characters occur from 1840 to 1878. And when Browning decided to use the sonnet for occasional purposes, his characters ironically make no further mention of that verse form.

The only sonnets Browning published in a collection of his verse were the three in the footnote to "Jochanan Hakkadosh." They form a sequential arrangement indicated by their Roman numerals. The first sonnet recounts Moses' leaping ninety cubits in the air only to discover that he then reached barely to the giant Og's ankle bone. The second sonnet, beginning "And this same fact has met with unbelief!" recounts the speaker's experience walking the length of Og's thigh bone—a four hours' walk. The sonnet ends "respect to Moses, though!" The humor of the second poem, while it can be read and understood separately, is not entirely apparent without the first. Browning emphasizes this unity by beginning the sonnet with *And*, by referring to Moses' exploit of Sonnet I, and by duplicating the exact Petrarchan rime pattern in both. The third sonnet begins, "Og's thigh bone—if ye deem its measure strange," and goes on to tell of an even stranger tale of a stork wading in a "tank" whose bottom has not been reached by a stone that was dropped seventy years ago! Here again the sonnet is intelligible in its own right, but its real point of exaggeration *in extremis* is lost unless the sequence is read as one poem, though the relationship of the third is not so close as that of the first and second. And the rime scheme with the same octave (*abba abba*) in all three varies the sestet from *cdcdcd* of I and II to *cdecde* in III with just the right shade of riming similarity and difference.

For one who wrote few sonnets and disliked the form, Browning demonstrates in these sonnets that he is aware of some of the nuances of the sonnet sequence. With his skill in oblique narration one wonders if he were ever tempted to use the techniques of this basically lyric medium to suggest narration by the skill of the juxtaposition of its parts. The truth is that in "James Lee's Wife" Browning actually wrote his sonnet sequence without benefit of sonnets. The poem is a series of dramatic lyrics that tell a story of the marital relations of Mr. and Mrs. Lee. The immediate subject is James Lee—the original title of the poem—and the point of view is strictly that of Mrs. James Lee. Most recent commentators on the poem have begun to see it as somewhat more than another of Browning's dramatic psychological studies.[21] One of the latest of these commentators in " 'James Lee's Wife'—and Browning's" makes a convincing case for "a remarkable likeness of theme and imagery in 'James Lee's Wife' and Elizabeth's *Sonnets from the Portuguese*."[22]

An equally good case could be made for "a remarkable likeness" to Meredith's *Modern Love*. Both poems concern marriages that are falling apart because of too divergent personalities in too exclusively close range of each other. And in each case the woman sacrifices herself, in *Modern Love* by suicidal poison and in "James Lee's Wife" by fleeing on shipboard. In each poem the point of view is confined: in *Modern Love* it is the husband who speaks when the omniscience is shifted; in "James Lee's Wife" the wife speaks throughout. Both poems use much nature imagery, a practice unusual for Browning. In fact, it is difficult not to see Meredith's images in

> We saw the swallows gathering in the sky,
> And in the osier-isle we heard them noise.
> . . .
> Love, that had robbed us of immortal things,
> This little moment mercifully gave,
> Where I have seen across the twilight wave
> The swan sail with her young beneath her wings.
>   (XLVII.1–2, 13–16)[23]

lurking behind Browning's

> The swallow has set her six young on the rail,
>   And looks sea-ward:
> The water's in stripes like a snake, olive-pale
>   To the leeward,—
> On the weather-side, black, spotted white with the wind.
> "Good fortune departs, and disaster's behind,"—
> Hark, the wind with its wants and its infinite wail!
>   (III.53–60)

Both poets depart from the usual sonnet metrics: Meredith slightly into fifty sixteen-line lyrics, and Browning radically into nine lyrics of varying lengths and metrics.

There can be little doubt that in the summer of 1862 one of the books Browning took with him to the coast of Brittany, where "James Lee's Wife" was primarily written, was Meredith's *Modern Love*.[24] It had been published in the spring of that year, and Browning, we know, was curious about the methods both Rossetti and Meredith were using in writing about the deaths of their wives. Whether Browning was more influenced by *Sonnets from the Portuguese* or *Modern Love* may be debated. Both of these influences, however, as well as what Rossetti seemed to be planning in his songs and sonnets, point to the fact that Browning was aware of the narrative-lyric ambiguities of a sonnet sequence, while at the same time he was determined not to be caught in his readers' eyes as one who unlocks his heart with a sonnet-key. So he did two things, both of which were typical Browning procedures: he wrote from the feminine point of view, as he had done in other poems like "The Glove"; and he transferred some of the features of the sonnet sequence, like off-stage action and implied narration, to a sequence of dramatic lyrics, much as Arnold had done in his "Switzerland" and "Faded Leaves" poems.

Browning's relationship to the sonnet is a series of "satires of circumstance." Though he wrote no sonnets in his most productive middle years, he is the inspirer of the most popular series of the period. When he spoke ill of putting one's loves into sonnets, Mrs. Browning postponed showing him her sonnets about their love. After the publication of *Sonnets from the Portuguese*, when he felt that some public acknowledgment was due her, he tried thanking her with the rather hastily written "One Word More." Gallantly he put his foot in his mouth by praising Rafael for keeping his sonnets, written to the women he loved best, both private and unprinted. From 1840 to 1878, when Browning wrote his greatest poems, his numerous *men and women* speak surprisingly often and disparagingly of the sonnet, particularly in *The Inn Album*. But when he himself begins to find the sonnet a useful vehicle for certain occasions, his characters fall silent. Ironically Browning chooses to record these occasions in the Inn Albums of the world while an admiring public reads over his now famous shoulder. Publications in *The Shakespeare Show-Book, The Century, Pall-Mall Gazette, The World*, and *Why I am a Liberal* breached his private prejudice to full public circle.[25]

NOTES

1. See Dougald B. MacEachen, "Tennyson and the Sonnet," *VN*, No. 14 (1958), 1–8. In accounting for Tennyson's "failure" as a sonneteer, MacEachen might well have intimated more strongly that to the poet the sonnet was the special province of his friend Hallam and his brother Charles, the latter of whom wrote more than 300.
2. The most productive decade of sonnet writing both in quantity and quality was probably 1590–1600. According to estimates of Sidney Lee in *Elizabethan Sonnets* (London: Archibald Constable, 1904) and *A Life of Shakespeare*, 4th ed. (London: John Murray, 1925), and of Janet G. Scott in *Les sonnets elisabethains* (Paris: Librairie Ancienne Honore Champion, 1929), the Elizabethans produced somewhat over 2,000 sonnets in and out of series. Because of the proliferation of poets and printing presses, the number of Victorian sonnets in my own representative list of only those in sequence exceeds 2,600, while the number of single sonnets would probably more than double this figure.
3. The term *sonnet sequence* itself is Victorian. See my articles "The Term Sonnet Sequence," *MLN*, 62 (1947), 400–402, and "Gascoigne and the Term 'Sonnet Sequence,'" *N&Q*, NS 1 (1954), 189–91.
4. The standard references on this subject state the number as nine: Karl Lentzner, "Robert Browning's Sonettdichtung," *Anglia*, 9 (1899), 500–17; and Harlan H. Hatcher, *The Versification of Robert Browning* (Columbus: Ohio State Univ. Press, 1928), 132–34. Lentzner did not know of "Eyes

Calm Beside Thee" or the Zappi translation; Hatcher does not mention the Zappi; though he includes "The Founder of the Feast" in his metrical list of sestet rimes, he apparently does not entirely accept the poem as a sonnet even after Browning corrected the original fifteen lines to fourteen. See William C. DeVane, *A Browning Handbook,* 2nd ed. (New York: Appleton, 1955).

5. DeVane, p. 470.

6. Hatcher, p. 113, makes this suggestion, but he does not state how he sees the "evolution." The text of "Sonnet" is taken from *The Complete Works of Robert Browning,* ed. Roma A King, et al. (Athens: Ohio Univ. Press, 1969), I, 57; the text of "Rawdon Brown" is from *The Complete Works of Robert Browning* (Arno Edition), ed. Charlotte Porter and Helen A. Clarke (New York: George D. Sproul, 1899), XII, 276. All subsequent quotations from Browning's poems are from this edition unless otherwise noted.

7. Ibid., p. 132.

8. Though information about the composition of this sonnet is not known, Griffin and Minchin in *The Life of Robert Browning* (London: Methuen, 1938), p. 309, suggest that it was occasioned by Browning's devotion to Eliza Flower.

9. DeVane, p. 472.

10. *New Poems by Robert Browning and Elizabeth Barrett Browning,* ed. Sir Frederic G. Kenyon (New York: Macmillan, 1915), p. 26. Probably unknown to Browning, Sir Aubrey de Vere had translated this same sonnet in 1842, calling it "The Statue of Moses: From Zappi."

11. *Robert Browning and Julia Wedgwood: A Broken Friendship as Revealed by Their Letters,* ed. Richard Curle (New York: Stokes, 1937), pp. 99–100.

12. See *The Complete Poems of John Milton,* ed. F. A. Patterson (New York: Crofts, 1934), p. 55 of "Notes."

13. DeVane, p. 560.

14. In a letter to Furnivall, reproduced in *Letters of Robert Browning, Collected by Thomas J. Wise,* ed. T. L. Hood (New Haven: Yale Univ. Press), p. 197, Browning writes, "William Macready's oldest boy . . . asked me to give him some little thing to illustrate; so, I made a bit of a poem out of an old account of the death of the Pope's legate at the Council of Trent." Browning did not publish "The Cardinal and the Dog" until his last volume *Asolando* (1889), when the poem appeared mainly at the insistence of the Browning Society; the poem was revised and now in a sense "belonged" again to the poet, for Willie Macready had been dead several years. On the other hand, "The Pied Piper," an afterthought, was not presented to Willie in answer to his original request; the poem therefore "belonged" to them both. In this respect it resembles "One Word More," which was written for, not requested by, E. B. B. in 1855.

15. DeVane, p. 400. See also DeVane's "The Harlot and the Thoughtful Young Man: A Study of the Relation between Rossetti's *Jenny* and Browning's *Fifine at the Fair," SP,* 24 (1932), 463–84.

16. The deaths of the three wives occurred in a space of nine months: E. B. B. in June 1861, Mary Meredith in Oct. 1861, and Elizabeth Rossetti in Feb. 1862.

17. *Letters of George Meredith,* ed. by his Son (New York: Scribners, 1912), I, 73.

18. The first two of these quotations from *Sordello* (as well as those to follow from other poems) were suggested by L. N. Broughton and B. F. Stetler, *A Concordance to the Poems of Robert Browning* (New York: Stechert, 1924–25). The third one, "twice twelve sonnets," was apparently over-

looked by the editors, and it is Browning's most specific reference to the
tedium of sonnets in series.

19. Edmund Gosse, *Critical Kit-Kats* (London: Heinemann, 1896), p. 3.
Though Gosse is unreliable in some of his statements about *Sonnets from
the Portuguese* (particularly those having to do with the forged Reading
Edition), the spirit of this statement attributed to Browning is doubtless
true enough. At least Mrs. Browning said much the same thing when she
wrote to her sister Arabel on Jan. 12, 1851, that when Robert saw the
manuscript of the sonnets, he was "much touched and pleased" and thought
so highly of the poetry that he "could not consent that they be lost" to her
volumes. This information is contained in an unpublished letter in the
Berg Collection quoted by Gardner B. Taplin, *The Life of Elizabeth Barrett Browning* (New Haven: Yale Univ. Press, 1957), p. 233.

20. Roma A King, Jr., *The Focusing Artifice: The Poetry of Robert Browning*
(Athens: Ohio Univ. Press, 1968), p. 196.

21. Following the lead of C. H. Herford in *Robert Browning* (London: Blackwood, 1905), H. C. Duffin in *Amphibian: A Reconsideration of Browning:
A Portrait* (London: Bowes & Bowes, 1962) sees it as connected with the
frustration of Robert's and Elizabeth's marriage.

22. Glenn Sandstrom, *VP*, 4 (Autumn 1966), 259–70.

23. *The Works of George Meredith,* Memorial Edition, XXIV (New York:
Scribners, 1910), p. 227.

24. DeVane, *Handbook*, p. 285. Frederic E. Faverty's "Browning's Debt to
Meredith in *James Lee's Wife*" in *Essays in American and English Literature Presented to Bruce Robert McElderry, Jr.*, ed. Max F. Schulz, with William D. Templeman and Charles R. Metzger (Athens: Ohio Univ. Press,
1967), pp. 290–305, discusses Browning's indebtedness to Meredith in considerable detail. I was unable to consult Professor Faverty's essay in time for
the writing of this section. Since my argument is similar to his, but with
different illustrative statements, I prefer it to stand on its own.

25. William Sharp included two of Browning's sonnets ("Helen's Tower" and
"Why I am a Liberal") in his *Sonnets of This* [Nineteenth] *Century* (London: Walter Scott, 1886), a carefully edited collection of 300 sonnets.

Southern Illinois University, Edwardsville

PHILIP RAISOR

THE FAILURE OF BROWNING'S CHILDE ROLAND

The last stanza of Robert Browning's "Childe Roland to the Dark Tower Came" reads:

> There they stood, ranged along the hillsides, met
> To view the last of me, a living frame
> For one more picture! in a sheet of flame
> I saw them and I knew them all. And yet
> Dauntless the slug-horn to my lips I set,
> And blew. *"Childe Roland to the Dark Tower came."*[1]

There is no mistaking the sense of power that erupts at the end of the poem and the sense of resolute and apparently clear-sighted aim of the protagonist—Roland would struggle with the forces that assail him. For most critics, Roland's comparison of his condition with that of the "sick man very near to death" becomes the gauge of his conduct, and his final defiance in contrast to the sick man's submissiveness is viewed as a heroic act.[2] But Roland's final perception is the product of grief, anger, and a disillusionment born of the reversal of his previous assumptions about his condition, and his final act cannot be divorced from the shock of his awareness.

I believe Roland's final act links him with those literary heroes whose response to human violation is as outrageously excessive as the violation itself. Ahab, if struck by the sun, would strike back; Ivan Karamazov, convinced that God is unjust, returns his entrance ticket to his creator; and Lear, assured that chaos has returned, that "unaccommodated man" is no more than a "poor, bare, forked animal," sheds his garments in defiance of an unreasonable existence. To place Roland in this group of metaphysical rebels[3] is to assume, first, that

99

Browning's apparent affirmation of one interpretation of the poem is not conclusive. When asked if he meant "He that endureth to the end shall be saved," Browning replied, "Yes, just about that" (an answer to a question asked some thirty years after the poem was written).[4] Much earlier, and for a long time, he maintained that the poem came to him as "a kind of dream. I had to write it . . . . I did not know then what I meant beyond that, and I'm sure I don't know now."[5] In neither case was Browning precise (as he was, for example, with "Bishop Blougram's Apology"[6]), and the equivocal "just about that" is characteristic of Browning's reticent acknowledgment of quite different interpretations.[7] Second, considering "Childe Roland" a dramatic monologue (Imperfect, in Ina B. Sessions' classification[8]), I assume that though the grotesque landscape and the movements of the questing knight vie with each other for the reader's attention, it is not, as William B. DeVane suggests, "the gloom and the horror of the landscape that makes the poem possible at all."[9] It will be part of my purpose to show that the protagonist's mind is the poem's *raison d'être*. Third, another interpretation is justified, perhaps, by critics' persistent reading of Childe Roland as an essentially admirable character whose blast on the slug-horn, in either victory or defeat, further ennobles the hero. As I hope to show, Childe Roland's battle-cry is a blind rebellion in defense of a negative perception.

It has not been observed previously that Childe Roland's mind is the cynosure of his physical and moral progress, and that the progress is dependent upon the quality of his mind. From his first thought to his last Roland remains a "childe"—quick to see, and quick to draw conclusions; basically unreflective, and yet creative; persistently expedient, and rashly principled. He is a mental novice who pushes hard to bring past, present, and future together. To understand the context of Roland's final act, it is necessary to understand his mind.

In illuminating respects, Childe Roland reflects the type of mentality Browning had described in his *An Essay on Shelley*:

I conjecture, from a review of the various publications of Shelley's youth, that one of the causes of his failure at the outset was the peculiar *practicalness* of his mind, which was not without a determining effect on his progress in theorizing. An ordinary youth, who turns his attention to similar subjects [oppression], discovers falsities, incongruities, and various points for amendment, and, in the natural advance of the purely critical spirit unchecked by considerations of remedy, keeps up before his young eyes so many instances of the same error and wrong, that he finds himself unawares arrived at the startling conclusion, that all must be changed—or nothing: in the face of which plainly impossible achievement, he is apt (looking perhaps a little more serious by the time he touches at the decisive issue) to feel, either carelessly or considerately, that his own attempting a single piece of service would be worse than useless even, and to refer the whole task to another age and person—safe in proportion to his incapacity. Wanting words to speak, he has never made a fool of himself by speaking. But, in Shelley's case, the early fervor to *see* was accompanied by as precocious a fertility to *contrive*: he endeavored to realize as he went on idealizing; every wrong had simultaneously its remedy, and out of his strength of his hatred for the former, he took the strength of his confidence in the latter—till suddenly he stood pledged to the defense of a set of miserable little expedients, just as if they represented great principles, and to an attack upon various great principles, really so, without leaving himself time to examine whether because they were antagonistical to the remedy he had suggested, they must therefore be identical or even essentially connected with the wrong he sought to cure,— playing with blind passion into the hands of his enemies, and dashing at whatever red cloak was held forth to him, as the cause of the fireball he had last been stung with—mistaking Churchdom for Christianity, and for marriage, "the sale of love" and the law of sexual oppression.[10]

This "low practical dexterity"[11] which resulted, implies Browning, in the content and "delirious notes of Queen Mab"[12] is an unconsidered key, perhaps, to Roland's vigorous trumpeting.

Granted that the passage from Browning's *Essay* is from a context that ultimately praises Shelley's mind and moral character, and granted that Browning was not indebted to any single source,[13] it does not follow that the poet was working from remembered or available[14] sources to his purpose. If his purpose was more subtle than simple allegorizing a moral philosophy (as his fragmentary use of sources would indicate), then it is possible that he was utilizing the conventional framework of the quest and utilizing details from romances, popular children's tales, allegories, paintings, and personal observations to achieve as much breadth of dramatic effect as possible, while at the same time maintaining a controlled aura of feeling appropriate, on all levels, to his purpose. If part of his intention was to reveal a type of mind confronted by overwhelming oppression,[15] then the passage from his recently completed *Essay*[16] would be appropriate to this aim.

In conjunction with his *Essay*, Browning may have recalled or, perhaps, had near him Shelley's "Queen Mab" and the notes (specifically to Sections VI and VII). The conflicting doctrines of free will and necessity (the deterministic element) are quietly central to "Childe Roland," and details from Shelley's material are echoed in Browning's poem: the protagonist's restlessness and endless roving, the early timorousness and desire for death, the skull-like face, Nature's yawning and grotesque threat, the Apollyonic guide, images of war and implements of torture, the trampled earth and the hoof of the fiendish steed, the failures of previous heroes, the deepening of despair and the speaker's final determination to wage war against the supernatural tyrant.[17] Perhaps it is not unjustified to contend that the youthful Roland ends where Shelley's Ahasuerus begins:

> But my soul,
> From sight and sense of the polluting woe
> Of tyranny, had long learned to prefer
> Hell's freedom to the servitude of Heaven.
> Therefore I rose, and dauntless began
> My lonely and unending pilgrimage,
> Resolved to wage unweariable war
> With my almighty Tyrant, and to hurl
> Defiance at His impotence to harm
> Beyond the curse I bore.[18]

But if Browning had Shelley's material in mind, he clearly molded it to his own purpose—perhaps used it as a foil—for Childe Roland's outrage is not keyed on the same scale as Ahasuerus'. If Roland's dauntless rebellion brings to mind Shelley's hero or, as Golder argues, the two Jacks of the Beanstalk and the Giant Killer,[19] it also brings to mind Poor Tom and "Fie, foh, and fum." I am not particularly impatient to read Browning in the refracted light of Shelley's antireligious intentions, nor do I feel that Browning was overtly concerned in this poem with moral philosophy, but it is apparent that Browning (as an objective, though not neutral, poet[20]) moved closer to Shelley's atheism for a particular reason. As I see it, Browning's broad concern with "the manifested action of the human heart and brain" (the only action which he felt worth presenting)[21] led him in "Childe Roland" to portray a youth who made a foolish mistake.

Roland's first assumption is that the "hoary cripple's" answer to his question is firmly rooted in tyrannical intent:

> What else should he be set for, with his staff?
> What, save to waylay with his lies, ensnare
> All travellers who might find him posted there,
> And ask the road?

If, as Curtis Dahl avers, Roland "is dedicated from the start to seek out the Dark Tower,"[22] then it is reasonable to assume that he requests the proper path. The old man's guidance, then, is not false and Roland's impulsive judgments are openly suspect. Nor is the cripple lying if Roland, exhausted by the pursuit of his original goal, submissively requests the path that "all agree, / Hides the Dark Tower." Only if Roland asks, "Which way to the Light Tower?" is the old man a false counselor. Roland's judgment, no doubt, is accurate, and the falsity of the old man does reflect his tyrannical intent. But Roland has arrived at this conclusion by assuming that appearance reveals purpose. If there are other answers to his question "What else should he be set for, with his staff?" Roland does not consider them. He follows his first thought and guesses at the result of his action:

> I guessed what skull-like laugh
> Would break, what crutch 'gin write my epitaph
> For pastime in the dusty thoroughfare,
> If at his counsel I should turn aside . . . .

It is characteristic of Roland's mind that it *sees* intensely and attempts to congeal all elements into a single, unified perception. His mental ardor (he questions, answers, exclaims, criticizes, judges), though it reflects a vibrant mind, is directed toward synthesis rather than analysis. His observation of effects is specific, occasionally microscopic; and not content with mere observation, he persistently conceives (or attempts to conceive) a cause for each effect that confronts him. Absence of evidence ("No footprint leading to that horrid mews, / None out of it") does not thwart him; through his sensuous imagination, he strives, by analogy or passion, to reduce all that he regards (either in past, present, or future) to concretely inflexible visions.

Though intimidated by the old man, it is basically his heart, responding to his "first thought," that directs Roland to endure his failure nobly. It is important to recognize that there are two towers involved and that Roland believes he turns aside from his original goal of his own free will. His heart, "finding failure in its scope," offers a solution to his "world-wide wandering," one that accords with his limitations and those voices which have always prophesied his doom; his mind responds with supporting argument—"that just to fail as they [the Band], seemed best." That he turns aside believing he could not "cope / With that obstreperous joy success would bring," though it may be an accurate and realistic analysis of his inner condition, is nonetheless reductive. It is clear that in his early idealism, at the very beginning of his quest, Roland would have rebuked his heart considerably for its present willingness to accept failure as an end in itself, and I think that Roland, whose search has been insufferably long, would have previously considered the possibility of failing if he doubted that perseverance and fortitude would finally prevail. If he maintains that attitude, he does so residually, for in turning aside and expecting an end (any "end [that] might be"), he indicates less about his perseverance than his limitations. The thinking Roland does is clearly practical and consistent with his motive and expectations. But his heart truly reflects his capacities.

In his passion for synthesis, Roland creates his own landscape. Possessing a studied (though not scientific) knowledge of plant life, Roland is sufficiently familiar with normally arid countrysides to know that cockle and spurge should proliferate "according to their law." Since, in his first observation of the barren landscape, he can perceive no material cause for its condition, he is unable to comprehend that condition in terms of natural law. But his drive for meaning and certainty is undaunted, and, though unaware of it, he views nature, to his own satisfaction, in a way commensurate with his own mood:

> No! penury, inertness and grimace,
> In some strange sort, were the land's portion.

We are not to assume, I think, that Roland, as C. C. Clarke suggests, "is reporting, dispassionately."[23] The countryside Roland perceives, imbued with natural, human, and supernatural activities, functions only in terms of his conception of its "portion" and the law of cause and effect he imagines to operate. The common denominator in his perception is oppression. The "portion" he envisages is a representative composite of what his knowledge and experience allow him to imagine of tyranny—its effects and its causes. Thus, the "ragged thistle stalk," "the dock's harsh swarth leaves," "the mud," both the "Low scrubby alders" and "Drenched willows," the "galley-slaves," and "men's bodies" are all victims of oppression—of a tyrant's jealous or brutish or spiteful or sportive or disease-fostered malice; and if unable to imagine a cause in human terms, Roland completes his image by reference to the Devil and his votaries. The appearance of the "stiff blind horse," for example, is, to Roland, materially unaccountable ("however he came there"), but in terms of Roland's impression of the land's portion, the grotesque condition as well as his presence is explained— "Thrust out past service from the devil's stud!" The act of synthesis results in a re-shaping of the natural landscape, and though, no doubt, Roland does see thistle stalks, leaves, spots of grass, and so on, his ardor for resolution adds both content and dimension to the countryside.

It would be a mistake to believe, however, that Roland transforms the landscape into a Devil's playground just for his own entertainment. His hatred of tyranny (as well as his fear of being victimized) possesses his mind, and from his encounter with the cripple it is clear that Roland's concern is not only with the end, but also with the oppressive forces that tend to thwart men's freedom. Engaged as he is in a quest that he believes he has freely chosen, he is necessarily concerned with the relationship of those forces to himself.

But at the beginning, in spite of his doubts about his fitness, Roland is intuitively certain that he can withstand the present threat and that the scope of horror is temporary. First, as a soldier, he is confident that the "soldier's art" can sustain him. The central question "should I be fit?" is a question of conduct, and in stanza XV he indicates both his conception of that conduct and the means by which he expects to endure his trial:

> I shut my eyes and turned them on my heart.
>   As a man calls for wine before he fights,
>   I asked one draught of earlier, happier sights,
> Ere fitly I could hope to play my part.
>   Think first, fight afterwards—the soldier's art:
>   One taste of the old time sets all to rights.

The tone of prayerful invocation is both mocking and self-mocking, the soldier half-swaggering and momentarily, perhaps, half-knowing that he swaggers. But the following "Not it!" and his disgust with his failure to fasten himself in his past innocence indicate that beneath the witty facade is the serious intent to find in his heart the "earlier, happier sights" he believes necessary to fight against the pervasive sense of tyranny that threatens to overwhelm him. Second, though one of Nature's prisoners, Roland assumes that the law that controls Nature is not applicable to him. Confident of a "better country" ahead and of his own moral rectitude, he mocks the landscape with facile phrases—"As for grass, it grew as scant as hair / In leprosy" or "Will the night send a howlet or a bat?"—while earnestly hating the oppression he sees. Though he believes he is in the Devil's playground, Roland predicts a short session with evil.

To the point that "Here ended, then, / Progress this way," Roland's practical reasoning advances him on the plain ("naught else remained to do. / So, on I went"; "Better this present than a past like that") but at the recognition that he is "just as far as ever from the end!" his mind is confronted by a problem that, apparently, it cannot solve. The stay, however, is momentary. Though aware that he is trapped on the plain (the "safe road" disappears as the day shoots "one grim / Red leer to see the plain catch its estray"), it is not until he arrives at the enclosing entrapment ("came a click / As when a trap shuts— you're inside the den!") that he fully realizes that ignoble Nature's dictum, "See / or shut your eyes, / . . . It nothing skills," is true: he has seen (XII–XIV) and shut his eyes (XV) and seen again (XVIII–XXIX), and, indeed, in neither the natural world nor his own heart does he find the solution to his imprisonment. At this point, in Browning's terms, an ordinary youth, perceiving the impossibility of altering either or both objective and subjective conditions, would, like Nature itself, "refer the whole task to another age and person—safe in proportion to his incapacity." But Roland who, at the beginning, acts on incomplete knowledge to remedy, if possible, his prolonged suffering, whatever the "end might be," undergoes no basic change in either his motive or his expectations or his mental processes, and the knowledge that he is trapped only precipitates another attempt at remedy.

Roland's response to the "round squat turret" is foreshadowed in his belief that "Mad brewage" must have been the cause of the "savage trample" that took place in the "fell cirque." To Roland, the "Mad brewage" is the result of the oppressive imprisonment of the "strugglers" whose freedom ("with all the plain to choose") has been maliciously denied. There is no humor in Roland's report, only the conjecture that in Nature ("Toads in a poisoned tank, / Or wild cats in a red-hot iron cage") or in men's experience (the internecine war of Christians and Jews), the loss of liberty has a maddening effect. If we recognize that Roland's solution, in part, to the problem of his entrapment is similarly a call to warfare, that the battle he would wage would "pad the dank / Soil to a plash," then the analogous conditions imply that the final blast on the slug-horn is, ironically, the "Mad brewage" at work in his own mind.

But the "Mad brewage," for Browning, was not the result of apparently unending tyranny. It was the product of the attempt to solve the problem by "the soldier's art." Once Roland sees that he is "just as far as ever from the end," he begins to turn against the previous assumptions. Centrally, his conception of the freedom he assumed he had begins to vanish with his belief that a "trick / Of mischief" has been played on him. I doubt if the prank relates to the old man's lie (since Roland never doubts that the cripple has lied), but relates more generally to Roland's previous attitude that he could be a noble failure. Roland, who, at first, believes he freely chooses to fail, discovers, when the trap shuts, that he does not govern his own freedom, and in fact that his freedom to fail (or succeed) is an illusion. Eugene R. Kintgen's comment that Roland's "victory is assured in reaching the tower rather than in anything he might do there"[24] does not account for the actions of Roland's mind. Roland's concern is with solving the problem of how to get from the "ugly heights and heaps." At first, he sees no alternative to submission. But with his belief that he is trapped comes a new vitality. It is *because* he believes he is trapped that he sees the Tower and finds a solution to his problem. The victory Roland achieves is, paradoxically, a defeat, and only if we miss the irony in Roland's solution can we consider his arrival at the Tower a victory.

The first part of his solution is in recognizing that the goal itself is, on the one hand, "blind as the fool's heart"—a mirror-image of his own heart which had "failure in its scope." Since the blindness also reminds us of the "stiff blind horse," and the "fool's heart" of the inconstancy of the fool who "finds mirth / Makes a thing and then mars it, till his mood / Changes and off he goes!," the Tower manifests both a "law within" and a "law without"—a blindly creative, inconstant and brutish force. Roland also speaks of the Tower as "without a counterpart / In the whole world." Has Roland forgotten his original goal? More likely, Roland's solution rests on denying the existence of the "Light Tower." Roland, with his passion for synthesis and his ardor for solution, finds his remedy in recognizing the cause of his entrapment. The force of malice, within and without, is the only governing principle in the universe. A principle of good does not exist.

This conviction leads Roland, in the last three stanzas, to dismiss all guides, all forms of knowledge, except that which comes through his senses and his own personal experience: "Not see? . . . / Not hear? . . . / one moment knelled the woe of years." In his awareness that the strong and the bold and the fortunate knights (Giles and Cuthbert apparently included) have all been lost, and in his certainty that he knows why ("I saw them and I knew them all"), Roland is trapped not only by his own sense of victimization but also by his sorrow. When he sees the day return and hears noise toll "Increasing like a bell" (perhaps the fire of the Last Judgment and the bell that tolls for him), Roland, having had one last taste of the old time, strikes at the fireball he believes is the sign of his enemy's presence. Unwittingly, Roland's hatred of tyranny and his chain of perceptions have led him to concentrate only upon the failure of the good to prevail over the evil, and in his passion to remedy this condition he finds his solution the only alternative to submission.

For Browning, however, the first step in the elimination of wrongs was not the "soldier's art," but " 'A worship of the Spirit of good within, which requires [before it sends that inspiration forth, which impresses its likeness on all it creates] devoted and disinterested homage.' "[25] Roland rebukes his heart and denies its value as a sustaining force and a guide. Roland's mind, which gathers data unreflectively and is more accumulative than incisive, and which is possessed by hatred of tyranny (and of the death and destruction which it embodies), is led to the conclusion that all is maliciously determined. God and soul stand in the Tower. He cannot see the light which illuminates the good, only the light which illuminates its failure. The "hoary cripple" is both the beginning and end of his perception, and Roland's response is a crazed (not heroic) dash for the source of it all. The mistake Roland makes is an impatience to put into action intellectual powers not yet mature, and as Browning, perhaps, would have it, Roland's failure is in this impatience when his intellectual perception is limited. In a later poem, "La Saisiaz," Browning established a central point in his conception of truth:

> I have questioned and am answered. Question, answer
> presuppose
> Two points: that the thing itself which questions,
> answers,—*is*, it knows;
> As it also knows the thing perceived outside itself,—
> a force
> Actual ere its own beginning, operative through its
> course,
> Unaffected by its end,—that this thing likewise
> needs must be;
> Call this—God, then, call that—soul, and both—
> the only facts for me.[26]

In "Childe Roland" Browning suggests that error and distraction— a distortion of both the objective and subjective thing (God-soul) itself—are the result of Roland's quest.

NOTES

1. All quotations from Browning's writings are taken from *The Complete Poetic and Dramatic Works of Robert Browning*, Cambridge Edition (1895; rpt. Boston: Houghton, 1947). Hereafter cited as Browning, *Works*.
2. The following list is not exhaustive; it simply represents the persistence of this type of interpretation. See John T. Nettleship, *Essays and Thoughts* (London: Elkin Matthews, 1890), pp. 89–113; Harold Golder, "Browning's 'Childe Roland,'" *PMLA*, 29 (1924), 963–78; William C. DeVane, *A Browning Handbook*, 2nd ed. (New York: Appleton, 1955), p. 232; C. C. Clarke, "Humor and Wit in 'Childe Roland,'" *MLQ*, 23 (1962), 323–36; John W. Willoughby, "Browning's 'Childe Roland to the Dark Tower Came,'" *VP*, 1 (1963), 291–99. Although a few commentators find that the poem ends in a personal disaster, they feel that Roland's defeat is without despair. Edward Berdoe, C. H. Herford, Betty Miller, and Donald J. Gray (again I'm being representative) consider the defeat ameliorative; it serves, states Mr. Berdoe, "as a warning to others . . . that the way to the Dark Tower was the way of destruction and death." In this approach the redemptive feature of Coleridge's "The Rime of the Ancient Mariner" is obvious, and Roland remains a hero with a message for mankind. See Ed-

ward Berdoe, *The Browning Cyclopaedia*, 2nd ed. (London: George Allen & Unwin, 1897), p. 105; C. H. Herford, *Robert Browning* (Edinburgh: William Blackwood and Sons, 1905), pp. 95–96, 263–64; Betty Miller, *Robert Browning: A Portrait* (New York: Scribners, 1952), p. 180; Donald J. Gray, "Arthur, Roland, Empedocles, Sigurd, and the Despair of Heroes in Victorian Poetry," *Boston University Studies*, 5 (1961), 1–17.

3. See Frederick J. Hoffman, *The Mortal No: Death and the Modern Imagination* (Princeton: Princeton Univ. Press, 1964), pp. 154–57; 179–201. Hoffman suggests that "The full range of modern violence may be comprehended in terms of the metaphor of assailant and victim" (p. 154), and that the conventional formulas for rendering this metaphor may be understood to work on five basic levels: the assailant as person, the assailant as an ideological instrument, the assailant as mob, the assailant as machine, and the assailant as landscape. If one reads "Childe Roland," with Clarice Short, as "the distorted vision of a distracted mind," Browning's poem incorporates Hoffman's fifth level, and the scene of violence is a reflection of the protagonist's moral and psychological condition. Metaphysically, then, the protagonist creates his own landscape and is primarily responsible for the outrage he creates. If such a view is uncharacteristic of Browning's use of landscape (as Francis Howard Williams or H. M. McLuhan would argue), it is nonetheless consonant with Roland's gradual assumption of many of the peculiarities of the assailant, culminating in the final merger of assailant and victim. See Clarice Short, "John Keats and 'Childe Roland,' " *N&Q* (1955), 216–18; Francis Howard Williams, "The Relation of Nature to Man in Browning," *Poet Lore*, 4 (1892), 238–43; H. M. McLuhan, "Tennyson and Picturesque Poetry," *Essays in Criticism*, 1 (1951), 278–82.

4. Berdoe, p. 102.

5. Ibid.

6. See F. E. L. Priestley, "Blougram's Apologetics," in *The Browning Critics*, ed. Boyd Litzinger and K. L. Knickerbocker (Lexington: Univ. of Kentucky Press, 1965), p. 167. When Browning *was* precise, it created a different kind of problem than we have here.

7. See Richard D. Altick, "The Private Life of Robert Browning," in *The Browning Critics*, pp. 250–51.

8. "The Dramatic Monologue," *PMLA*, 62 (1947), 503.

9. "The Landscape of 'Childe Roland,' " *PMLA*, 40 (1925), 427.

10. Browning, *Works*, pp. 1012–13.

11. Ibid., p. 1013.

12. Ibid.

13. Most recent critics of "Childe Roland," in the spirit of Irene Hardy, have not accepted Browning's statement that "My own performance was wholly suggested by the line from 'Lear' in connection with a tower I happened to see among some hills near Carrara in Italy," as the only source for the poem. The list of possible influences is inexhaustible, ranging from a Danish ballad of "Childe Roland" to the opening stanza of John Donne's "A Valediction: Forbidding Mourning."

14. It has often been noted that, at the time he wrote "Childe Roland" (Jan. 2, 1852), Browning did not have his little "yellow book" at his sleeve nor a roomful of books in his apartment in Paris to work from.

15. As Betty Miller suggests, the immediate impulse for the composition of "Childe Roland" may have come from the conjunction of Browning's work on the *Essay* and the entrance of Louis Napoleon into Paris. Miller, pp. 178–80.

16. Browning completed his *Essay* on Dec. 4, 1851.

17. See *The Complete Poetical Works of Percy Bysshe Shelley*, ed. Thomas Hutchinson (1905; rpt. London: Oxford Univ. Press, 1965), pp. 788–92; 818–19. Hereafter cited as Shelley, *Works*.
18. Shelley, *Works*, pp. 790–91.
19. Golder, p. 966.
20. It is admittedly difficult to establish the extent to which Browning considered himself an objective poet—"one whose endeavor has been to reproduce things external [whether the phenomena of the scenic universe or the manifested action of the human heart and brain] with an immediate reference, in every case, to the common eye and apprehension of his fellow men assumed capable of receiving and profiting by his reproduction" (Browning, *Works*, p. 1008). But Philip Drew's article demonstrates, I think, that the *Essay* itself is a defense of Browning's own method of producing a certain kind of poem that is "substantive, projected from himself and distinct" (Browning, *Works*, p. 1008). Since the *Essay* was finished less than a month before the writing of "Childe Roland," it seems unlikely that in his imaginative process the distance between himself and his poem would have dramatically narrowed. See Philip Drew, "Browning's *Essay on Shelley*," *Victorian Poetry*, 1 (1963), 1–6. Cf. Thomas J. Collins, "Browning's *Essay on Shelley*: In Context," *VP*, 2 (1964), 119–24.
21. Browning, *Works*, p. 1008.
22. "The Victorian Wasteland," in *Victorian Literature: Modern Essays in Criticism*, ed. Austin Wright (New York: Oxford Univ. Press, 1961), p. 36.
23. P. 332.
24. "Childe Roland and the Perversity of the Mind," *VP*, 9 (1966), 258.
25. Browning, *Works*, p. 1013.
26. Ibid., pp. 852–53.

Old Dominion University

KENT PATTERSON

A TERRIBLE BEAUTY:
MEDUSA IN THREE VICTORIAN POETS

One of the most extreme instances of the nineteenth century's obsession with the theme of the "dark woman" is a fascination with the image of the Medusa. As a symbol of deadly beauty, she appears in poems by Dante Gabriel Rossetti, William Morris, and Algernon Charles Swinburne. A study of the manner in which these three very different poets interpreted and altered the original image provides insight into differences in the aesthetic assumptions which lie behind much of their poetry. All three poets were part of the broad movement which might be called Victorian Romanticism, and in their early works both Morris and Swinburne were strongly influenced by Rossetti. One might expect some similarity in their treatment of an identical image, but their use of the Medusa shows three very different concepts of the purpose of art. Rossetti stresses the power of the artist to create an ideal beauty from even a terrible reality. In compliance with his theories of the importance of popular art, Morris makes Medusa a conventional heroine and sees her as an object of pathos rather than horror. Swinburne, the most subjective of the three, uses Medusa's snaky hair and general frightfulness as a symbol of his private sexual obsessions.

The story of Medusa, like other Greek myths, has long been a part of the poets' stock of standard allusions. Before the nineteenth century, most of the allusions are either to the glory of Perseus, who killed Medusa by means of a charmed reflecting shield, or to the horror of Medusa as a conventional poetic monster. Though the myth of the Medusa can be found in other works, most of the allusions in

111

English literature are based on the version of the myth found in Ovid's *Metamorphosis*. There Ovid has Perseus narrate his adventures to the admiring court of King Cepheus. Since the story is told from Perseus' point of view, Medusa gets scant sympathy. She is a monster who deserves whatever punishment the gods choose to give her. Ovid tells her story in a few terse lines:

> She was very lovely once, the hope of many
> An envious suitor, and of all her beauties
> Her hair most beautiful—at least I heard so
> From one who claimed he had seen her. One day Neptune
> Found her and raped her, in Minerva's temple,
> And the goddess turned away, and hid her eyes
> Behind her shield, and, punishing the outrage
> As it deserved, she changed her hair to serpents,
> And even now, to frighten evil doers,
> She carries on her breastplate metal vipers
> To serve as awful warning of her vengeance.[1]

From the viewpoint of a modern reader, Medusa's punishment seems entirely out of proportion to her crime. It might be argued that her beauty is more than mortal and thus she has committed the sin of excessive pride, but Ovid does not really give us enough information to decide. As for the "outrage" against Minerva, one would think that Neptune's lust more than Medusa's beauty led to the desecration of the temple. The Greek gods frequently show a truly divine indifference to the elementary laws of human justice, though, and this incident is no exception. It might be noted, too, that the point of view is entirely masculine. Medusa is raped, but she, not Neptune, is guilty. She is individualized no more than the hapless women captured as prizes in the *Iliad*; they are traded from one man to the next with only the briefest reference to their own emotions or desires.

On the whole, Medusa seems to play about the same role in Ovid's account of Perseus as the dragon does in the story of St. George. Though Medusa had once been a beautiful woman, Minerva's curse transforms her into a repulsive monster with nothing to engage our human sympathies. Ovid tells her story with the disengaged objectivity one might expect of a modern historian. He is neither attracted nor repelled emotionally by his subject matter, and certainly there is little of his own personality expressed. Most later poets followed Ovid's example. In the period beginning with the Renaissance and continuing throughout the eighteenth century, allusions to Medusa or to the Gorgons are fairly common, but the Medusa is invariably depicted as a monster without beauty or even any human attributes at all.

With the coming of romantic theories of aesthetics, the tale of Perseus, like other Greek myths, was considerably altered. In his "On the Medusa of Leonardo Da Vinci in the Florentine Gallery," Shelley makes the Medusa a symbol of the "loveliness of terror." Ovid describes the Medusa as a monster who was once a beautiful woman, but Shelley describes her as a beautiful woman who is also a monster. The beauty and the terror are inseparable and mutually complementary; it is "less the horror than the grace / Which turns the gazer's spirit into stone." (ll.10–11) In Shelley's hands, the Medusa becomes a symbol for the romantic aesthetic doctrine that the truly beautiful contains an element of the terrible. The poetic imagination fused the "terror" and the "beauty" into the "tempestuous loveliness of terror." Thus the treatment of the Medusa becomes both more subjective and more complex, and the emphasis of the tale is placed upon the feminine power of Medusa to seduce and destroy rather than upon the masculine courage of Perseus.[2]

Dante Gabriel Rossetti's fascination with the "dark woman" motif, which can be seen very well in such paintings as "Lilith," shows a deep concern with the theme of the deadly beauty. Like Shelley's Medusa, the dark woman is both fascinating and deadly and is often used as a symbol of moral ambiguity. Frequently she is associated with snakes or is a snake herself. The type is virtually as old as the beginnings of mythology, but the Romantics revived it and gave it new meaning. Coleridge's "Christabel," with its aura of mysterious evil in a medieval setting, and Keats's "Lamia," with its romantic moral and exotic imagery, both appealed greatly to Rossetti, and the more contemporary example of Tennyson's Vivien, who "clung like a snake" to Merlin,[3] helped create a literary convention which colored Rossetti's treatment of women in general and the Medusa in particular. As the most extreme manifestation of the dark woman theme, the Medusa provides an especially good example of Rossetti's attempt to handle the potentially dangerous theme of the dark woman without falling victim to the sensationalism implicit in the subject. Unlike some other artists who handled versions of this theme, Rossetti committed himself to work within the bounds of Victorian decorum. While rejecting the most extreme and absurd manifestations of prudery, he remained within the tradition that regarded the artist's proper object to be not the object itself but the object idealized by the judicious selection of detail coupled with proper aesthetic distance. The necessity he and most of the Victorians felt for making art reflect "reality" while simultaneously avoiding any reference to the sordid or ugly led to what might be called an aesthetic of implication. At its best, such art could be powerful and effective; clumsily handled, it led to that combination of prudery and puerile suggestiveness which marks the worst of nineteenth-century sentimentalism.

The Medusa gave Rossetti a symbol for such a theory of art. The severed head could not be looked upon directly; only its reflection in Perseus' shield was safe for mortal eyes. An obvious moral can be drawn. The terrible beauty of horror could only be safely seen through the purifying and idealizing medium of art. The "Aspect of Medusa," a painting commissioned by a Mr. C. P. Matthews, was to have pictured Perseus showing the severed head of Medusa to Andromeda. In the preliminary sketches, the head is not shown directly, but is reflected in water. Swinburne felt the design for the painting was "wonderful for grace and force" and thought that it would "assuredly be one of the painter's greatest."[4] Mr. Matthews, a respectable brewer, seems to have had different views of art, though, and canceled the commission because he feared the indecency of the severed head. Rossetti sprang to the defense of his subject in a statement which reveals much about his view of art:

the head, treated as a pure ideal, presenting no likeness (as it will not) to the severed head of an actual person, being moreover so much in shadow (according to my arrangement) that no painful ghastliness of colour will be apparent, will not really possess when executed the least degree of that repugnant reality which might naturally suggest itself at first consideration. I feel the utmost confidence in this myself, as the kind of French sensational horror which the realistic treatment of the severed head would cause is exactly the quality I should most desire to avoid.[5]

For both Shelley and Rossetti, the Medusa symbolized the beauty which the artistic imagination could create from even a terrible reality, but to Shelley the reality possesses beauty even in its terror while to Rossetti the reality possesses beauty only if the terror is hidden and indirectly suggested. Perhaps the differences lies in what seems to be Shelley's faith in the imagination as a force to reveal the beauty and terror which are inherent in reality while Rossetti sees the imagination as a force which can extract beauty from the terror of reality. Rossetti's poem written about the painting and called similarly "Aspecta Medusa" makes the point clearer:

> Andromeda, by Perseus saved and wed,
> Hankered each day to see the Gorgon's head:
> Till o'er a fount he held it, bade her lean,
> And mirrored in the wave was safely seen
> That death she lived by.
>   Let not thine eyes know

> Any forbidding thing itself, although
> It once should save as well as kill: but be
> Its shadow upon life enough for thee.

To some extent, Rossetti must have shared Shelley's idea that in the Medusa beauty and terror were inextricably mixed. His ambivalence toward the Medusa appears in the line "it once should save as well as kill." However, that he also feels the "death she lived by" cannot be seen in all its dread reality is made rather clumsily obvious. The imagination which Shelley saw as a way to "truth" to Rossetti is almost a protection from the "truth."

William Morris, though influenced both by Rossetti personally and the Pre-Raphaelite movement generally, treats the myth of the Medusa very differently. Unlike Shelley and Rossetti, he sees no terror in the Medusa but makes her a sentimental heroine doomed to a pathetic fate:

> . . . a third woman [Medusa] paced about the hall,
> And ever turned her head from wall to wall
> And moaned aloud, and shrieked in her despair;
> Because the golden tresses of her hair
> Were moved by writhing snakes from side to side,
> That in their writhing often times would glide
> On to her breast, or shuddering shoulders white!
> Or, falling down, the hideous things would light
> Upon her feet, and crawling thence would twine
> Their slimy folds about her ankles fine.[6]

Only the snakes are called "hideous"; Medusa herself is seen as an innocent victim of Neptune's lying flattery. Like any number of pathetic Victorian heroines, she has met the "fate worse than death." Seduced and abandoned, she prays constantly for "the rest of Death, and full forgetfullness." Only after death does her head become terrible, though even then its power is used only in the service of right. Morris follows the general outline of Ovid's narrative closely, but the iconographic meaning of Medusa has been changed from terror to pathos. Rossetti's terrible beauty has been domesticated into a Victorian abandoned female.

If the Medusa of *The Earthly Paradise* resembles the heroine of a sentimental best seller, the reason is not hard to find. In contrast to most of his contemporaries, Morris worked to bring art back to the understanding of the common people. He was among the very last of the English poets who succeeded in being very popular with the general public without sacrificing all hope of literary acclaim among more learned readers. Since his time, art in general and poetry in particular have become more and more the exclusive province of an educated elite. During Morris's own life, it was still possible (though difficult) to appeal both to the common people and to the intellectual elite, but even then the division between the masses of semi-educated readers and the elite of highly educated and critical artists was already very evident and was rapidly widening. A socialist in aesthetics as well as in politics, Morris deplored this trend and remarked with sadness that "it is impossible for anyone who is not highly educated to understand the higher kind of pictures." In spite of his respect for the talent of the modern painters, Morris felt that modern artists "cannot fill the gap which the loss of popular art has made . . . ."[7]

Since the time Morris made his appeal for a revival of popular art, the idea that the higher forms of art do not, or even should not, appeal to the general public has become a common assumption, but Morris strongly distrusted any form of art intended only for an elite.[8] His distaste for the increasingly elitest nature of late nineteenth-century art was so intense that he argued that art would eventually either return to the common fold of humanity or cease to exist. The "present state of things" in 1880, which allowed elitest art to flourish while popular art was "asleep or sick," led him to believe that art had reached "a transitional state, which must end at last either in utter defeat or utter victory for the arts."[9] He warns that the position of an artist who fails to make his work accessible to the common people must be one of neglect and alienation:

if those who cultivate art intellectually were inclined never so much to wrap themselves in their special gifts and their high cultivation, and so live, happily, apart from other men, and despising them, they could not do so; they are, as it were, living in an enemy's country; at every turn there is something lying in wait to offend and vex their nicer sense and educated eyes; they must share in the general discomfort—and I am glad of it.[10]

Determined that he would not be one wrapped in a private "high cultivation," Morris insisted that "Art will not grow and flourish, nay, it will not long exist, unless it be shared by all people; and for my part I don't wish that it should."[11] In light of his view of art, it is not surprising that Morris made the Medusa a suffering Victorian abandoned woman. The theme of the betrayal of a basically innocent young woman was not only an enormously popular theme in Victorian literature, but even after the sterner views of Marxism had begun to influence Morris's political thought the abandoned female remained perhaps the most important symbol of economic desperation conceivable by early reform-minded novelists. Without the insight gained from the more modern concepts of society and economics, the early reformers tended to interpret what would now be considered strictly economic problems in terms of individual morality, and thus the innocent young woman driven to absolute despair by cold-blooded exploitation provided an objective human symbol by which the shortcomings of the new industrial society could be measured. Even as late as Steinbeck's Rose of Sharon in *The Grapes of Wrath*, the abandoned woman serves as a powerful symbol of injustice and economic degradation.

Sentimental novelists made much of the victimized young women not so much because of their urge to reform society as because of their urge to sell books; the abandoned woman offered a splendid opportunity for very overt moralizing and some less overt sexual titillation—a best-selling formula then as now. While Morris does not descend to the level of the vapid sentimentality which frequently accompanies the popular treatment of the abandoned woman, the influence of such works is apparent even in his brief treatment of Medusa. She mourns her pathetic condition and prays for death. A minor, but telling, detail which underlines how much Morris relied upon the conventions of sentimental literature is that he has made Medusa, supposedly a Greek woman, into a blonde. On the other hand, it is only fair to stress that the popularization of Medusa was not merely an attempt to gain money. Morris strove to bring the classic art of the past into contact with the popular mind of the present. Critics who attack his reputation for the superficiality of much of his poetic work must recognize his purpose and the aesthetic reasoning which lies behind his work. He wrote "superficial" poetry not because he lacked ability to write otherwise but because his whole theory of art insisted that popular art not only was valuable, but also was the necessary basis for all art and for all civilization. Critics must direct their effort against his theory of art as an integrated whole if they intend to deal with the apparent superficiality of his poetry.

As might be expected, Swinburne's treatment of the Medusa is both more subjective and more explicitly sexual than either Rossetti's or Morris's. While he did not write his own "Medusa," her image haunts his poetry. He knew and admired Shelley's poem,[12] Rossetti's picture, and the original painting from which Shelley got the idea for his poem.[13] In Swinburne's work, the Medusa's iconographic meaning seems to be somewhat narrowed. The Medusa becomes one of a number of manifestations of an obsession with what might be called the "lady of pain." The Medusan image retains all of its ambivalence of beauty and terror, but it is endowed with a far more specifically sexual kind of fascination than even Rossetti's dark lady. It would be quite possible to give Rossetti's poem a sexual significance, but unless one is somewhat excessively Freudian there is no need for such an interpretation. In Swinburne's poetry the sexual interpretation is virtually forced. He is more concerned with the Medusa as a sexual object than as an aesthetic symbol. Much of the notoriety of his poetry stems from his celebration of masochistic and sadistic love, and his Medusan allusions exhibit the masochistic side of the nineteenth-century obsession with the ambivalent female.

Although Swinburne published no description of the Medusa, he saw the same painting in the Uffizi Gallery which Shelley saw and very probably another "Medusa" (by Caravaggio) as well. At the time he was gathering information for his "Notes on the Designs of the Old Masters at Florence," and references to snaky-haired beauty are rife throughout this extremely subjective critical work. The most significant is in the critique of Leonardo da Vinci's study of a female head. According to Swinburne, she "wears a head-dress of eastern fashion . . . plaited in the likeness of closely-welded scales as of a chrysalid serpent . . . ." Her dress and "ornaments seem to partake of her fatal nature, to bear upon them their brand of beauty fresh from hell . . . in touching her flesh they have become infected with deadly and malignant meaning." To Swinburne the beauty of the painting exists because it is terrible:

Her eyes are full of proud and passionless lust after gold and blood; her hair, close and curled, seems ready to shudder in sunder and divide into snakes. Her throat, full, and fresh, round and hard to the eye as her bosom and arms, is erect and stately, . . . her mouth crueller than a tiger's, colder than a snake's, and beautiful beyond a woman's. She . . . is divested of all feminine attributes not native to the snake . . . Cleopatra, not dying but turning serpent under the serpent's bite; or that queen of the extreme East who with her husband marked every day as it went by some device of a new and wonderful cruelty.

The association of the snaky-haired Victorian Medusa with Cleopatra, another frequent icon for the terrible female, is especially striking, for Swinburne continues to describe Cleopatra as snaky-haired too:

Here also the electric hair, which looks as though it would hiss and glitter with sparks if once touched, is wound up to a tuft with serpentine plaits and involutions; all that remains of it unbound falls in one curl, shaping itself into a snake's likeness as it unwinds, right against a living snake held to the breast and throat.

Swinburne continues to suggest that the painting represents a "mystic marriage as that painted in the loveliest passage of 'Salammbo,' between the maiden body and the scaly coils of the serpent and the priestess alike made sacred to the moon . . . ."[14] Few critics other than Swinburne would have used the word "loveliest" to describe such a marital union, but the meaning of the passage is clear enough. Swinburne has merged the Medusa and Cleopatra with his own personal icon of "our lady of pain." The combination becomes a symbol of his homosexual attraction to the phallic imagery of the serpent and his sado-masochistic obsession with pain, especially pain caused by biting. In the poem "Cleopatra," Swinburne describes her love showing "the slow looks of a snake or dove!" Innocence and terror, love and hate, beauty and pain—Swinburne sees them all in the same image. The Medusa persists, for "through her hair the imperial / Curled likeness of the river snake, / Whose bite shall make an end of all." The Medusa-Cleopatra is beyond all time, all knowledge, and all men are doomed to fall prey to her terrible power. "Shall she not have the hearts of us / To shatter, and the loves therein / To shred between her fingers thus?" the poet asks, and the answer goes without saying.

After the Romantics and their late-blooming Victorian heirs, the use of Greek mythology in the intense and personal way which marks much of their work lost its originality and vigor. Perhaps because of its very popularity and perhaps because of a new mutation to the "bitch-goddess" of the twentieth century, the Medusa as a subject seems to have lost much of its direct appeal, though occasionally it still appears in a psychological context. As a serious aesthetic symbol, it seems to have become totally outdated. The reasons for this are complex and certainly lie far beyond the scope of this paper, but it is tempting to speculate that the very intensity of nineteenth-century feeling to Greek mythology eventually destroyed its symbolic value. Not, of course, that modern writers have stopped using Greek mythology; but they use it as public mythology rather than as personal revelation. Perhaps the greater objectivity of modern writing in general works against the kind of subjective symbolic identification with mythological figures which is so apparent in Swinburne's poetry. Perhaps too, the greater freedom given to a modern writer's choice of subject may be a factor; a contemporary poet with Swinburne's sexual obsessions would not need even the transparent veil of Medusa to hide his subject. In any case, in Swinburne's work the Medusa icon has already lost much of its aesthetic significance. Swinburne is far too intent upon capturing images for his subjective emotional states to use mythology as much more than a source of metaphor. This complete subjectivity couples with Swinburne's characteristic emotional diffuseness to make Greek mythology simply an extension of his private world. The Medusa's two most striking attributes, snaky hair and the power to destroy by sight alone, become icons in their own right and are almost totally isolated from the original myth. Swinburne knew the myth of Perseus perfectly well, but he was intent only on its meaning as a sexual symbol. There is nothing Greek in Swinburne's Medusa; there is no Perseus or magic shield, nor is there any real attempt to create a conscious symbol of an aesthetic doctrine. The sexual significance of the Medusa is so much stronger than any aesthetic or mythological one that the phallic imagery of the snaky hair can become a symbol completely detached from Medusa. In "Fragoletta," a poem to a "being sexless" who is asked, entirely appropriately, "Wilt thou be Maiden or boy?" Medusa has even her gender confused:

> Thou has a serpent in thine hair,
> In all the curls that close and cling;
> And ah, thy breast-flower!
> Ah love, thy mouth too fair
> To kiss and sting!

NOTES

1. Rolfe Humphries, trans. (Bloomington: Indiana Univ. Press, 1957), p. 106.
2. Shelley was mistaken in attributing this painting to Leonardo da Vinci. It was also accepted as genuine by Swinburne and by Pater in *The Renaissance*.
3. "Merlin and Vivien," *Idylls of the King, Works*, ed. Lord Hallam Tennyson (New York: Macmillan, 1908), XI, 192.
4. "Notes on Some Pictures of 1868," *The Complete Works of Algernon Charles Swinburne*, ed. Sir Edmund Gosse (New York: Wells, 1925–27), XV, 215.
5. *Rossetti Papers, 1862–1870*, ed. William Michael Rossetti (London: Sands, 1902), pp. 281–82.
6. *The Earthly Paradise*, in *The Collected Works of William Morris*, ed. May Morris (London: Longmans, 1910), III, 203.
7. Ibid., XXII, 164.
8. Jessie Kocmanova, "The Aesthetic Opinions of William Morris," *Comparative Literature Studies*, 4 (1967), 422.
9. Morris, *Works*, XXII, 56.
10. Ibid.
11. Ibid., p. 165.
12. See his comments in "Notes on the Text of Shelley," *Works*, V, 365.
13. See Sir Edmund Gosse's *Life* included in Swinburne's *Works*, XIX, 97–98.
14. Swinburne, *Works*, XV, 160–61.

Glassboro State College

CORA ROBEY

IN THE YEAR OF JUBILEE:
A SATIRE ON LATE VICTORIAN CULTURE

Virtually neglected in our time, George Gissing's *In the Year of Jubilee* deserves attention as a satiric commentary on the intellectual "progress" of England in the 1880s. Using the idea of the Jubilee year, an effective setting, and Dickensian comic character vignettes, this work frequently focuses on a subject treated masterfully in the critical prose of Matthew Arnold, the culture of nineteenth-century England.

The idea of the Jubilee itself is Gissing's starting point. The event commemorates the fifty successful years of Victoria's reign, a reign which brought growth and wealth to the English nation. But Gissing uses the title ironically. One can almost hear in the boasts of England's progress Matthew Arnold's familiar quotations from the Philistine oratory of Mr. Roebuck or Mr. Lowe. Recall this favorite of Arnold's, for example:

See what you have done! I look over this country and see the cities you have built, the railroads you have made, the manufactures you have produced, the cargoes which freight the ships of the greatest mercantile navy the world has ever seen.[1]

And just as Arnold exposes a misdirected mid-Victorian pride, so Gissing shows us effectively in the first part of his novel that England in its Jubilee year has a few reasons not to be jubilant. She has railroads, newspapers, disinfectants, popular education: for these things, perhaps, she is to be commended. But the intellectual climate of a civilization that boasts of these accomplishments also fosters vulgarity, mediocrity, and materialism. It is appropriate that Samuel Bennett Barmby, the English businessman who represents most clearly these

121

defects of *fin-de-siècle* British progress, should serve as spokesman for the Jubilee:

It's to celebrate the fiftieth year of the reign of Queen Victoria—yes, but at the same time, and far more, it's to celebrate the completion of fifty years of Progress. National Progress, without precedent in the history of mankind! . . . Compare England now, compare the world with what it was in 1837. It takes away one's breath.[2]

During the evening of the Jubilee festivities, Gissing uses the setting to comment critically on English "progress." The characters being jostled about on the crowded trams read the following advertisements:[3]

Somebody's "Blue"; somebody's "Soap"; somebody's "High-class Jams"; and behold inserted between the Soap and the Jam—"God so loved the world, that He gave His only begotten Son, that whoso believeth in Him should not perish, but have everlasting life!"   (pp. 54–55)

In this scene Gissing illustrates that advertising so conditions people, even sensitive individuals like Nancy Lord, that they become indifferent to its vulgarity. An increase in literacy, the availability of reading matter to the middle classes in the absence of any real means of educating or civilizing them, leads only to a perversion of education and to a blunting of the sensibilities of the educated.

The first several scenes of the novel all allude to the Jubilee celebration. They demonstrate through setting and especially through satirical character sketches that England's progress is not really progress at all. The work begins with a glimpse at the residence of the French sisters who are preparing for the festivities. It expresses the spirit of self-satisfaction of the Jubilee itself: "Each house [in their quarter] seems to remind its neighbour with all the complacence expressible in buff brick, that in this locality lodgings are not to let" (p. 1). The furnishings in the French residence are new, pretentious, and lacking in taste: "The pictures were a strange medley—autotypes of some artistic value hanging side by side with hideous oleographs framed in ponderous gilding" (p. 2). A glimpse at the French sisters preparing for the festivities reveals their "sham education and mock refinement grafted upon a stock of robust vulgarity" (p. 6). They feel that they know French, piano, and political economy while they have actually learned only a few superficial things. Through their conversation, Gissing comments ironically on the "progress" which has been made in education.[4]

One of Gissing's best comic characters appears early in the novel. In an effort to seek some diversion, Nancy Lord accepts, as a companion for the evening of the Jubilee festivities, Luckworth Crewe, a young man who hopes to make his fortune through advertising. In the festive atmosphere of the Jubilee, he charms Nancy completely, and she finds that the evening she spends with him is worth "whole oceans of 'culture' " (p. 89). But of course he is as much a product of the fifty years of "progress" as are the French sisters, and the scene between Nancy and Luckworth Crewe is another indictment of Victorian society. Crewe might be regarded as the most American of Gissing's characters in that he combines the most likeable qualities we associate with the American businessman at the turn of the century—ingenuousness, a sense of equality, humble origins, and basic decency in spite of his lack of education and vulgar ambitions. He is an English precursor of Howells' Silas Lapham, Lewis's Dodsworth and Babbitt, or Dreiser's Drouet. He is not impressed by the royalties, calling them "Expensive humbugs" (p. 57), but he is very much impressed with the possibilities the Jubilee affords for making money.[5] He tells Nancy enthusiastically about an acquaintance who made nearly a hundred pounds a day by inventing a Jubilee perfume. In an amusing narrative, he describes his harassment of a man who wouldn't allow an advertisement to be put up in his garden: "My dear sir, you're impeding the progress of civilization. How could we have become what we are without the modern science and art of advertising? Till advertising sprang up, the world was barbarous" (p. 67).

But Luckworth Crewe does not receive Gissing's most pointed barbs. Unquestionably, the novel's most effective satire on the deficiencies of England in its Jubilee year appears in the person of the businessman Samuel Bennett Barmby. He is actually a descendant of that enemy of culture, Mr. Podsnap of *Our Mutual Friend*.[6] As the reader will remember, Mr. Podsnap's idea of the arts is:

Literature; large print, respectively descriptive of getting up at eight, shaving close at a quarter-past, breakfasting at nine, going to the City at ten, coming home at half-past five, and dining at seven. Painting and Sculpture; models and portraits representing Professors of getting up at eight, shaving close at a quarter-past, breakfasting at nine, going to the City at ten, coming home at half-past five, and dining at seven. Music; a respectable performance (without variations) on stringed and wind instruments, sedately expressive of getting up at eight, shaving close at a quarter-past, breakfasting at nine, going to the City at ten, coming home at half-past five, and dining at seven. Nothing else to be permitted to those same vagrants the Arts, on pain of excommunication. Nothing else To Be—anywhere![7]

A few decades later Podsnap becomes Barmby, a man of no more basic cultivation but one who, through greater educational opportunities, believes himself "far on the way to attain it" (p. 193). Barmby has inherited a habit of assumed gravity, pretentiousness, and glowing self-satisfaction from his father, who loves to write letters to the newspaper concerning overcrowded railway carriages, indecent bathing or littered pavements, signing himself "Urban Rambler," "Otium cum Dignitate" or "Paterfamilias," yet Barmby considers himself far ahead of his family in matters of culture. During his father's Sunday readings of *Paradise Lost,* Barmby's superior education makes him shudder when he hears: "Ail orrors, ail! and thou profoundest Ell / Receive thy new possessor!" (p. 192). Unlike his sisters who are religious dissenters, Barmby is "broad" in matters of faith; in fact, "having read somewhere that Tennyson's *In Memoriam* represented this attitude, he spoke of the poem as 'one of the books that have made me what I am'" (p. 193). His religious convictions, like all his convictions, are very flexible, however. In sceptical circles, he smiles condescendingly at older conventional beliefs. When trying to convince Nancy Lord of his lofty religious "ideal of life" (p. 292), he tells her that he has formed his own religion which he will present in the form of an essay to be called "The Religion of a Man of Business," reconciling business and religious faith. He describes the businessman as a moral leader. Barmby's preachings may suggest to American minds our own Andrew Carnegie's Gospel of Wealth or Bruce Barton's statements on the economy. In one passage bemoaning the lack of integrity among many disinfectant manufacturers, Barmby declares earnestly: "People who make disinfectants ought to regard themselves as invested with a sacred trust" (p. 273).

Barmby considers himself an authority on philosophy and aesthetics as well as religion. He is at work on a pamphlet to be called (he always names his treatises before writing them) "The Influence of Culture on Morality."[8] Barmby feels that the "popular taste" needs to be improved and suggests that Burne-Jones, William Morris, "and people of that kind" give lectures on "the elements of art" (p. 60).[9]

His own education, as Gissing illustrates in several amusing passages, is actually only slipshod. He has learned a few names, phrases, and titles which he jumbles up in his mind: "Herbert Spencer jostled with Charles Bradlaugh, Matthew Arnold with Samuel Smiles; . . . from puerile facetiae he passed to speculations on the origin of being, and with equally light heart" (p. 193). His familiarity with the English classics is based on the actual reading of only two, *Pilgrim's Progress* and *Robinson Crusoe.*

From the account Gissing gives us of Barmby's actual reading habits, we learn that the daily newspaper is to a large extent responsible for the Barmbys of the world. His "diet of newspapers" makes him incapable of concentration. It encourages his smugness and provincialism. Barmby's citations from the newspapers may remind the reader of the statistics which impressed Arnold's immortal Bottles of *Friendship's Garland* whose tastes and opinions were formed entirely by the British newspapers. National greatness, Barmby feels, can be measured by numbers; therefore, England is already at its apex. He quotes for Nancy Lord a startling newspaper revelation to the effect that the Chinese Empire, with a population of four hundred million, has only ten daily papers. Barmby has also learned from the newspapers that if all the cabs in London were put end to end, there would be forty miles of cabs, an obvious indication of progress.

Barmby is unquestionably Gissing's most devastating indictment of Victorian progress in educational matters, but he is far from the only indictment. Nancy Lord's friend Jessica Morgan illustrates bitingly just how unsatisfying are the results of mass education in late Victorian England and how few are its real contributions to the cultivation of the individual. Jessica represents above all the grubbiness of mass education: its emphasis on cramming for examinations and its function as status symbol, encouraging people who lack real ability yet who see in education a hope for improving their social position.[10] Her grand aim is to graduate from London University, an aim which gradually becomes an obsession. Jessica centers her entire existence around her examinations. She is frantic when she cannot understand some formulas involving geometric progression. She talks only of her exams and stuffs her pockets with scraps of paper to be memorized. Her brain becomes "a mere receptacle for dates and definitions, vocabularies and rules syntactic, for thrice-boiled essence of history, ragged scraps of science, quotations at fifth hand, and all the heterogeneous rubbish of a 'crammer's' shop" (p. 15).

Gissing is successful in contrasting in a comic manner Jessica's mechanically acquired education with the vague, superficial, and equally inadequate education of Barmby. The scenes in which they are brought together are some of the best in the novel. Each considers the other lacking in cultivation. Jessica, who looks upon herself as educated, scorns Barmby's enthusiasm for art lectures by Morris and Burne-Jones, declaring her lack of faith in "popular education." (It is a nice touch that Jessica falls in love with Barmby, an episode that Gissing might have put to even greater comic and thematic use). Barmby, in turn, finds Jessica lacking "broad culture"—something which he already possesses to perfection.

The feeling that one has already reached perfection, that there is no longer a need for developing and growing, is one of the qualities which, as Arnold tells us, gives the Philistine character its stamp. It makes Dickens' Podsnap and Podsnap's descendant Barmby enemies of culture in any real sense. Provincialism or the ignorance of any real excellence in literature and thought and a consequent self-satisfaction and inability to view oneself and one's society judiciously or to develop all of one's powers harmoniously and steadily characterize the French sisters, Luckworth Crewe, Jessica Morgan, and, above all, Samuel Bennett Barmby. As a novelist, Gissing has chosen to view the occasion of the Jubilee, his setting, and his memorable characters as Arnold surely would have, in a comic sense. A few years ago, a noted critic speculated about the kind of novel Arnold might have written.[11]

In many ways, *In the Year of Jubilee* is a novel Arnold might have enjoyed writing. Its lively commentary on the cultural progress of England in the fiftieth year of Victoria's reign may appeal especially to American readers who still find in H. L. Mencken and Sinclair Lewis something of relevance to their own culture.

NOTES

1. Matthew Arnold, *Culture and Anarchy* (New York: Macmillan, 1913), pp. 31–32.
2. George Gissing, *In the Year of Jubilee* (New York: Appleton, 1895), p. 51. Hereafter, references to this work will not be documented.
3. Gissing had what amounted to an almost pathological fear of crowds and mob vulgarity. This fear becomes an obsessive concern in Richard Mutimer's victimization in *Demos* and does frequently undermine the air of objectivity necessary for successful satire.
4. Gissing explores the "type" the French sisters represent in an earlier novel. The Denyer sisters of *The Emancipated* all have cultural pretensions. One sister, for example, pretends to adore "only those writers who find inspiration South of the Alps." See *The Emancipated* (London: Richard Bentley and Son, 1890), I, 73.
5. Jasper Milvain of Gissing's *New Grub Street*, a cynical producer of slick literature, is Gissing's more unpleasant study of a man who has profited materially from the vulgarity and taste for mediocrity of his time.
6. Arnold, incidentally, praised Dickens for his knowledge of the middle class and specifically for satirizing the British Philistine in *David Copperfield*'s Murdstone. See Arnold's *Five Uncollected Essays*, ed. Kenneth Allott (Liverpool: Univ. Press of Liverpool, 1953), p. 16.
7. Charles Dickens, *The Works of Charles Dickens*, XII (New York: Crowell [n. d.]), 143–44.
8. Gissing frequently has fun at the expense of would-be authors of pretentiously conceived documents. Elgar in *The Emancipated*, for example, is planning to write a history of the English mind in relation to Puritanism.
9. Actually, since Morris did give lectures for working men, Gissing is prob-

ably also expressing his lack of faith in "popular" education—a theme which occurs in many of his novels.

10. Thomas Hardy treats the relationship between education and social status also but with a different emphasis. He shows, in *Jude the Obscure* most obviously, that education is really only a mockery since it serves principally as a painful reminder to the individual of the impossibility of improving his position in society.

11. A. Dwight Culler, " 'No Arnold Could Ever Write a Novel,' " *The Victorian Newsletter*, 29 (Spring 1966), 1–5.

North Carolina State University at Raleigh

WILLIAM J. SCHEICK

MAN'S WILDRED STATE AND THE CURIOUS NEEDLEWORK OF PROVIDENCE: THE SELF IN EDWARD TAYLOR'S *PREPARATORY MEDITATIONS*

Edward Taylor's verbal piety, as expressed in the *Preparatory Meditations*, represents the assertion of a self in quest for divine Love, for that true identity of sainthood proceeding from the experience of conversion.[1] Hence, throughout his poetry the will or heart—Taylor used the terms interchangeably to signify that faculty of the rational soul primarily associated with the self and most centrally engaged in the drama of conversion—necessarily remains prominent. Although it was voluntarily dedicated to serve Christ in every way, Taylor's will maintained its distinctness and was never lost in mystical union with the divine Will. As numerous images of human activity in his verse suggest, Taylor's self, like the expression stemming from it, was firmly rooted in the temporal world. Recognizing that all men live in an experiential context—even Christ "learnd Obedience in his Suff'ring-Schoole. / Experience taught him (though a Feeble toole)" (2.41, 35–36)—Taylor, in the dual but related vocations of poet and minister, conducted his search for self-identity within the vicissitudes of time. As a Christian pilgrim he did not seek escape from the divinely decreed progress of life's trials. Rather, in accordance with the design of Providence, he sought to ferret out of his "Wildred state" and the apparent "Crooked Passages" of his daily existence the essential meaning of and the key to his real identity either as a loving child of God or as a degenerate heir to hell. His was an inward quest which, as a facet of the regenerative process, was to be completed only in Heaven. In

129

Taylor's meditations we discover, therefore, an individual and unique will or self creating pious poetry in imitation of, and hopefully in response to, Christ's love or grace. Through the venting and simultaneous working out of this introspective search as well as through the suspension of judgment regarding his spiritual fate, Taylor derived from his love for and his devotion to Christ as much of a sense of regenerate self-identity as one can arrive at in this world.

I

The question of Taylor's mysticism is important in regard to this matter. For Norman Grabo, the chief exponent of the mystical reading of Taylor's work, not only is the poet's "theory of poetry . . . derived from his mysticism," but "the mystical process is the subject" of his verse.[2] One of the difficulties of such a position lies in the word *mysticism*. Owing to its reference to a wide range of beliefs and practices, the term is not easily defined. However, usually two types of mystical thought are identified: the one, according to which God is utterly outside and transcendent to the universe man inhabits; the other, according to which God is immanent and dwells within creation, indeed within the very soul of man.

Certain particulars of both notions were incorporated in New England Puritan thought, and this is why Perry Miller concluded that "at the core of the theology there was an indestructible element which was mystical, and a feeling for the universe which was almost pantheistic."[3] Miller is careful, however, to temper his comment concerning New England Puritan mysticism. There existed an *element* of it in their thought. This qualification, it seems to me, is likewise applicable to Taylor's verse, in which various particulars of mysticism occur. Besides his belief in God as Perfect Being, as the only reality informing but separate from the universe, Taylor's effort to look within himself for truth, as well as his tendency to reflect the Salesian spirit of meditation (emphasizing love and mental union),[4] supports a mystical interpretation of his poems. It is also true that one can comb his verse and single out passages which can be made to conform with the five traditional stages of mystical ascent. Similarly, Taylor's fondness for metaphor and the circularity of so many of his images, if considered aside from his poetic decorum, buttress the mystical reading of his work; for one of the implications of these two devices is that some underlying unity permeates all things.

Nevertheless, contrary evidence argues against a mystical interpretation of the *Preparatory Meditations*. For one thing, the purpose of meditation is not necessarily the preparation for a mystical experience.

As Louis Martz has noted, meditation "is not, properly speaking, a mystical activity, but a part of the duties of every man in daily life."[5] In other words, meditation, the religious practice designed to move the will or heart toward God, is an outgrowth of, as well as an inducement to, the exercise of *practical* piety as the basis for the conduct of one's life in the temporal world.

The temporal world was not for Taylor an inherently demonic realm. He discerned there a progressive hierarchy of degrees of perfection (*C*, pp. 159–60, 220; *TCLS*, pp. 142–43) and an innate goodness (*C*, pp. 117, 403) which denied the notion of a gap separating the order of nature from that of heaven (2.90, 37–42). He perceived that since the order of nature participates in the order of grace, that grace works through natural means (*TCLS*, p. 157); time itself is in some sense a part of eternity. Moreover, the universe is no mere shadow. It is real insofar as it is pervaded by God's Being or Love (2.15, 33–34), is divinely ordained for man's use (*C*, p. 312), and serves as the vehicle for the Incarnation (2.90, 59–60).

With such a view of the temporal realm, Taylor never advocated the abandonment of earthly things. All objects, rightly seen and properly used, point back to God (*TCLS*, p. 54), the source of their origin and their daily containment in being (2.17, 2). This point of view is opposed to that of the mystic whose aim remains "wholly transcendental and spiritual" and whose vision "is in no way concerned with adding to, explaining, re-arranging, or improving anything in the visible universe."[6] Although Taylor certainly remonstrated against any disproportionate concern with or any abuse of the world and although he often lamented the effects of man's fall on nature, his poetry evidences a conspicuous absence of the *contemptus mundi* motif usually associated with the thought of the mystic.

Taylor's conception of nature includes the human body. Because he discerned no real gap between heaven and earth, he necessarily rejected the Platonic notion of a separation between the soul and its bodily instrument:

God in the Creation of Man designed, that all those Glorious Qualifications, and all those admirable Organs of the Bodie of man, so curiously made, and that imortall Soule, that is Seated in the Whole of these, should in a most regular way act to the glory of God.   (*C*, p. 314)

To be sure, he often deplored the post-lapsarian state of the fallen body and the readiness of the sin-ridden will to play lackey to the flesh and thereby subvert the proper hierarchical relationship between them. He indeed knew that "the ill humors in the body will abide till this earthly tabernacle be dissolved," that as long as these ill humors persist as a result of the residence of sin in our wills, "we shall find these vermin crawling in our souls ofttimes, as worms in our bowels, infesting our thoughts and sometimes crawling out in our discourse, and flyblowing our works, both civil and sacred concerns" (*TCLS*, p. 152).

Yet Taylor is clear, even in this metaphoric passage: it is its ill humors, its *fallen state,* not the body itself, which is to be disparaged. The body always retains its original radical goodness, continues to share in the divine Love pervading all creation; sin resides in the rational soul, which is superior to and the regulator of the body (*C*, p. 100). In Taylor's thought, "Fallen Nature is not Sinfull Nature before it is Rationall nature" (*C*, pp. 12–13). In fact, the desires and senses of the body are basically excellent; initially, in Adam, they contributed to the expression of man's love for God (1.31, 1–6), and presently they are unruly owing only to their misguidance by an unregenerate rational soul.

With this perspective it would have been unreasonable for Taylor to have advocated a mystical transcendence of the body. Chocking off, repressing, or seeking detachment from the senses and affections of the body were alien to Taylor's thought.[7] It would have been utterly inconsistent for the poet who devoted his entire adult life to singing the glory of the Incarnation—the event which, among other things, reasserted creation (*C*, p. 91) and elevated the dignity of the flesh (*C*, p. 25)—to espouse mystical release from the body. That would seem contrary to the practice of *imitatio Christi*, the practice Taylor explicitly emphasizes throughout his sermons and poems (e.g., *C*, p. 167; 2.15, 38–40).

Likewise, though Taylor's central theme of his quest for divine Love may seem at times to verge on the mystical, he always recognized that the pure love he was celebrating is unattainable on earth, that it is achieved only when the saint's regenerative process is completed in heaven. Thus Taylor's introspective search for this love never encouraged his withdrawal from the world or his escape to a "paradise within." Although his meditations represent inward dramas, they actually reveal a self which remains fixed within a temporal context. I do not mean that these poems reflect a specific time and place—there are no overt references to Westfield—but they are permeated by man's world, his concerns, his handiwork, and the like. It is interesting to recall, in this regard, that Taylor assigned an exact date to most of the poems in the *Preparatory Meditations*.

The point to be drawn from these comments is that this context—

it might be termed a *historical* context—undercuts any sense of the loss of the mystical poet's self. In the mystical experience "the self . . . surrenders itself, its individuality, and its will, completely" as "consciousness of I-hood and consciousness of the world disappear."[8] The will becomes totally passive, entirely overcome by the divine Will.

This, however, is not the sort of surrender Taylor meant in regard to the regenerate relation of the saint's converted will to God's Will. By the attunement of a saint's will to that of God, Taylor never implied that conversion negates or expunges the saint's volitional faculty. On the contrary, in conjunction with its passive disposition to grace, the will is always to be actively exerted.[9] When attuned by Christ's act of Love or grace, the will is renewed; that, in fact, is the whole point. Renewal or conversion constitutes the saint's true self or identity; through the artistry of grace the love of God is engendered in the heart, thereby giving the saint's self a basis for meaning, for true identity.

This renewed self is not to retreat into mystical silence. On the contrary, in order to respond to and imitate Christ, the Poet of poets, Taylor asserted his will or self verbally. Not silence, but words (the primary mode of this assertion of the will) express and define the poet's self.[10] Thus the *Preparatory Meditations* represents an autobiography of Taylor's self. If he were one of Christ's elect, the very words of his poems would become the narrative of his conversion, of the turning of his heart. This relation between language and the self underlies the sense of the following lines: "I am Tonguetide stupid, sensless stand, / And Drier drain'd than is my pen I hand"; with Christ's art, His all-filling waters of grace, "I then shall sweetly tune thy Praise, When hee / In Whom all Fulness dwells, doth dwell in mee" (1.27, 11–12, 47–48). The pen is an extension, a tool of the poet's will. The words it writes by his hand simultaneously discover and express his self. As Meditation 2.35 makes clear, Taylor suspended this expression of his self in a verbal "Golden bridg" founded in Christ, the mediating *Logos* and "Golden Linck" to God. There, he hoped, this expression ("this small ship") bearing "a mutuall Intrest" was conveyed over the waters of grace and arched within the mediating crosscurrents of a reciprocal love. There too lay the key to his spiritual state, his temporal judgment of which likewise hung suspended.

II

Poem after poem in the *Preparatory Meditations* concludes in future tense, in subjunctive mode, in petition rather than in resolution, for Taylor eschewed a simple or easy deciphering of the complex matter of his spiritual condition. Because he believed that "we are in the way of ordinary dispensations, and therefore are not to expect extra ordinary communications" (*TCLS*, p. 157), Taylor saw that the converted self undergoing the regenerative process must remain in time, in which state it tends to vacillate between the earthly polarities of presumption and despair. Consequently the saint must forswear any sense of certitude and assurance: "Doubtings and faith may stande and will stand together."[11] In the temporal world God's ways are continuous and progressive;[12] Christ is forever beginning in the soul (2.38, 43–44) as that soul progressively experiences "all Degrees of Love" (2.40, 39–40). Though divine fullness "runs to and fro" in a manner quite different from the ebb and flow of the tides (2.51, 31–34), man's response to and reflection of Christ's Love—grace is depicted as a fluid, as *Aqua Vitae*, throughout Taylor's verse—does fluctuate. Because it is less perfect than Christ's Love, the saint's love appropriately reflects the ocean's tidal movements. On earth no one evidences a constant response (see Taylor's "The Ebb and Flow"), and the affections of the will seem very much like the tides.[13]

But just as the earthly tides represent a uniform or fixed rhythm, the saint's alternation between hope and despair signifies an underlying constancy in God's scheme. It reflects the continuation of the process initiated at the time of creation, when divine Love flowed or ran from God's hand in a fluid genesis (2.15, 33–34), henceforth pervading everything (1.1, 7–9). So the apparent inconsistency of the saint's heart may in reality be "blessed motions" in disguise (*GD*, p. 432). In *Gods Determinations* even Satan, unaware that he is a mere pen in the hand of Providence, seizes upon this very image, thereby inadvertently explaining God's ways to the very saints he is trying to torment:

> What's thy Repentance? Can'st thou come and show
> By those salt Rivers which do Ebb, and Flow
> By th' motion of that Ocean Vast within,
> Of pickled sorrow rising for thy Sin?   (p. 412)

The saint, of course, cannot answer this question. He must always contend with doubt and a distraught conscience in the temporal world. Only God knows for certain who is saved.

This same inconclusiveness or incompleteness is, in Taylor's view, a part of the divine plan. The very *drama* of conversion in fact lies in this process. By making this drama progressive God avoids violating a man's self or will; in spite of the "Sea of Electing Grace, and Love" (*C*, p. 305), therefore, the saints continue to toss amid the

"Worlds wild waves" (2.111, 12). The saints continue to experience in their temporal life an ebb and flow of their affections. This rhythmic restlessness of the anguished conscience carries men to God, with whom true peace of mind resides; for it is the intent of Providence to reserve "something that is most concerning, as the *ultima lima* of glory last attained unto, as an allurement" (*TCLS*, p. 143). It is this attraction, this drama of the self wrestling for true identity in Christ, which is at the vital core of Taylor's poems. Through the willed assertion of his love for God, Taylor struggled in his poetry to perceive by degrees over the years the fundamental "Golden Theame" or "Golden Web" which would give identity to the "Linsy-Wolsy Loom" of the poet's self (1.26, 7–10).

III

Thus, in spite of the fact that he had experienced a spiritual awakening at an early age, that he felt called as a minister of Christ, and that he believed some degree of assurance of his election could eventually be attained, Taylor realized that decisive insight into "that Ocean Vast within" was known with certainty only by God. Of the three stages of the "instituted order that God attends in converting souls from sin to Himself" (*TCLS*, p. 99), he had experienced a partial "enlightening" of his reason and a "convicting" of his conscience. But he continually inquired as to the "turning" of his heart or will. Even in his public "Spiritual Relation" delivered on August 27, 1679, Taylor admitted, concerning the turning of his heart, that he could discover only "Something of this nature," that the affection of love was "more Sensible at one time than at another."[14] Thus his meditative explorations of the heart always left the issue of his spiritual state, of the true nature of his self, unresolved, especially since a sense of confidence might testify to damning presumption. The judgment of the moral condition of his soul had to be held in abeyance. Consequently he suspended his expectations across his verbal bridge to God, hoping that they were carried in a current of mutual love.

When the reader of Taylor's verse realizes that the poet wrote the *Preparatory Meditations* over a span of about forty-three years (1682–1725), he is struck by their static quality. There is, generally speaking, no development, no divergence, no progress in the thought or artistry of his poetry. Tedious as it often becomes, this unchanging character of the entire corpus of the *Preparatory Meditations* derived from the poet's basic irresolution.[15] It grew out of his refusal to decide whether or not the ebb and flow of his love, as evidenced in the rhythm of his verbal piety, mirrored the influence of the regenerating waters, the *Aqua Vitae* of the Word's art of grace. He awaited, albeit not without anxiety, the unfolding of God's plan. After death, each man's

> Wildred state will wane away, and hence
> These Crooked Passages will soon appeare
> The Curious needlework of Providence,
> Embrodered with golden Spangles Cleare.
> Judge not this Web while in the Loom, but stay
> From judging it untill the judgment day.
>
> For while its foiled up the best Can see
> But little of it, and that little too
> Shews weather beaten but when it shall bee
> Hung open all at once, Oh beautious shew!
> Though thrids run in, and out, Cross snarld and twinde
> The Web will even be enwrought you'l finde.
>
> (*GD*, pp. 449–50)

This anchoring of his will in God's mysterious but certain design and the consequent suspension of his individual and assertive self across a bridge of verbal piety founded on the mediation of the *Logos* or Christ, in Whom all true identity lies, are what the *Preparatory Meditations* is finally about.

Although he stressed the dependence of the will upon grace for the power to express itself in pious art, Taylor never obscured the importance of the active efforts of the self. Grace does not rape the will but weds the heart (2.133) in such a way that the saint achieves identity. Taylor did not seek to escape this earthbound self through mystical transcendence; for the self must assert its love verbally, not in spite of but *because* of its conversion and attunement to the divine Will. And in conjunction with this unrelenting effort to express his love in verse, Taylor kept the question of his spiritual condition open. What emerges from the heart of the *Preparatory Meditations* is a portrait of Taylor's continual endeavor to assert his self and to appraise, through that assertion, the relation of his self to Christ, the Sacred Self. He never crossed the bridge of his verbal piety into the blinding light and numbing silence of mystical union and assurance.

NOTES

1. Page references to the prose of Edward Taylor will appear in parentheses in the text and will be identified by *C* for *Edward Taylor's Christographia*, ed. Norman S. Grabo (New Haven: Yale Univ. Press, 1962); and *TCLS* for *Edward Taylor's Treatise Concerning the Lord's Supper*, ed. Norman S. Grabo (East Lansing: Michigan State Univ. Press, 1965). Quotations from his verse are from *The Poems of Edward Taylor*, ed. Donald E. Stanford (New Haven: Yale Univ. Press, 1960). Individual poems of the *Prepa-*

ratory Meditations will be referred to by number (2.3, 10, for instance, to designate the tenth line of the third poem of the Second Series); those of *Gods Determinations* will be signified by *GD* followed by the appropriate page number.

2. *Edward Taylor* (New York: Twayne, 1961), pp. 43, 87. In "The Veiled Vision: The Role of Aesthetics in Early American Intellectual History," *William and Mary Quarterly*, 19 (Oct. 1962), 505, Grabo asserts that in the *Preparatory Meditations* "visions (imagined and actual) and sexual images abound, evidencing that Taylor reeled and staggered." In spite of these comments, Grabo senses Taylor's refusal to identify with the consummation of a mystical union with Christ (*Taylor*, pp. 82–83). Michael J. Colacurcio, on the other hand, has remarked: "Taylor the pastoral rhetorician convinces me in a way that Taylor the would-be mystic does not" ("*Gods Determinations Touching Half-Way Membership*: Occasion and Audience in Edward Taylor," *American Literature*, 39 [Nov. 1967], 313).

3. *Errand into the Wilderness* (New York: Harper, 1964), p. 192.

4. Louis L. Martz, *The Poetry of Meditation: A Study of English Religious Literature of the Seventeenth Century*, rev. ed. (New Haven: Yale Univ. Press, 1962), pp. 145–47.

5. Ibid., p. 16.

6. Evelyn Underhill, *Mysticism* (London: Methuen, 1919), p. 96.

7. For the mystic's attitude toward the flesh, see Underhill, pp. 205, 255, 264–65.

8. Underhill, pp. 206, 371, 374.

9. This point and related issues are discussed in "A Viper's Nest, the Featherbed of Faith: Edward Taylor on the Will," to appear in a forthcoming issue of *Early American Literature*.

10. This idea is presented in detail in "Nonsense from a Lisping Child: Edward Taylor on the Word as Piety," to appear in a forthcoming issue of *Texas Studies in Literature and Language*.

11. "Theological Notes" (MS, Redwood Athenaeum), p. 27ᵛ.

12. Speaking of Augustine's view of this matter, Roger Hazelton remarks: "Relatedness to God is not a position but a movement, not a point but a process. No static confrontation but a dynamic interaction of the soul and God is its substance, realized with a moving, growing experience" ("The Devotional Life," in *A Companion to the Study of St. Augustine*, ed. Roy W. Battenhouse, New York: Oxford Univ. Press, 1955, p. 401).

13. John Cotton used the same image: "Though you might thinke the sands would soone be fretted through by the boysterous waves, yet God by his word hath made the sand a perpetuall Bulwarke against the sea, that it cannot prevaile against it; but the heart of man is more unruly then the great sea, and more illimitable then the sea" (*The Way of Life*, London, 1641, p. 204).

14. Donald E. Stanford, "Edward Taylor's 'Spiritual Relations,'" *American Literature*, 35 (Jan. 1964), 469, 474.

15. Charles W. Mignon discusses "the unchanging character of the speaker's attitude" in the *Preparatory Meditations* in relation to Taylor's wavering between doubt and certitude in "A Principle of Order in Edward Taylor's *Preparatory Meditations*," *Early American Literature*, 4, No. 3 (1970), 110–16.

University of Texas, Austin

WILLIAM H. GRAVELY, JR.

NEW SOURCES FOR POE'S "HANS PFAALL"

Foremost among those works which have been either suggested or actually treated as sources for Poe's "Hans Pfaall" are Sir John Herschel's *A Treatise on Astronomy*[1] and George Tucker's *A Voyage to the Moon*.[2] There can be no question about the extent of Poe's indebtedness to Herschel. Not only did Poe himself freely acknowledge this debt, but Professor Meredith N. Posey has clearly shown that some ten or twelve passages from "Hans Pfaall" may be traced to Herschel's *Treatise* and that several passages of considerable length are mere paraphrases of it.[3] I am convinced, however, that Poe's indebtedness to Tucker, though not insignificant, is much less heavy than some scholars have held it to be. My purpose in this study is not only to establish new sources for "Hans Pfaall" but to demonstrate to those interested in examining former studies that these sources contain passages which, in some instances, more closely parallel passages in Poe's tale than those previously pointed out in Tucker's narrative.

Both James Harrison[4] and Hervey Allen[5] conjecture that Poe's interest in moon-hoaxes and lunar voyages may have had its origin in Tucker's work. But neither Harrison nor Allen attempts to prove that Poe used it as a definite source. Such an attempt was first made by Professor Posey in the same article in which he so clearly demonstrates Poe's debt to Herschel (p. 501). Here he lists a series of details common to both Poe's story and numerous excerpts from Tucker's book as reproduced in an elaborate review of it. Posey's language is confusing, for he leaves the impression that Tucker's work was published in magazine form when he speaks of Poe's having mentioned "among other stories dealing with a trip to the moon a tale from the *American Quarterly Review* of March, 1828, entitled *A Voyage to the Moon*" (p. 501). Actually, Poe's reference is not to the book, firsthand, but to the lengthy review.[6] The reference occurs near the end of the long note appended to "Hans Pfaall,"[7] and nowhere does Poe mention the book by its title or intimate that he knew who wrote either the book or the review.

In an article published in the June 1942 number of *PMLA*,[8] Professor J. O. Bailey seeks to demonstrate that Poe's main source for "Hans Pfaall" is not the review but the book itself. Although Bailey acknowledges that the review "contains much of the material used in 'Hans Pfaal,' " he eliminates it as a direct source on the ground that he has discovered "items common to both Tucker's book and Poe's story, but not in the review" (p. 523). He then proceeds to draw certain "tentative conclusions—or surmises" which he feels are suggested by his re-examination of "Hans Pfaall" (p. 529). One of these tentative conclusions is that, contrary to Poe's own statements, the central part of the tale was written earlier than 1835, the period of writing covering possibly more than two years (pp. 530–31).

Finally, in a brief article published in the September 1966 number of *Notes and Queries*,[9] Roland S. Wilkinson persuasively argues that "Poe follows the plot of Tucker to a much greater extent than has been realized" and concludes that he does so "in such manner to suggest that 'Hans Pfaall' was designed as a subtle satire upon Tucker's *Voyage* in particular, and previous 'moon-voyages' in general" (p. 334). I am willing to concede that after Poe abandoned his original design of "imparting very close verisimilitude" (*Works*, XV, 128) to a description of the lunar scenery as viewed through an extraordinary telescope and decided, instead, to write a "voyage to the moon" in a half-plausible and half-bantering style, he may well have decided also, as one feature of his altered plan, to direct some sportive ridicule at Tucker's romance and other works, perhaps, of the same genre. I do not, however, believe that satire was his principal intent or that *A Voyage to the Moon* was his inspirational source. His inspirational source, I am convinced, was Herschel's *Treatise*; and when he sought to achieve his main object—that of imparting as much verisimilitude as he could to an actual journey to the moon—he not only drew copiously from Herschel's work but also searched for other scientific sources that would help him to accomplish his purpose.

Because of his interest in the science of aeronautics it may be safely assumed that Poe familiarized himself with many accounts of the famous balloon ascensions which took place near the end of the eighteenth century and the beginning of the nineteenth. At any rate, there can be little doubt that he drew important material for "Hans Pfaall" from at least two books dealing with such journeys: Vincent Lunardi's *An Account of the First Aërial Voyage in England*[10] and Thomas I. M. Forster's *Annals of Some Remarkable Aërial and Alpine Voyages*.[11] I am also certain that Poe's debt to Herschel's *Treatise* is even greater than evidence produced heretofore has shown it to be. New parallels which may be drawn between passages in these three works and passages in "Hans Pfaall" tend to lessen the importance of Tucker's romance as a major source. At times, even though Poe may have been originally indebted to Tucker for suggestions, he evidently turned, in developing these suggestions, to works which exerted a more positive influence upon him.

Poe probably owed something to Lunardi's famous ascension from London in 1784 and possibly to an account in Forster's *Annals* for the method that Hans Pfaall employed to produce balloon gas for his lunar journey. The account in Forster's book describes in detail Professor Robertson's ascension from St. Petersburg during the year 1804. It is a translation of an account originally written in Russian by the Academician Sacharof, who accompanied Robertson on the voyage. I quote first from "Hans Pfaall":

I then took opportunities of conveying by night, to a retired situation east of Rotterdam, five iron-bound casks, to contain about fifty gallons each, and one of a larger size—six tinned ware tubes, three inches in diameter, properly shaped, and ten feet in length—a quantity of *a particular metallic substance or semimetal* which I shall not name—and a dozen demijohns of *a very common acid*. The gas to be formed from these latter materials is a gas never yet generated by any other person than myself—or at least never applied to any similar purpose. The secret I would make no difficulty in disclosing, but that it of right belongs to a citizen of Nantz in France, by whom it was conditionally communicated to myself. The same individual submitted to me, without being at all aware of my intentions, a method of constructing balloons from the membrane of a certain animal, through which substance any escape of gas was nearly an impossibility.[12]

Lunardi describes two methods of obtaining balloon gas. He rejects the method which yields elastic gas because it "requires a constant application of fire to the contents of the Balloon" and is therefore exceedingly dangerous, as well as difficult to use (p. 11). He says:

I have chosen inflammable rather than elastic air for my guide. It is a substance produced by the action of vitriolic acid on metals or semi-metals, and is similar to that vapour which takes fire in mines, and carries terror and destruction wherever it approaches.   (p. 12)

He then goes on to say that the advantage of this inflammable air is that it is *"seven* times lighter than atmospherical air," whereas the other kind is "not more than *three* times lighter" (p. 12). Again, somewhat later in his account, he tells how his planning to use inflammable air led to an acquaintance with Dr. George Fordyce, a distinguished physician and probably without an equal in the field of chemistry. This man, he writes, "has offered in the kindest manner to fill the Balloon, in a method which is an improvement on that of the French philosophers, as he contrives the tubes for conveying the inflammable so as to prevent the admission of any atmospheric air. He is also of the opinion, that air produced by the vitriolic acid and zinc alone, is the lightest of any that has been yet used" (p. 12).

The action of vitriolic (i.e., sulfuric) acid on zinc has long been a common method of producing hydrogen gas, although it was not, as the following description reveals, the method employed by Sacharof and Robertson:

The decomposition of the water was effected by sulphuric acid and iron filings, mostly from cast iron. The chemical apparatus consisted of twenty five vessels, from each of which a tin plate tube was conveyed to a tub. For separating the carbonic acid gas, unslaked lime was thrown into the water. Into each vessel were put three pood of iron filings with fifteen pood of water, and three pood of sulphuric acid were poured over them.   (pp. 44–45)

Now these excerpts from the accounts of Lunardi and Sacharof—especially those from Lunardi's account—surely suggest some influence upon the passage from "Hans Pfaall" quoted above. Compare, for instance, Poe's *"a particular metallic substance or semi-metal"* and his *"very common acid"* with Lunardi's "a substance produced by the action of vitriolic acid on metals or semi-metals." Moreover, when Hans Pfaall says that the gas generated by himself is unique, that he owes the secret of its generation to "a citizen of Nantz in France," and that this same citizen told him of a method of constructing balloons which would make it almost impossible for any air to escape, I feel that there at least a suggestion of Lunardi's account of his meeting a physician—probably the world's greatest chemist—who offered to fill the balloon "in a method which is an improvement on that of the French philosophers, as he contrives the tubes for conveying the inflammable so as to prevent the admission of any atmospheric air." Finally, Poe's "five iron-bound casks, to contain about fifty gallons each, and one of a larger size"; his "six tinned ware tubes, three inches in diameter"; and his twelve demijohns of acid may well have been suggested by the apparatus that Sacharof and Robertson used in making their gas—their "twenty five vessels, from each of which a tin plate tube was conveyed to a tub." I give weight to the last of these parallels only because evidence yet to be produced in this paper will clearly establish Poe's indebtedness both to Sacharof's account and to other accounts in Forster's *Annals*.

In the final revision of his tale Poe was somewhat less indefinite in describing the kind of gas used by Hans Pfaall, for he inserted in the passage quoted above the following additional observations by his voyager: "I can only venture to say here that it is *a constituent of azote* [i.e., nitrogen], so long considered irreducible, and that its density is about 37.4 times *less than that of hydrogen*. It is tasteless, but not odorless; burns, when pure, with a greenish flame; and is instantaneously fatal to animal life" (*Works*, II, 51–52). Here Poe may have been consciously trying to improve upon the efficacy of Lunardi's hydrogen gas, which "is *seven* times lighter than atmospherical air," two and one third times lighter than elastic air, and so inflammable that it "carries terror and destruction wherever it approaches."

Again, in his final revision of "Hans Pfaall," Poe is unquestionably indebted to Sacharof for many of the articles which Hans Pfaall decided to take with him on his journey. According to the tale in its original form, Hans Pfaall bought, during the course of his preparations, "a quadrant, a compass, a spy-glass, a common barometer with some important modifications, and two astronomical instruments not so generally well known" (p. 568). Then, after completing preparations, he attached his car and put in it all his articles, "not forgetting the condensing apparatus, a copious supply of water, and a large quantity of provisions, such as pemmican, in which much nutriment is contained in comparatively little bulk" (p. 568). In revising his story, Poe modified and enlarged upon these items. After mentioning his "purchase of numerous instruments and materials for experiment in the upper regions of the atmosphere" (p. 51), Hans Pfaall says:

In about four hours and a half I found the balloon sufficiently inflated. I attached the car, therefore, and put all my implements in it—a telescope; a barometer, with some important modifications; a thermometer; an electrometer; a compass; a magnetic needle; a seconds watch; a bell; a speaking trumpet, etc., etc., etc.—also a globe of glass, exhausted of air, and carefully closed with a stopper—not forgetting the condensing apparatus, some unslaked lime, a stick of sealing wax, a copious supply of water, and a large quantity of provisions, such as pemmican, in which much nutriment is contained in comparatively little bulk.   (p. 55)

Nearly all the items for experimental purposes listed in the last of these excerpts were unquestionably borrowed from Sacharof's account of his journey with Robertson. After mentioning various experiments to be made on the voyage, including "the filling with air, flasks exhausted by Torricelli's method, at each fall of an inch in the barometer," Sacharof continues:

The instruments I carried with me for these experiments were: 1st. Twelve flasks in a box with a lid; 2nd. A barometer and thermometer; 3rd. A thermometer; 4th. Two electrometers, with sealing wax and sulphur; 5th. A compass and magnetic needle; 6th. A watch that beat seconds; 7th. A bell; 8th. A speaking trumpet; 9th. A prism of crystal; 10th. Unslaked lime, and some other things for chemical and philosophical experiments.   (p. 44)

Besides food, drink, and implements of various kinds, Hans Pfaall carried with him two pigeons and a cat (p. 568). In Forster's *Annals* are several accounts of voyages on which pigeons and other birds were taken for experimental purposes. At various heights the birds were released and their reactions observed. Lunardi, who created a tremendous sensation when he ascended from London in 1784 before a huge crowd that included the Prince of Wales, took with him a pigeon, a dog, and a cat (p. 31).

The nearly fatal accident that Hans Pfaall met with as the result of an explosion which occurred just after he began his ascent was probably suggested to Poe by M. Windham Sadler's tragic death, recorded in Forster's *Annals*. Hans Pfaall's mishap is described in part as follows:

The balloon at first collapsed—then furiously expanded—then whirled round and round with horrible velocity—and finally, reeling and staggering like a drunken man, hurled me with great force over the rim of the car, and left me dangling at a terrific height, with my head downwards, and my face outwards from the balloon, by a piece of slender cord about three feet in length, which hung accidentally through a crevice near the bottom of the wicker-work, and in which, as I fell, my left foot became most providentially entangled. It is impossible—utterly impossible—to form any adequate idea of the horror of my situation.   (p. 569)

Compare the foregoing description with what happened to Sadler:

Wednesday, Sept. 29, 1824, M. Windham Sadler met with a fatal accident with a balloon today, and it is the second which happened this year. He had gone up, accompanied by one of his men, from Bolton: when nearly over a place called Church, near Blackburn, they prepared to descend, and coming down rather too rapidly, and with too much wind, the balloon brushed against a tree, which threw Sadler out of his car, to which he hung by one leg, the balloon moving on, while the aëronaut was suspended in this dreadful situation with his head downwards, struck again on a chimney, against which it dashed poor Sadler's head with so much violence that he was knocked down with his skull and several bones fractured, and died early the next day.   (pp. 89–90)

In developing a rather long episode recounting the painful sensations that Hans Pfaall and his animal companions experienced before the former was compelled to make use of his condenser, Poe is chiefly indebted, I think, to some of the accounts of balloon ascensions described in Forster's *Annals*. After the balloon had ascended to a height of at least nine and a half miles, the problem of respiration became acute, as Hans Pfaall thus observes:

I began to find great difficulty in drawing my breath. My head too was excessively painful; and having felt for some time a moisture about my cheeks, I at length discovered it to be blood, which was oozing quite fast from the drums of my ears. My eyes, also, gave me great uneasiness . . . . I was suddenly seized with a spasm which lasted for better than five minutes, and even when this, in a measure, ceased, I could catch my breath only at long intervals, and in a gasping manner—bleeding all the while copiously at the nose and ears, and even slightly at the eyes. The pigeons appeared distressed in the extreme, and struggled to escape . . . .   (p. 572)

Later Hans Pfaall records that his uneasy sensations continued even after he had opened a vein in his arm in order to lose some blood: "The pains in my head and ears returned, at intervals, with violence, and I still continued to bleed occasionally at the nose . . ." (p. 573). Compare the foregoing excerpts with two which I quote from Forster's *Annals* describing the sensations of Professor Robertson and his companion, M. Lhoest, after they had reached a very high altitude on a voyage begun at Hamburg in the middle of July 1803, about a year before Robertson's flight with Sacharof:

In the middle of July, of the same year, M. Robertson, accompanied by M. Lhoest, went up in a balloon from Hamburg, and having attained a great height, he could scarcely endure the cold; his teeth chattered, his head became swelled, and the blood came from his nose. M. Lhoest, his companion, was violently affected, but in a different way; it was simply such a swelling of the head that he could not bear his hat on. They both had singing of the ears all the way down, but the other sensations of pain disappeared on getting towards the earth . . . . A bird, taken up with them, was killed by the extreme rarefaction of the air.   (pp. 39–40)

The second excerpt from the *Annals* is from a later account, by Robertson himself, of the same voyage:

At that height the cold of the car was insupportable, though the thermometer was only one degree below the freezing point. We were obliged to respire faster, and our pulse beat with extreme rapidity. We could scarcely resist the strong inclination to sleep with which we were seized. The blood rushed to our heads, and M. Lhoest remarked that it had entered my eyes. My head was so swelled that I could not put on my hat.   (p. 40)

But there is stronger evidence than the matter contained in the last two passages to prove that Poe, in developing the long episode under discussion, is heavily indebted to accounts of balloon ascensions recorded in Forster's *Annals*. Included in the episode is a detailed description of how the pigeons carried aloft by Hans Pfaall reacted to the extreme altitude. I am certain that Poe again drew upon Sacharof's account of his voyage with Robertson for specific details of this description, as well as upon a report of one of Robertson's earlier voyages. Apparently, too, he relied on a description of an ascension by M. Sadler and M. Beaufoy, begun at Hackney, England, on August 29, 1811. The last-mentioned account is described as coming from contemporary journals, although Forster does not say which ones. I quote first from "Hans Pfaall":

The pigeons about this time seeming to undergo much suffering, I determined upon giving them their liberty. I first untied one of them—a beautiful gray-mottled pigeon—and placed him upon the rim of the wicker-work. He appeared extremely uneasy, looking anxiously around him, fluttering his wings, and making a loud cooing noise—but could not be persuaded to thrust himself from off the car. I took him up at last, and threw him to about half a dozen yards from the balloon. He made, however, no attempt to descend as I had expected, but struggled with great vehemence to get back, uttering at the same time very shrill and piercing cries. He at length succeeded in regaining his former station on the rim—but had hardly done so when his head dropped upon his breast, and he fell dead within the car. The other one did not prove so unfortunate. To prevent his following the example of his companion, and accomplishing a return, I threw him downwards with all my force, and was pleased to find him continue his descent, with great velocity, making use of his wings with ease, and in a perfectly natural manner.   (p. 573)

Next, I quote two excerpts from Sacharof's account:

About 20 minutes past nine we were at a height where the barometer stood at 23 inches, and the heat was 6½ degrees. At this height I filled the seventh flask with air, and suffered to escape two canary birds and a dove. One of the canary birds, when let loose from the cage, would not fly; but when thrown into the air, it fell down with precipitation. The dove also, when thrown from the car, flew down almost in a curved line to a village that lay below us.   (p. 47)

About 30 minutes past nine the barometer had fallen to 22 inches, and the thermometer indicated 4½ degrees of heat. I now filled the eighth flask with air. Before this I suffered the other dove to escape, or rather threw it from the car, as it sat on the edge of it and would not fly away. For two or three minutes it flew around the car at the distance of thirty fathoms, and again perched upon it. I then took it in my hand, without its making any resistance or showing the least fear, and threw it down; but it flew violently round in a circular manner, either because it was not able to rise, or because it saw no objects before it.
(pp. 47–48)

The following extract is from an account of another ascension by Robertson:

When the thermometer indicated one degree above freezing, and the barometer stood at 15 inches, M. Robertson set at liberty two pigeons, which descended with the rapidity of lightning, without moving their wings, and in a plane slightly inclined. When the barometer stood at 14 inches he let off a third pigeon, which, having fluttered about for a moment with difficulty, perched on the net work, and would not quit it.   (p. 42)

Finally, I quote two passages from an account of the ascension by Sadler and Beaufoy:

At this time placed a pigeon on the edge of the car; the poor animal seemed excessively alarmed: standing on the edge of the car and looking round. The earth was concealed from the view by the clouds beneath. After some little time the observer precipitated the pigeon gently from its perch, when it fell like a stone until lost in the haze, which was almost in an instant. As long as it remained in sight it did not make any attempt to assist itself with its wings.

(p. 65)

Turned off a pigeon, which would not leave the car, but continued to look frightened, and then turned its head inward without attempting to escape. When pushed off the side of the car, it fluttered and used the most violent exertions to regain the car, but as notwithstanding all its exertions it continued to sink rapidly below the car, it at length extended its wings, keeping them apparently immoveable, and darted towards the earth, at an angle considerably inclined, with the rapidity of a hawk making his swoop.   (p. 66)

In the light of the foregoing evidence there can be no doubt, I feel, that Poe owed much to accounts of various balloon ascensions in developing the long episode describing the suffering of Hans Pfaall and his animal companions during the early stages of their voyage. But I am inclined to think that Poe's reading of Herschel's *A Treatise on Astronomy* suggested to him the idea of having Hans Pfaall take with him a condenser for the purpose of making the rarefied air fit to breathe. Herschel says: "When we ascend to any considerable elevation above the earth, either in a balloon, or on mountains, we are made aware, by many uneasy sensations, of an insufficient supply of air" (p. 28). After mentioning that air "is compressible, i.e., capable of being condensed, or crowded into a smaller space in proportion to the incumbent pressure" (p. 28), he goes on to say:

Arguments, however, are not wanting to render it, if not absolutely certain, at least in the highest degree probable, that the surface of the aërial, like that of the aqueous ocean, has a real and definite limit, as above hinted at; beyond which there is positively *no* air, and above which a fresh quantity of air, could it be added from without, or carried aloft from below, instead of dilating itself indefinitely upwards, would, after a certain very enormous but still finite enlargement of volume, sink and merge, as water poured into the sea, and distribute itself among the mass beneath.   (p. 30)

Now there can be no doubt that Poe weighed in his mind the foregoing passages from Herschel's *Treatise* when he was at work on the first published version of "Hans Pfaall" and was seeking a means of enabling his voyager to overcome the difficulties of breathing at a great height. Near the beginning of the actual account of the voyage Hans Pfaall digresses to explain how he had earlier speculated on the problem of breathing in a rarefied atmosphere, a problem which he had known he must face after attaining a certain altitude. Contrary to what Herschel held almost certainly to be true, he had finally concluded that it would be impossible to "arrive at a limit beyond which no atmosphere is to be found" (p. 570), even though he "was aware [and here he paraphrases Herschel] that arguments have not been wanting to prove the existence of a real and definite limit to the atmosphere, beyond which there is absolutely no air whatsoever" (pp. 570–71). After thus resolving the matter to his satisfaction, he had further concluded that "by means of the very ingenious apparatus of M. Grimm," upon which he had "spent some money and great labor" to adapt it to his purposes, he could condense enough rarefied air during the course of his journey to enable him to breathe satisfactorily (p. 571). By rejecting, for the purposes of his story, the likely theory that most of the space between the earth and the moon is altogether devoid of air, Poe found a way of making Hans Pfaall's journey seem more plausible than it would otherwise have been; for no matter how rarefied the air became, so long as it existed in some form throughout the journey, it might—in the mind of the unscientific and gullible reader, of course— conceivably be made fit for respiration by means of a condenser such as Poe describes.

Poe seems to be indebted to Herschel for another detail in "Hans Pfaall" not previously pointed out. After landing on the moon, Hans Pfaall contemptuously turned away from the lunar inhabitants and, looking toward the earth, "beheld it like a huge, dull, copper shield, about two degrees in diameter, fixed immoveably in the heavens overhead, and tipped on one of its edges with a crescent border of the most brilliant gold" (p. 579). This passage is clearly, in part, a paraphrase of the following observation by Herschel in his *Treatise*: "If there be inhabitants in the moon, the earth must present to them the extraordinary appearance of a moon nearly 2° in diameter, exhibiting the same phases as we see the moon do, but *immoveably fixed in the sky . . .*" (p. 220).

The foregoing examination of new sources for "Hans Pfaall" has revealed, in my judgment, that Poe's most significant sources are scientific rather than fictional. Granted that he is indebted to *A Voyage to the Moon* for some suggestions and that he may have intended to hold up to some degree of ridicule not only Tucker's romance but also other works in the moon-voyage genre, it seems clear that when he sought to achieve the effect of verisimilitude by making Hans Pfaall's journey as plausible as he could, his obligation to Tucker was relatively small. Nor should it be overlooked that Poe considered the distinguishing feature of his own story to lie in the achievement of precisely that effect which, in his opinion, the author of *A Voyage to the Moon*, as well as the authors of other lunar voyages antedating "Hans Pfaall," had failed to achieve.

NOTES

1. *A Treatise on Astronomy* (Philadelphia: Carey, Lea, and Blanchard, 1834).
2. *A Voyage to the Moon* (New York: Elam Bliss, 1827). Tucker was Professor of Moral Philosophy at the University of Virginia when this book was published.
3. "Notes on Poe's 'Hans Pfaall,' " *MLN*, 45 (1930), 502–504.
4. Poe, *Complete Works*, ed. James A. Harrison (New York: Crowell, 1902), I, 55. This edition is hereafter referred to as *Works*.
5. *Israfel* (New York: Doran, 1926), I, 175.
6. The author of this anonymous review was Professor Robley Dunglison of the University of Virginia. For the review itself, see *The American Quarterly Review*, 3 (1828), 61–88.
7. *Works*, II, 108.
8. "Sources for Poe's *Arthur Gordon Pym*, 'Hans Pfaal,' and Other Pieces," *PMLA*, 57 (1942), 513–35.
9. "Poe's 'Hans Pfaall' Reconsidered," vol. 13, 333–37.
10. London: printed for the author and sold by J. Bell, 1784.
11. London: Keating and Brown, 1832.
12. "Hans Phaall—A Tale," *Southern Literary Messenger*, 1 (1835), 568. All excerpts quoted from Poe's story for the purpose of establishing parallels are taken, unless otherwise specified, from the original version appearing in the *Messenger*. At various times Poe spelled the last name of his voyager in several different ways.

University of Maryland

JOHN M. DITSKY

UPROOTED TREES: DYNASTY AND THE LAND
IN FAULKNER'S NOVELS

Dynasty, here defined as the use of the land for purposes of familial establishment, is generally assumed to have been a major theme of Faulkner's novels. Certainly the presence of great "houses"—Sutpens, Sartorises, Compsons, etc.—is an apparent and significant element in the constitution of the Yoknapatawpha saga. Less clearly understood, however, are the terms under which dynastic themes operate in Faulkner: their organization and development. A survey of the whole body of Faulkner's novelistic output, therefore, should assist us in measuring the degree to which issues of dynasty were of *actual* importance to Faulkner, and enable us to note the nature and evolution of his attitudes on the subject.

I

The concept of dynasty and the significance of familial establishments in general did not greatly concern Faulkner during the earliest, "apprenticeship" period of his career. One likely reason is that of scale: Faulkner had not yet realized the value of a consistently utilized setting, nor had he therefore been able to conceive of the novel as saga. Though there are few indications of what would follow in the early prose, Carvel Collins' *William Faulkner: Early Prose and Poetry* (1962; all books referred to throughout this article are the standard editions) contains a drama review with the statement that art ought to be "provincial" in nature (pp. 86–89). Such a concept readily leads to the idea of "rooting" characters in their native settings, yet Faulkner seems to have been unaware at first of the inevitability of the dynastic institution as a fixture of his fiction. Again, his suggestion that native dramatic materials should be exploited (pp. 93–97) implies some awareness of the way in which a given family—such as Faulkner's own—might be related to a literary treatment of regional concerns. And finally, Faulkner's stated isolation from "contemporary poets" is the result of his having "fixed" his "roots in the soil," a circumstance which he says led him to an even greater discovery:

the splendor of fortitude, the beauty of being of the soil like a tree about which fools might howl and which winds of disillusion and death and despair might strip, leaving it bleak, without bitterness; beautiful in sadness.   (p. 117)

Furthermore, Faulkner's early attachment to themes of sexuality and fertility suggests a natural future involvement with the concept of dynasty. For instance, one of the *New Orleans Sketches* (1961), called "The Longshoreman," takes its sense of the tie between a people or race and a given area of land—and the corresponding isolation of a member of that people when away from his own land—out of the "dark forces" of the blood:

These cities are not my cities, but this dark is my dark, with all the old passions and fears and sorrows that my people have breathed into it. Let this blood sing: did I make this blood?   (p. 44)

The other sketches "Sunset" and "Yo Ho and Two Bottles of Rum" also use the race-land link; and though their handling is not recognizably Faulknerian, they confirm a growing awareness on his part of the sources of his own emerging artistry.

Yet Faulkner's acknowledgment of that awareness was slow in coming: his first two novels evidence a certain abiding distrust for the literary possibilities of Lafayette County, while Faulkner himself continues to experiment with the more fashionable themes of postwar disillusionment and the emptiness of interpersonal relationships. In *Soldiers' Pay* (1926), the spectacle of Donald Mahon coming home to die might have had a greater impact if Faulkner had shown just what "home" meant to Donald, and why the war caused such a loss or achieved such a distancing between a man and the world he had once called his own. What might have been is hinted at in the scene in which the vegetating Donald, confronted by his old black "mammy" for the first time since the war, suddenly announces "I've got to go home, Joe" and dies shortly thereafter, having made the only possible sort of reconciliation with his own past (p. 172).

Mosquitoes (1927) might have become much more significant, or seemed less silly, had Faulkner used a contrasting world of order and stability grounded in Nature as a yardstick of loss. But both *Soldiers' Pay* and *Mosquitoes* are interesting chiefly for what *might* have been, and *Sartoris* (1929) is the measure of their lacks. Although the latter work is not Faulkner's most comfortable use of dynastic thematic materials, it is a partially successful effort—a third try with the same fictional elements. His limited but apparent success can be traced to his deliberate adoption of Mississippi as a locale and of dynastic establishment upon the land as a standard by which the book's hero might be understood.

Sartoris begins by establishing the interconnection between the Sartoris family and its lands (p. 6), an association so intimate and a bond so durable as to provide the novel's basis in character, conflict, and theme. When evening prompts memories, they are recollections of the landed past (pp. 42–43). Yet the novel's larger statements on the subject of dynasty display its author's ambivalence: if the past was so very silly, after all, it was very splendid too:

> Old Bayard sat for a long time, regarding the stark dissolving apotheosis of his name. Sartorises had derided Time, but Time was not vindictive, being longer than Sartorises. And probably unaware of them. But it was a good gesture, anyway.
> "In the nineteenth century," John Sartoris said, "genealogy is poppycock. Particularly in America, where only what a man takes and keeps has any significance and where all of us have a common ancestry and the only house from which we can claim descent with any assurance is the Old Bailey. Yet the man who professes to care nothing about his forebears is only a little less vain than the man who bases all his actions on blood precedent. And I reckon a Sartoris can have a little vanity and poppycock, if he wants it."   (p. 92)

In the end it is Miss Jenny who, having been torn away herself from "that soil where her forefathers slept trusting in the integrity of mankind," is best able to reflect upon the meaning of dynasty: the fatal charm of "rash and heedless men" who, by stretching themselves across history like a chain, are able to make at least a doomed but noble impression upon it (p. 357).

Negroes, whose position in Faulkner's work is special because of their assumed closeness to the soil—without either rights of ownership or tendencies toward land abuse—are shown (in the argument between Simon and Miss Jenny over the proper planting of flowers) as sharing in the dynastic trait of stubbornness (pp. 50–51) and (through the returning soldier Caspey) as being just as capable of estrangement from the land as their employers (p. 66). Though love of the land without the desire to possess, alter, or despoil it preserves the integrity of Faulkner's Negroes as a fictional class, exempting them from the corruption and decay of the spirit to which his whites are prone, the modern reader may find it difficult to appreciate their situation as one of comic irony: that is, by "knowing their place" they may acquire more actual power than their decadent white masters (p. 83). Still, Faulkner's method is prescriptive only *after* it has been descriptive, and there is no gainsaying the honesty of his attempt to discover a personal truth in an existent social system.

II

In *The Sound and the Fury* (1929), the dynastic concept is so related to proprietorship of land that its earliest Indian owners become part of the inheritance of guilt which finally destroys the last generation of Compsons (pp. 403–408). Misuse of the land is, of course, the source of the guilt; the land is subjected to human rapacity without respect for its intrinsic value. Deprived of the association with Nature that opposes human greed, the Compsons are unable to cope with decline. Just as Benjy fails to understand the loss of the pasture which had been his birthright (p. 22), so the dynastic legacy of a mounting necessity for expiation of many crimes of property is only dimly perceived.

On the other hand, *As I Lay Dying* (1930) uses the Bundrens to explore the possibilities of a non-dynastic relationship with the soil; the covenant is essentially the same. For the landless, or for those whose proprietary rights are minimal, familial tensions still find expression in Nature. Thus Addie, disgusted with Anse and his passionless mode of existence, sets great store by the wish to have her body returned to her own people for burial in the family plot, symbolically rejecting all that her husband represents (p. 18). To Anse, man's purpose is the achievement of a treelike stability—and inactivity (p. 35). Between these poles of parental attitude the several characters of the novel position themselves, always in terms of Nature.

In *Sanctuary* (1931), a third possibility is considered: the anti-dynasts, who neither strive to possess land to fix themselves upon nor try to exist in and with Nature in some vital way, are either oblivious to or contemptuous of the land. The lives of such people are predictably patterns of selfish and cheap emotionality, establishing a sort of negative *moral* dynasty. Lacking commitment to the soil, the younger generation in *Sanctuary* expresses itself in meaningless gestures (pp. 204–205); a new breed, born of the land but no longer its own, emerges—the Snopeses. (Faulkner contrasts a Negro and a Snopes to judge the value of the new ruling class [pp. 213, 239].) Against the backdrop of such societal change, the gangster element central to the novel exercises its power to pervert; the rape of Temple Drake and the strikingly symbolic instrument of its accomplishment are double indications of the seriousness of the perversion of Nature involved.

Light in August (1932) is the least "dynastic" of Faulkner's major novels, its characters representing neither decaying aristocracy, enduring peasantry, nor usurping barbarians. Its treatment of Joe Christmas' alienation from humanity and Lena Grove's confident childbearing, however, does involve an orientation to a vaster human dynasty in which ancestor and descendant are positioned by historical priorities— much like the resolution of *The Grapes of Wrath*. But the fact that the "rootless" Joe seems able to call "no square of earth his home" (p. 27) is in itself a reason why *Light in August* does not belong to this discussion as initially defined.

"Dynasty," after all, is not Faulkner's term, nor is it relevant to Southern society except by special application. Yet the notion of setting up an ongoing family unit on a parcel of land is essentially more Southern than American in general; as an idea, it is quite natural to a land-based society of limited mobility. Mobility and changed setting often accomplish a radical transformation of Faulkner's fictional patterning; *Pylon* (1935), its society in constant flux, presents an essentially nightmarish world out of Eliot's *Waste Land* in which normal human relationships are distorted or perverted by circumstance—a whole run of Christmases. Thus the reporter, near the novel's end, can only lament that he doesn't "know the family's habits yet" (p. 301). The reason is that this is no ordinary family, but one free of the influence of "roots" and therefore unpredictable. Its dynastic structure is like the Shumann house: built in a Hollywood "mud-and-chickenwire tradition," wearing "an air of dilapidation and rot," with an "immediate disintegration . . . inherent in the wood" (p. 304). It is not a world which implies futurity; its ending posits the hope of "peace," remote even at the cost of grief (pp. 306–307).

Although *Absalom, Absalom!* (1936) is the novel most directly and extensively concerned with dynasty, its treatment of the leading families of Jefferson suggests that Faulkner had concluded that dynasty, by reason of intrinsic selfishness, was a fundamentally negative concept. Sutpen fails to bring his dreams to fulfillment because they are initially corrupt, as end and in chosen means, and cause their possessor to violate the Nature-covenant and thus become evil, unnatural, and accursed. Sutpen is godlike, accomplishing the creation of his estate by lesser genesis, as if by fiat; but the proper analogy in epic is neither

Hector nor Odysseus, but Satan: Sutpen is called "demon" (pp. 8–11), one of Faulkner's villains of pure will. It is Rosa Coldfield who identifies this damned lineage and damned soil as a "fatality and curse on the South and on our family as though because some ancestor of ours had elected to establish his descent in a land primed for fatality and already cursed with it" (p. 21). Faulkner offers Rosa's bitterness as one result of the "black foundation" whose doom and destruction were inherent in its creation (p. 78). During the war, the Sutpen house gradually becomes a "shell" and a "skeleton" in more than one sense (p. 132). Later, Sutpen is seen as an "ancient varicose and despairing Faustus" maintaining only the possibility that some "dragon's outcropping of Sutpen blood" might still work "the hereditary evil" (p. 182). But the family curse remains operative, and with the marriage of Charles Etienne to a woman described as "ape-like" and zoo-born, the fall of the dynasty is assured (pp. 205, 209). The house itself becomes a Gothic horror, a house of Usher filled with the ghost of the man who gave up his "innocence" over an obligation to his dead ancestors and ghosts of the sons whose father's acts accomplish their own disinheritance (pp. 220, 316). What finally burns had long been scorched.

III

After *Absalom, Absalom!* and the end of his major period, Faulkner's interest in dynastic themes declines markedly. As he develops a conception of Nature as metaphor rather than as actual presence in the later work, the idea of dynasty is partially transformed into a spiritual lineage alongside. Thus *The Unvanquished* (1938) extends the usual pattern by having Bayard reassert his right to use his father's land, an act coextensive with his own coming-of-age. *The Wild Palms* (1939) is occupied with persons specifically cutting themselves off from posterity, except in a spiritual sense. *Intruder in the Dust* (1948) develops the idea of a symbolic dynasty further, as the individual is enabled to look upon past generations of his townspeople as his relations in Nature—a connection that, if made, might have saved the burdened mind of Quentin Compson considerable anguish and prevented his suicide. Thus the thought of former hunting days, prompted by the necessity of digging up a grave in the present, causes reflection upon all the members of the old hunting parties and upon what it means to be "the sum of your ancestry" (p. 93). Tales such as the earlier "The Bear," which exploit the mystique of hunting, show Faulkner developing a relatively new conception, the dynasty of deed, ritual, and attitude which requires neither blood link nor land ownership. This genuine though metaphorical kind of dynasty is based on a transmitted affinity for Nature, the opposite of *Absalom, Absalom!*'s heritage of guilt and violence and its effects on Quentin. By making possible an active involvement with the past out of a felt "familial" attachment, Faulkner has "redeemed" the consistently tragic concept of landed dynasty from its usual selfishness. Thus for Chick, the "strong heady vivid living smell of the pines" in a graveyard produces an intoxication in which "ridge on pine-dense ridge" of mountains, rolling back to Scotland in his imagination, creates sympathetic kinship with the dead who were formerly only part of another anonymous "Face" to him (pp. 100–101). Dealing with the reality of what one is, and with the past out of a realistic understanding of one's people and their abiding ties with the soil, yields a concept of dynasty for the twentieth century. Therefore, *Requiem for a Nun* (1951) and *A Fable* (1954) simply carry further the idea of a dynasty of traditional effort to the optimistic abstraction, however land-based, of a world-view of each man as Son of Man.

Originating in materials first worked over during his major period, Faulkner's Snopes trilogy stays with the earlier formulation of the meaning of dynasty. Anti-dynasty in nature, the rise of the Snopes clan in *The Hamlet* (1940) is no fulfillment of dynastic ambitions but a savage emergence from unpropertied bondage for the sake of being king of the scrap heap of the old society. Appropriately, the work opens with a glimpse of dynastic ruins, the Old Frenchman's place (p. 3). Property to Flem, however, is merely power, a fact evident in Will Varner's joint role as largest landowner and judge (p. 5). But even the idyllic episode of Ike and the cow emphasizes the impossibility of a positive dynasty and involves characters such as Jack Houston's childless wife and the owner of the feed barn whose children have deserted the hard life of their parents (pp. 189–98). Themes of dynasty lie dormant in *The Town* (1957) and reappear in *The Mansion* (1959) with the return of Mink Snopes. Mink's resentment of his lot has dynastic implications: he and his kind labor upon the land until worn out in mind and body, yet they never possess it or its fruits. Instead, they accumulate debts which make their children eventual inheritors of their thralldom (pp. 90–91). The tenant system forces hatred of the earth on Mink, while his kin ignore him as just another "pillar, rock-fixed, of things as they are" (p. 222). Rock instead of tree, Mink represents a negative version of the man-land relationship. And the Snopeses themselves are never the sort of mutuality of flesh and name which might constitute the makings of a dynasty; instead, there are the communal integrity of the pack and the social inclinations of the swarm. The climax of anti-dynastic Snopesism comes when Flem seems swindled by that Snopes-like Compson, Jason, over the property which has already embodied a family's dissolution in *The Sound and the Fury*; Flem triumphs over Jason, however—twentieth-century land-rapacity besting the earlier version of the same spirit. Selfish dynasty gives way to anti-dynasty, culminating in the unspeakable irony with which Flem shows the mockery and contempt he holds for land values: the renaming of the Compson place "Eula Acres" (pp. 322–33). Mink's killing of Flem reasserts the earth's dominion, and Mink's right to a piece of it, while Flem's burial is said to resemble a gathering of wolves to scavenge the remains of the head wolf (p. 421). The Snopes trilogy completed, Faulkner left the theme of dynastic establishment for good and all.

The Reivers (1962), therefore, is not directly concerned at all with land-ownership, returning instead to the notion of a transmission of a heritage of deeds and responsibilities from one generation to another. Familial ties are indirect as well as regular: a prostitute's redemption to motherhood is emblem of the new sort of legacy, represented by the boy-hero's name being given to the ex-whore's child (p. 305). Chucking the older, literal form of dynastic establishment—a movement I think Faulkner found necessary because of the realities of our time discussed in *Intruder in the Dust* and *A Fable*—Faulkner changed modes as well, from the tragic to the comic.

Therefore, though Faulkner made use of a triple division of dynastic considerations in his earlier novels (a division I have labeled dynastic, anti-dynastic, and non-dynastic), the concept of dynastic establishment, especially as the saga of "great families," has not finally proved as important to Faulkner's thinking as is often supposed—at least insofar as the land-basis for dynasty is concerned. Without its consistent soil-referent, the theme of dynasty becomes something else: group morality, heredity, social relationships—any of several topics which may involve blood ties without land ties. There is a definite shift in Faulkner's interest from the propertied to the unpropertied and to a later development of the metaphorical conception of dynasty as a spiritual heritage of traditional values. At last, a man finds his birthright in the country of his own heart, Nature herself having become to the eye the landscape described in *A Fable*:

the entire earth one unbroken machined de-mountained dis-rivered expanse of concrete paving protuberanceless by tree or bush or house . . . .   (p. 353)

University of Windsor

VICTOR A. KRAMER

JAMES AGEE'S UNPUBLISHED MANUSCRIPT
AND HIS EMPHASIS ON RELIGIOUS EMOTION
IN *THE MORNING WATCH*

Unpublished notes and manuscripts for *The Morning Watch* clarify Agee's concentration upon the evocation of a pinnacle of religious fervor which the twelve-year-old protagonist, Richard, attempts to sustain. The futility of Richard's effort to prolong a doomed emotion is the core of the book, and clarification of this explains the almost static quality of his watch. This semi-autobiographical novella was planned to evoke emotion, an emotion largely conveyed by attention to details imaginatively recalled about a particular atmosphere: St. Andrew's, the boarding school near Sewanee, Tennessee, as remembered by Agee.[1] Real persons are the basis for much of the characterization.

Rufus of *A Death in the Family* might well be remembered as one reads *The Morning Watch* because the method employed in that later novel is an extension of the technique used in *The Morning Watch*. Thus, six-year-old Rufus does not develop; rather he beholds events which will influence his later development. Essentially the same thing occurs in *The Morning Watch*, even though more change might be expected with its older protagonist. *The Morning Watch* resembles Agee's *Let Us Now Praise Famous Men* where he concentrates upon intersections of space, time, and consciousness and is not particularly occupied with character development. Commentary on *The Morning Watch* often either expresses dissatisfaction with the lack of a clear development in Richard's character or explains his development in terms of the symbolism incorporated into the work.[2] Agee's emphasis, however, is more simply upon the evocation of a particular moment than some readers expect, or admit.

As he planned his book, Agee wrote that its focus was to be on religious emotion, but mixed with the "beginning of intrusions of [a] sense of beauty and a sense of science" while the general "watershed" about which the story was to flow was to remain the "age of faith at its height."[3] Neither in these preliminary notes nor in the finished novella is there emphasis on development of Richard's character. The boy's growing awareness of the complexity of his consciousness is the vehicle, but the desire to feel his faith, and how that desire is crushed by other influences, is the core to which all events of *The Morning Watch* are related.

Agee is concerned with catching a fleeting moment of childhood. But that moment is doomed to expire in the same way as the candles which are so elaborately described as part of the atmosphere of the boarding school chapel which kindled Richard's emotion Good Friday morning. Attention, therefore, to the particularities of what Richard sees is the way of evoking what he feels. Good Friday's experiences cause him to become more knowledgeable about suffering and death, as he becomes more aware of a consciousness which is beginning to impair the ability to feel religious. But while what he experiences, both inside and outside the chapel, alters his consciousness, he still feels at the end of his Good Friday's experience that he and his schoolmates are "children."[4] Those few hours are a crucial time for Richard, but they are relatively static hours.

Holy Week was a special time for everyone at St. Andrew's; and for Richard the events of the week were the culmination of an elaborate series of attempts to foster religious emotion. The entire preceding year had been devoted by him to an intensification of religious fervor. As the narrative opens he lies awake waiting to be called by Father Whitman, and he tries to meditate on Christ's Passion. But his attempts are broken by the happiness and blasphemy of other boys in the dormitory and by his own mental distractions.

The dominant pattern within *The Morning Watch* is made up of the attempt to meditate, an attempt always quickly intruded upon by something else. Good Friday's morning prayer vigil is the high point of expectations, yet during that time he is constantly distracted. These hours should be, he imagines, the best of times to cultivate religious emotion; and so it seems ironic that nothing much comes of his fervor. Such frustration is precisely what Agee emphasizes.

Materials written in conjuction with the novella support a reading which emphasizes the futility of the young protagonist's attempts to sustain his simple faith as it is intruded upon by all manner of things from sex to skepticism. In several notes Agee asked himself what he hoped to accomplish. From his answer, and unused introductory and concluding passages as well, it is clear he felt his story should imply that innocence would yield to other ways of experiencing the world, but that the height of religious emotion was to be his focus in this narrative. Both notes and unused passages convey insights into the complexity of what the young protagonist experiences. Agee asked himself the following:

What really am I after in this story, and is it worth doing? Religion at its deepest intensity or clarity of childhood faith and emotions; plus beginnings of a skeptical intellect and set of senses; how the senses themselves, and sexuality, feed the skeptical or non-religious or esthetic intellect; efforts at self-discipline. Religious-esthetic-biological experiences carrying with them above all, religious experience of an unusually fine kind, and the innocent certainty that it is doomed. To be done in terms of: the watching in the chapel; wanderings of the mind and efforts at prayer; memories of the dead father; imaginations of sex and sport; workings of guilt; excesses of religious intention and complications of guilt and pride; the excitement of . . . dawn . . . the locust hull; . . . the snake. Is [the snake] too obvious a symbol, and the locust? They seem so.
    Is this worth doing? I can't get any solid hold of it or confidence in it.
    A much gentler way of seeing and writing it? Or more casual? Mine is very dry and very literary.[5]

Although he had doubts about method, he knew that the emphasis was to be on "childhood faith . . . doomed." There is no mention of characterization or plot. The concern, as in the finished book, is with the evocation of religious emotion as intruded upon by other concerns.

The fact that Agee expresses doubt about uses of symbolism is significant because the book has been criticized for its weak ending where there is a reliance upon symbolism. Richard Chase argues that in place of "relaxed and perspicacious biography of spiritual change" the concluding part of the book provides "spectacular semantic gestures."[6] Perhaps there is an excess of symbolism within the concluding section of the book; but that part of the book is small, in quantity and import, in comparison with the dominant second part where Richard's futile attempts at prayer are the major concern. And even the concluding section, which describes Richard's adventures with other boys during the pre-dawn hours, remains fundamentally concerned with a boy's intently religious attitudes during hours of the most solemn religious feast of the year. Agee's fear that his method of writing was perhaps elaborate and too "literary" provides an insight into what he did accomplish—a sense of immediacy and an evocation of emotion, but an emotion almost ready to collapse. In still another note he suggested "R's waking emotion and the hollowness of the dormitory beds must be as nearly immediate and simultaneous as possible."[7] Any indirection, abstraction, or use of symbols, unless very carefully integrated into the experience as a whole, would tend to detract from the immediacy of that moment.

The emphasis upon the difficulty of Richard's sustaining religious emotion and the immediacy of what he does experience would have certainly been strengthened if the introductory section and alternate ending written for the novella had been retained. This introductory section is also about the difficulty of feeling religious emotion, but it is from the point of view of an adult. In the excluded passage Father Whitman, the priest who wakes the boys, also tries to feel, but cannot, the solemnity of the night. For him the meaning of the Passion is intellectually clear, but it is not something which he can feel. His disturbed thoughts provide an insight into Richard's dilemma. The implication of Richard's growing awareness, as qualified by this opening description of Father Whitman, is that with maturity, religious emotion becomes complicated by intellect and is easily distracted. But throughout the novella Richard is not particularly aware of what he is experiencing, although he senses the difficulty of what he tries to accomplish. He is yet unable to understand that religious emotion cannot be forced.[8] Such a realization can be made only by a wiser person: the reader, the artist, Father Whitman.

In the excluded passage the dull emotion of Father Whitman stands in contrast with the excitement of Richard. Father Whitman tries to meditate. He has been a member of his Order for twenty years, and, as he lies awake waiting to call the boys to their watch, he knows that Maundy Thursday and Good Friday have lost their special aura for him. If a priest who has been trying for decades cannot focus his attention on the mystery of God's coming and sacrifice, how then can a young person, with a mind wonderfully active, do so?

In conjunction with this unused introductory passage there is a "possible addition" for the conclusion which would have slightly altered further the emphasis of the book. This passage obviously was written for the same purpose as the introductory passage. These excluded words, which provide an alternate ending for the novalla, suggest Richard's kinship with Father Whitman. The unused passages are the following:

Between the middle of the morning on Maundy Thursday and the Mass of the Presanctified on Good Friday morning the Blessed Sacrament was exposed in the Lady Chapel and the boys, teachers and priests of the School, and some of the people who lived nearby on the Mountain, signed the list on the bulletin board for half-hour periods in the continuous watch that was kept before it. Since there was no compulsion, even of an invisible kind, it is probable that most of those who signed and watched were sincerely devout (though some signed perhaps ostentatiously often); but since no hour was forbidden to anyone, except through conflict of classes or other obligations, and since the opportunities for keeping irregular hours were particularly rare for the younger boys, the hours between midnight and daybreak were crowded with their semi-legible signatures. Older boys, like the grown people, were depended on to wake themselves, but it was felt that the younger boys would not manage to do this. The first year the watch had been kept, a prefect had been assigned to the job of waking them; but he had overslept a number of the watches and had failed to keep order and to see that those who finished their watches got back to bed promptly. It was felt that no layman among the teachers should be imposed on and the next year one of the monks, Father Whitman, volunteered; and because nobody else wanted the job, any more than he did, it became assumed from that year on that he would do it. So now again, for the tenth or yes, he remembered, the eleventh year, a cot was set up for him in the space at the stairhead nearest the little boys' dormitories, and from ten o'clock on he lay there, wondering between each performance of his duty whether to try to sleep (for tomorrow was a black fast, and the year's longest and hardest day) or whether to try not to (for to him, because despite their graveness they were without special distinction or celebration, these were also, of all the year, the hours most dear and most solemn). By three thirty in the morning he had still not slept; nor had he been sufficiently awake to use the wakefulness well.

The ticking of the alarm clock still tormented him; even from under the pillow, the pine walls and the hollow stairhead seemed to reflect it, and it came through the hard pillow and stirred in his ear and in the center of his brain almost the more strongly through being muffled; like the effort, he reflected, to stifle conscience; he tried to make that the subject for meditation. Yet on the floor it had been perhaps even worse; it had sounded like a wild beast at a night waterhole, drinking insatiably in stealthy but complete security; and he had thought of the beast as the Devil and had been as much tempted towards his wild, predatory supremacy, as drawn to God. Father Whitman was very sorry he had brought the clock along; but he knew he could not have trusted himself. He lay trying to pray, now formally and now extemporaneously, and to conduct a useful meditation, and to control the sinful and frivolous, fantastic straying of his weary mind, and most earnestly of all, to realize the solemnity of the event which was even now repeating itself; but however clearly he realized it in his dull, tired mind, he could not realize it in his heart. He remembered how the mother of one of the boys on the place, a widow who lived just off the grounds, had spoken once of that kind of reward, as rare, but wonderful, and compensating for all, and to be relied on, and how he had told her that in twenty years of hoping, it had never once happened to him. I only want to be a religious, he told himself quietly. I haven't got it in me to be, and in twenty years of trying, none of that has changed. He struck his breast three times and prayed for forgiveness if possible for his doubt of his avowed and long tested vocation, and for support in his faith and in his efforts to discharge his duties as best he might, whether or not his heart was ever for an instant rewarded. More and more often, after the second quarter of the hour, he interrupted his unhappy devotions to take his watch from his shoe beside the cot and to hold it close beside his eye, its face towards the pallor of the windows above the stairs. It was a fine ancestral machine, one of the few personal luxuries tolerated by his Order, and the only one in which he indulged himself. Only by holding it so close could he hear it; and each time its exact delicateness became audible he experienced a sense of comfort. When at last the watch marked sixteen minutes of four, he briefly and formulatically completed his prayers, made the long firm sign of the cross which usually for a little while deeply confirmed him in his faithfulness, shut off the alarm, got up from the cot, and went as silently as he could down the corridor into Number Twelve to wake three more boys.

. . . .

[Possible addition if this beginning is used; to be added onto present ending, no new paragraph:]
. . . and exactly as he had foreseen, there on the back steps was Father Whitman, and although his eyes too were just as Richard had foreseen, hard, sleepless, patient, eyes to be afraid of and ashamed before, it was not so very hard to meet them after all.[9]

Had Agee chosen to include these additional portions the design of his book would have been more immediately apparent. With a beginning which initially suggests the difficulty of sustaining religious emotion and a conclusion which again returns to Father Whitman, the emphasis upon an "age of faith at its height," but doomed to destruction, would have been more clearly evident.

NOTES

1. The Agee Family spent the summer of 1919 in a cottage at St. Andrew's, and since the cottage was vacant in the fall, Mrs. Agee "decided to stay on . . . and have the children attend the school." Agee remained a student at St. Andrew's through the spring of 1925. In 1924 the widowed Mrs. Agee married Rev. Erskine Wright, a teacher at St. Andrew's. An indication of Agee's concern about precision of detail is illustrated by his question to Father Flye, his teacher and lifelong friend from this school, about the exact time of dawn in spring in Middle Tennessee. *Letters of James Agee to Father Flye* (New York: Braziller, 1962), Introduction, pp. 12, 181.
2. Kenneth Seib, *James Agee: Promise and Fulfillment* (Pittsburgh: Univ. of Pittsburgh Press, 1968), pp. 69–73, argues this story of "initiation into life and the full flowering of that manhood" contains "some of Agee's most complex symbolism." See also Richard Chase, footnote 6.
3. The morning watch: pages of incomplete drafts (on sheet headed "notes"), n.d., University of Texas library. This material and all additional materials from the Agee Papers at Texas are gratefully used with the permission of The James Agee Trust.
4. *The Morning Watch* (Boston: Houghton, 1951), p. 119.
5. The morning watch: pages of incomplete drafts.
6. "Sense and Sensibility," *The Kenyon Review*, 13 (Autumn 1951), 691.
7. The morning watch: pages of incomplete drafts.
8. See Peter Ohlin, *Agee* (New York: Obolonsky, 1966), p. 190; and John S. Phillipson, "Character, Theme, and Symbol in *The Morning Watch*," *Western Humanities Review*, 15 (Autumn 1961), 367, for development of this ironic point.
9. The Morning Watch: Note, typed and typed carbon copy with autograph emendation (3 pp.), n.d., University of Texas library.

Georgia State University

RICHARD MARIUS

HISTORY AND LITERATURE:
SOME WHIMSICAL REMARKS*

When we speak of history and literature, I suppose we are really speaking of historians and writers, and we probably ought to include readers. For history and literature are both affairs of the mind. They possess no real existence outside the intellect of those who conceive them and those who appreciate them. I recall a problem in physics in high school: If a tree falls in a forest where there is no one to hear, does it make a sound? And of course the answer is "no." In the same vein we may ask if either history or literature may exist in libraries without living minds to appropriate what is there, and the answer is likewise a firm "no."

We may then ask why historians and writers do the things they do—write history and novels and poetry and plays? And why do readers spend their time on what is written? The answer to these questions is, I think, a simple one: Something in us delights in rising out of the world we "really" inhabit so that we may live for awhile in another world created strangely in our minds by words which work like some potent acid to eat away the walls set around us by our finitude. In a puritan culture like our own, we are often compelled to justify our work by its usefulness. So writers, historians, and readers are often sucked into the hypocrisy of claiming that we do what we do out of some profound wish to help other men. We prate about the civilizing idealism of our motives, and we like to believe that we are as useful to society as any engineer who ever built a sewer or a bridge.

*A paper delivered at the South Atlantic Modern Language Association meeting, Atlanta, Nov. 7, 1969.

But the truth is that we do what we do because we like to do it, because we love to travel in the realms of gold.

There is a narcotic factor in all this. The more we expand our consciousness of worlds beyond our own, the more we lust to live in them. Interest begets curiosity, and satisfied or even frustrated curiosity breeds more interest. And we awaken one morning to find ourselves hopelessly addicted to history or to letters, living in so strange a manner that we might as well be dreaming "reality" and living our dreams. The fortunate thing is that in our society we can make a living doing what we like. At times I feel a sense of oddity in that I am paid hard cash merely to dream.

And yet for all our dreams, we remain creatures bound by time and space. No matter how near we may be to the subject of history or of literature, we are always to be found separated from our dreams by a great gulf fixed. And it is this gulf which I wish to explore.

Historians have been quite aware of their problem for a long time. Leopold von Ranke posed it quite succinctly a century ago when he said that history should reproduce the past *wie es eigentlich gewesen ist*. That is to say, we should reconstruct the past not only in terms of events as they actually happened, but also in terms of the values which judged those events and gave them meaning for their time.

But we all know that this is impossible. The "past" happened to people in a way that no historian can recapture with mere words. At Gettysburg men smelled the smoke and the heat and the reek of blood, and they tasted fear, and chunks of fiery metal punctured their tender skin, and they died in all the ways men can die in battle, and some survived to spin fantastic yarns of how it was that terrible day. A century afterwards an excellent historian such as Professor Stewart or Professor Coddington or Mr. Catton can minutely describe the battle in words. But what they produce is not the same as the experience those men at Gettysburg endured because the words are not the same as smoke and fire and violent death.

Indeed, their words are devoid of meaning unless I the reader know what smoke and fire are and have some conception, however faint, of violent death. But even if I know these separate entities, I cannot really know what they are in war because I have never been to war. The historian must use *my* experience if *he* is to be understood, but he must also *expand* my experience with his words to include something that I have never known, namely the phenomenon of battle on a sultry afternoon in Pennsylvania a hundred years ago. And of course he must expand his own experience since he was not and never can be a part of the events he describes.

We all know that words have an awesome power in themselves, and the mastery of such power is the art of rhetoric. Our problem in history is to make those potent symbols truly represent something which on the one hand was quite "unwordy" in its happening, but may now be apprehended only by words. We are thrust into the logically terrible situation in which the symbol is all of reality which we possess. And no matter how adept we become at their manipulation, symbols leave us lacking something. We have long since been shorn of that sweet faith of primitive man who seemed to believe in a necessary relationship of the antelopes and the mammoths which he drew on the walls of his cave to the antelopes and the mammoths which roamed the world outside. Not only do words fail to bring us "reality," but they can often deceive us because of the way we apprehend them. Benedictus de Spinoza wrote of the difficulty a long time ago: "from the thought of the word *pomum* a Roman immediately turned to the thought of the fruit, which has no resemblance to the articulate sound *pomum*, nor anything in common with it, excepting this, that the body of that man was often affected by the thing and the sound; that is to say, he often heard the word *pomum* when he saw the fruit. In this manner each person will turn from one thought to another according to the manner in which the habit of each has arranged the images of things in the body. The soldier, for instance, if he sees the footsteps of a horse in the sand, will immediately turn from the thought of a horse to the thought of a horseman, and so to the thought of war. The countryman, on the other hand, from the thought of a horse will turn to the thought of his plough, his field, etc.; and thus each person will turn from one thought to this or that thought, according to the manner in which he has been accustomed to connect and bind together the images of things in his mind." So the historian must set the past into words learned according to *his* experience, and he must pass those words on to others who will hear them according to *their* experience. It is a distance of terrifying proportions if anyone takes history seriously at all.

Now I would submit that there is a similar "distance" to frustrate the writer. Partly it is a "distance" between those vague and lofty perceptions he may see as the goal of his work and the work itself as it finally appears in print. I may be here treading on the dangerous and slippery edges of Platonism. But in the way the writer experiences things, there is indeed something Platonic to the process. When he begins to work, the writer senses something that is beyond his immediate powers or perception. He may have a vague idea of a character he wishes to develop, and however irrational it may sound, there is a sense in which the character seems to exist "out there" dimly concealed in a haze of dreams. And by means of words the writer slowly extricates his man from the haze and commits him to paper.

Sometimes the character is captured with such a vengeance that he runs away from the writer's intentions and becomes an embarrassment. I rather agree with that critical judgment that Mercutio in *Romeo and Juliet* simply *had* to be killed off. Otherwise he would have made off with the whole drama on his back, leaving the two young principals to die with all the attention granted to a losing team in the World Series.

I surprise myself a bit by seeming to imply that there exists a kind of archetype, a transcendent form existing just beyond the writer's grasp, which he seeks to draw down to his matter of paper and ink. I shall say quickly to any nominalists among us that I am as unprepared to defend the autonomously transcendent as I am unprepared to defend the reality of man's immortal soul. And certainly I would not dream of making another Platonic assumption, namely that the writer communicates with the archetype by means of some divine frenzy or ecstasy. Frenzy does not rest well on the keys of the typewriter. I am simply talking about the way the writer feels about his work at the moment he is working. Something does seem to be "out there" which he is trying to copy. And surely anyone who has ever written and rewritten a sentence, trying to get it "right," will know exactly what I mean.

Now history, like the writer's conception, has no existence outside the minds of those men who labor at it—not unless we suppose a "God" who remembers everything and retains each historical event as a divine idea presently and eternally existing in His mind. Then historians might be priests, and I reject that. Nevertheless, when the historian works he has a very vivid perception of something called "the past" which *seems* to be very real to him. And he works to build a bridge from himself to it.

The writer is also striving to bridge distance, rising like Ikaros for the sun. It is dangerous business. How many writers have soared aloft on a vision of *War and Peace* only to fall to an *Exodus*. There is a sense in which every book represents a failure, and failure in these times is more terrifying than death. Yet our accomplishment in print establishes very neatly the limitations of our powers. To live a long life, as Cicero wrote, is only to be reminded constantly of our mortality. And to write a novel is to establish beyond any doubt that we have failed to grasp that world we reached for across the gulf of our imagination.

Because failure is so horrifying in this day when our gods are all as broken as Ozymandias, I would now submit that both history and literature in our time suffer from an acute case of acrophobia. I am thinking of how it once was, in the nineteenth century and before, when both historiography and the novel existed in something very nearly like a golden age. It was the epoch of the colossal imagination, roving at will over a vast scene—*Tom Jones* and *Pamela, David Copperfield, Bleak House, Moby Dick, War and Peace, Vanity Fair.* These were works in which writers undertook to observe, to plot, to create dozens and dozens of characters who swarm now through the collective memory of us all like so many dear friends out of a past misty with the nostalgia of our first meeting.

History knew a similar breadth. Gibbon's *Decline and Fall of the Roman Empire,* Macaulay's truly monumental history of England, Adolphe Thiers' *Histoire de la révolution* and its sequel, *Histoire du consulat et de l'empire.* There was of course Leopold von Ranke, and who can forget Thomas Carlyle? Each year I read to my freshman classes the account of the execution of Louis XVI which Carlyle wrote in his *French Revolution.* It is always a surprise to me to consider that though the room is quiet when I begin, the vast, breathless silence at the end is almost a spell.

Certainly there were faults in all this. I do get rather fatigued with all those precious young girls with hearts of pure gold who flit through the novels of Dickens, all the garrulous wise old men with odd habits and devotions, and I must admit that I have always wished Thackeray had chosen some name other than "Dobbin" for that character of his who represents horse-like fidelity. And what crimes were committed in history's name! Here is Ranke in his *Deutsche Geschichten im Zeitalter der Reformation* hoisting that old canard of Luther going up the *sancta scala* in Rome on his knees, standing erect suddenly in the middle and shouting, "The just shall live by faith," and walking triumphantly back down with the Reformation in his fist—all a decade before Luther really broke with Rome. And in Carlyle's *French Revolution* we never really understand why seagreen Robespierre the Incorruptible had such a power over his age. We could recite other flaws in this kind of history, and perhaps all of them are to be explained by a scholarly hubris, the ambition to do more than any historian really can do in imagining the past as it really was.

Still and all, these great works captured the educated imagination of their times. Both novelists and historians wrote in a sublimely unselfconscious daring which swept their age along with them. But what has happened to us in the twentieth century? I can speak more certainly for history than for literature, but I believe the trends are the same. The good historians, or at least those with sound technical training, have lost confidence in their power to cover a wide range of the past. They have all but abdicated general history except when they wish to turn a fast buck by writing a textbook. This is the age of the monograph, that heavy little treatise which undertakes to prove beyond a shadow of doubt that which nobody considered worth mentioning before. I do not intend to demean this necessary scraping and cleaning of the bricks of history so that they may be set firmly together in a structure both harmonious and strong. The trouble is that most monographs are left lying about in the muck of pedantry—unsynthesized, unattended, and usually unread. For historians this is the age of the university press.

This phenomenon of the subsidized university press deserves a remark or two, for it is symptomatic of what is happening to history. The educated public is not reading the work of the professional historian any more. Consequently no trade house can afford to handle much academic history because the public will not support it. How many professional, academic historians are known to the general reading public? You can probably count them on the fingers of one hand.

But this is not to say that the public has abandoned history. It is simply going outside the academy to find what it wants. I think especially of the work of Will Durant, whose sweeping books have tracked man from the ooze to the Enlightenment. And though it is a sickening thought, I must mention the colossal popularity of the late Thomas B. Costain, whose "gee-whiz, gosh, oh boy" versions of English history have sold in the millions. Hardly an issue of the *New York Times Book Review* does not bring us an account of some historical extravaganza—a new biography of Mary, Queen of Scots, a secret life of the founding fathers, a spine-tingling lie about the way Woodrow Wilson's wife really ran the country during the last days of his administration. However slight their scholarly weight, these books are avidly read by the public. Scholars view all this with such contempt that the very word "popularizer" has become an invective. If history is readable, they assume, it just can't be good.

Now it is very hard for me or anybody else to generalize about modern literature. There are literally thousands of novels being published every year, and people both known and unknown are working with an immense variety of styles, plots, characters, non-plots, and non-characters. But I personally sense that many writers have lost their nerve. In the same way that historians are doing monographs, so writers are delving ever deeper into the subjective consciousness of single characters so that both writer and historian seem to me to be focusing their attention on a narrowing slice of the human experience.

Again I must plead my own fallibility (which no doubt is evident enough to you), but I suspect that many writers are spending a great deal of time in writing about characters hardly different from the writers themselves. It seems to have become too difficult or too dangerous in our age to leap over that distance between our own being and some other being "out there." So the good writers seem to be content to do very little imagining and a great deal of reporting.

Many of you may shrug and say, "So what?" I suppose writing a novel should be like teaching a course in the university. If there is material, and if there is someone to do the job and someone to accept what is offered, then we ought to allow people to do what they like. If Philip Roth wants to write as he so brilliantly does about masturbation and fantasy and the constipation of a middle-class Jewish father, then he should do as he pleases. If Alberto Moravia wants to dwell on the way women dominate rather uninteresting and weakly men, then he should do so. If Ernest Hemingway was entranced by unhappy marriage and the necessity of men to prove their manhood by violent deeds, then he did right to stick to his last. And what of John Updike? In *Couples* his one-dimensional suburbanites grimly screw their tedious way from cover to cover with all the glassy-eyed ardor of a pimply adolescent who has won two-hundred and fourteen free games on a pinball machine and so must play them every one until the last rolling steel ball has gone to rest in that realm of darkness where all games end in absurdity. There *are* one-dimensional suburbanites, and if they do not commit adultery, most of them want to, and so somebody should write about them. And yet I feel uneasy about what seems to be a squandering of so much talent on so small a part of the human experience.

I am certainly aware of the argument that if one is to write truly, he must write about the things he knows best. But if that is the case, why then do writers not have the courage or perhaps the energy to know more? Why don't they try to leap across that gulf of distance and live for awhile in a world truly different from their own or to imagine people significantly different from themselves? Some do, of course. I think of Bernard Malamud's *The Fixer* and Nabokov's brilliantly conceived and executed *Lolita*, and I think also of that rather interesting failure of William Styron, *The Confessions of Nat Turner*. Then there is that wonderful book by Gunther Grass, *The Tin Drum*. But I must confess to a great fatigue in the sameness of book after book produced by some of our leading novelists. I just do not believe I can stand the monumental monotony of one more book by James Baldwin concerning the problems of the black queer. I worked my way through Saul Bellow's *Herzog* and found it a crashing bore, a pallid reflection of that grand and beautiful book, *Ulysses*, from which the name Moses Herzog is drawn, a book which, I feel, represents the model for much of Bellow's work. In what may seem to you to be an arrogant and tasteless way, I am saying that I sense a lack of something almost indefinable in modern writers, and I *think* it is a lack of audacity in the imagination.

Meanwhile the general reading public still seeks out those books which appear to expand the imagination by exposing great chunks of the human experience through a diversity of characters and a plot that goes somewhere. People who buy books like the so-called big books. But the good writers have virtually abdicated this field, leaving it to people like Jacqueline Susanne, Arthur Hailey, Leon Uris, Irving Wallace, Harold Robbins, Alan Drury. Now there is an old Latin aphorism, *de gustibus non disputandum*, which is to say that some like butterscotch and some like vanilla. But I believe most of us would agree that none of these people I have just mentioned is a Thackeray or a Dickens or a Tolstoy.

Irving Wallace has said that the critics really should pay attention to his works, seeing that millions of people read them. This must certainly provoke the scorn of Saul Bellow who remarked that he did not intend for *Herzog* to become a best-seller, the implication being that any book which was liked by the masses had to have something wrong with it. I need hardly point out that Mr. Bellow's attitude was markedly similar to that of professional historians toward popularity. Now I have never to my recollection read one word of the fictional prose of Irving Wallace, but I believe he is right, and I consider the implication of Mr. Bellow to be wrong. I also believe that historians of the academic professions should pay some small attention to Will Durant and to Thomas B. Costain.

I hope that you do not hear me as saying that writers should pander to the public whim or that historians should be sloppy with their standards so that the public will read them. Rather I am speaking out of a conviction that great art is a combination of two things—on the one hand an imaginative and yet precise mind and on the other a perception of impulses drawn from the people. I hope I do not seem to be trying to quantify taste, but it seems to me that the good writer and the good historian should inquire as to what it is which makes the people read the books they do.

I rather think that the people seek out those books which are somehow reflective of the public mythology, whatever that may be at the moment. There are the people, bearing their myths, groping in the forest for a pool where they may see a reflection of themselves and whatever it is they carry with them. In this, the new freedom in writing about sexuality is all to the good, for there is in many good writers a genuinely artistic impulse to explore a realm of the popular mythology. And yet I feel that in much modern writing, sexuality has been isolated and made the single driving impulse of human beings—which it simply is not. Writers are still Freudian long after psychologists have departed from the Freudian orthodoxy concerning the libido, for they have recognized its narrow limitations.

You may believe that the people threaten art, but I argue that in their clumsy and inarticulate way, the people push us to make a leap of the imagination and to carry them along with us. Merely because some pander to the tastes of the people does not mean that others should not try to work creatively with them. And I repeat my conviction that if the right imaginations respond to the impulses of the people at the right time, the result *may* be great writing and great history.

There is some justification in history for my claims. Dante combined the highly sophisticated theology and philosophy of the scholastics with some important elements of the popular imagination, and he produced the *Comedy* called by later ages divine. Dickens unabashedly designed characters which he thought would appeal to the public. But with that he combined a coherent view of human nature which was an expression and a critique of nineteenth-century values, and he wrote with a magnificence of language and rhythm unequaled since Shakespeare. Speaking of Shakespeare, I do not believe that the most aristocratic among us would dispute the fact that Shakespeare wrote to please the public. But in spite of this liability, he managed to express something of more than passing interest to the intellectuals of the earth.

I do not hold with that ancient Akkadian theory from the time of

Hammurabi, namely that writing was something so esoteric and so treasured that only a special clerical caste could be entrusted with it. Ours is not a democratic age, unfortunately, and most varieties of intellectuals today take a rather dim view of the prospects for strength from the people because we have experienced the fact that in politics the people have so often appeared to be wrong. But I rather believe in the ephemeral quality of politics when compared to the eternal quality of art, and in "art" I include history. I also believe that art involves a true lifting of our minds across a real distance between ourselves and the "world" or the experience which we wish to create. The people stand pressing us from behind to make that fearsome leap, and I think that we should, as both writers and historians, listen to their voices, gather about us our strength, look up and away from our own linty navels, and take the dazzling plunge.

The University of Tennessee, Knoxville

CONTRIBUTORS

WILLIAM BABULA, Assistant Professor of English at the University of Miami in Coral Gables, has published articles on Shakespeare and on modern drama.

ROBERT J. BLANCH, Associate Professor of English at Northeastern University in Boston, is the editor of three collections of critical essays dealing with Sir Gawain and the Pearl Poet, *Piers Plowman*, and Chaucer's *Merchant's Tale* and has published in various journals.

ROGER T. BURBRIDGE, Assistant Professor of English at Indiana University Northwest in Gary, has written articles for *Studies in English Literature, The Evelyn Waugh Newsletter,* and *Annuale Mediaevale.*

JOHN DITSKY, Assistant Professor of English at the University of Windsor, Ontario, has had articles published in a number of journals including *Southern Humanities Review, Walt Whitman Review,* the *Steinbeck Quarterly,* and *Modern Poetry Studies.*

WILLIAM T. GOING, Professor of Humanities at Southern Illinois University at Edwardsville, edited *99 Fables of William March* and *Regional Perspective: Essays in Alabama Literature* in addition to authoring some thirty-five essays on English and American literature in such journals as *Victorian Poetry, Modern Language Quarterly, Modern Language Notes,* and the *Victorian Newsletter.*

WILLIAM H. GRAVELY, JR., Associate Professor of English at the University of Maryland, has written articles on Edgar Allan Poe for *PMLA,* the *Poe Newsletter, Modern Language Notes,* and the *Princeton University Library Chronicle.*

VICTOR A. KRAMER, Assistant Professor of English at Georgia State University, has written about James Agee in the *Texas Quarterly* and in the *Library Chronicle* of the University of Texas. He is currently working on a book-length study of Agee's writings.

175

SAMUEL E. LONGMIRE, Assistant Professor of English at Vanderbilt University, manifests a continuing interest in Fielding (the subject of his dissertation at Indiana University) by an article on *Tom Jones* for *Texas Studies in Literature and Language* and in a forthcoming book on Fielding's fiction.

RICHARD MARIUS, Associate Professor of History at the University of Tennessee, Knoxville, is an editor of two volumes of the *Complete Works of St. Thomas More* and will be involved in a forthcoming edition of Erasmus. In addition to his work in the Renaissance, he has written a novel set in East Tennessee, *The Coming of Rain*, which was published in 1969.

KENT PATTERSON is teaching at Glassboro State College in New Jersey. He has written an article on Shelley for the *Keats-Shelley Journal*.

PHILIP RAISOR, Assistant Professor of English at Old Dominion University in Virginia, has written an article on Matthew Arnold for *Studies in English Literature*.

CORA ROBEY, Assistant Professor of English at North Carolina State University at Raleigh, previously published an essay on E. E. Cummings in *The Explicator*.

WILLIAM J. SCHEICK, Assistant Professor of English at the University of Texas, has done additional studies of Edward Taylor in *Early American Literature* and in *Texas Studies in Literature and Language*. He has also written about Henry Adams, H. G. Wells, Mark Twain, and Ralph Waldo Emerson.

WALTER SCHEPS, Assistant Professor of English at Ohio State University, has previously published essays on Chaucer, Shakespeare, the Scots Chaucerians, Middle English Romance, Middle English poetic diction, and *Beowulf*.

RUTH STEVENSON is a graduate fellow at Duke University. "The Influence of Astrophil's Star" is her first published article.

AUBREY WILLIAMS, Graduate Research Professor of English at the University of Florida, is the author of *Pope's Dunciad: A Study of Its Meaning* and the editor of the Riverside Edition of Pope's poetry and prose. He has co-edited two other volumes and has written numerous articles—principally on Pope—for such journals as *PMLA, Review of English Studies, Philological Quarterly,* and *ELH.* He was chosen to give the first John C. Hodges Memorial Lecture at the University of Tennessee, a series established to honor the former head of its Department of English.

ACKNOWLEDGMENT

The editors would like to express their appreciation to Professors Lorraine Burghardt, Barry J. Gaines, and Paul Merchant for the editorial assistance rendered in the preparation of this volume.

A SPECIAL EIGHTEENTH-CENTURY NUMBER

The 1974 volume of *Tennessee Studies in Literature* will be a special eighteenth-century number, devoted to the literature of the period 1660–1800. Essays for that issue are now being solicited. They may deal with the literature of any country and should be sent before March 1, 1973, to Professor Percy G. Adams, Department of English, University of Tennessee, Knoxville, Tennessee 37916.